THIS BOOK IS DEDICATED TO BRUCE RICKARD, KEN WOOLLEY, NEIL CLEREHAN, IAN MCKAY AND ENRICO TAGLIETTI

ICONIC

MODERN AUSTRALIAN HOUSES 1950 — 2000

KAREN McCARTNEY

PHOTOGRAPHY BY MICHAEL WEE

CONTENTS

INTRODUCTION

In 2000, we moved as a family into Bruce Rickard's Marshall House (1967) in Sydney's Clontarf. For me, it kickstarted an interest in residential Australian architecture from the 1950s onwards, which resulted in two books – *50/60/70 Iconic Australian Houses*, published in 2007, and its follow-up, *70/80/90 Iconic Australian Houses* in 2011. The 1970s features twice, as I managed to get two of the most influential houses of the period for the second book, the Kempsey House by Glenn Murcutt and the Palm House by Richard Leplastrier. The books formed the core content for a Sydney Living Museums exhibition which, for four years, travelled Australia-wide, and included not only images and text, plus video interviews with the architects and home owners, and selected models of the houses.

It is time to revisit these two volumes, to draw them into one book, redesign them in a new format and add one that got away the first time – the Jackson House, by Daryl Jackson in Victoria.

Part of the interest in these houses is the architectural lessons they provide: often modest in scale, they are inventive with site, materials and floor plan. The relationship to the outdoors starts tentatively, but gradually opens up to fully integrate gardens, courtyards and verandahs. This response to place, which began in the 1950s, is different to the 1940s where the model was British, with important rooms to the street front and a lack of connection to the back garden.

In the 10 years after World War II, more than 1.5 million migrants arrived in Australia; combine that with the numbers of returned servicemen, and there was a desperate need for housing. Building materials were scarce, and houses were subject to strict guidelines in terms of expenditure and size. The drive was often for quantity over quality, and aesthetics tended to give way to economics as the state controlled the process; architects, engineers, designers and town planners all fell under one bureaucratic umbrella.

To solve the housing crisis, the government looked to local as well as overseas companies, in Sweden and Great Britain, for quick-to-assemble housing. Set out in quarter-acre blocks, these houses had few of the refinements of previous decades – the plan consisted of boxy rooms with little thought given to the relationship between them, or to the link between indoor and outdoor space. Orientation was a given – the house faced the street regardless of sun or site.

While this was true of the broad sweep of development, it was also a time where young architects attempted to build a better world. There were plans by some, working within the restrictions, to maximise the sense of space by losing corridors and opening up kitchens and dining rooms. Notable is the Beaufort House, designed by Arthur Baldwinson in conjunction with the Beaufort Division of the Department of Aircraft Production, which was shown in prototype to the public in 1946. Using technology developed for aircraft manufacture, this steel-framed house was an innovative attempt to contribute to solving the housing problem.

THE SPIRIT OF THE FIFTIES

The arrival of the Fifties, with its economic prosperity, brought optimism and a strong consumer drive. Putting the war years behind them, Australians wanted the latest in mod cons and a style of home that reflected the spirit of the times. Magazines such as *Australian Home Beautiful* and *House & Garden* drove trends and influenced opinion. For a society that had made do, the desire for this new, ordered suburban life was irresistible. It is understandable that the state-of the-art kitchen at the Rose Seidler House, with its cutting-edge appliances, caused as much excitement as the radical building itself.

The Age RVIA Small Homes Service in Melbourne, launched in 1947, with Robin Boyd as director, showcased 40 architect-designed plans for homes that could be bought for £5. By 1951, they were providing plans for 10 percent of all new housing in Victoria. From 1957, plans were also available at the Home Plan Service Bureau at the Myer Emporium, Melbourne, and in 1962, Lend Lease's Carlingford Homes Fair in Sydney proved popular to the tune of two million visitors eager to see the latest in architect-designed project homes. This later morphed into Pettit & Sevitt, a company that, by 1963, was selling more than 200 houses per year. House plans were even published alongside knitting patterns in *The Australian Women's Weekly*.

A CRADLE OF MODERNITY

Postwar was a period of staggering creativity in Melbourne. Young architects were experimenting with shape and materials – Peter McIntyre, for instance, built his own house, an A-frame steel structure, with infill panels of Stramit, a compacted straw sheet material.

A shortage of materials had seen the introduction of lightweight steel frames and, as in Kevin Borland's Rice House, a series of thin concrete-sprayed shells. Cantilevered balconies and window walls; cable supports and plywood ceilings; colour and form; playfulness and theatre – experimentation knew no bounds.

A newly found affluence resulted in an interest in the holiday house. At one end of the spectrum was the commission from John and Sunday Reed for architects McGlashan and Everist to design a house right on the sand at Aspendale, a suburb outside Melbourne. At the opposite end, advertisements incorporating plans appealed to home builders to buy sheeting material and construct beach shacks themselves.

Another prominent architect designing beach houses (as well as country properties and city residences) in the Fifties for wealthy Melbourne clients was Guilford Bell, who had trained in London in the 1930s where he worked on a house restoration project for author Agatha Christie.

Melbourne's virtuoso performance was, however, short-lived. As Peter McIntyre admitted, it is hard to make a living out of radical thinking but, for a time, it was, as Robin Boyd said, Australia's 'cradle of modernity'.

TESTING POPULAR TASTE

In Sydney, an early pioneer of modernism was Sydney Ancher. He had spent time in Europe in the Thirties and returned to Australia filled with enthusiasm for the work of Ludwig Mies van der Rohe. In 1937, he designed what is considered one of Sydney's most important prewar buildings, the Prevost House, for his architectural partner Reginald Prevost. Ancher's experiences with local councils reveal something of the attitudes towards the new thinking in architecture. The 1945 design for his own house, Poyntzfield, in Killara, Sydney, was only approved after he altered the plan for a steel-framed building to a more traditional brick construction with a pitched roof. It still won the Sulman Medal in 1946.

INTERNATIONAL STYLE VS ORGANIC ARCHITECTURE

In Sydney in 1950, Harry Seidler, who had trained under Walter Gropius and Marcel Breuer, had completed the Rose Seidler House. Ancher's interpretation of International Style was tempered to suit local conditions and tastes; Seidler's house, in contrast, was in absolute adherence to its principles – so much so that it has been described by architectural writer Elizabeth Farrelly as 'built manifesto'.

Around the same time, there was another mood afoot, which drew inspiration from the work of American architect Frank Lloyd Wright (1867–1959), best known for the house Fallingwater (1935). For him, the relationship of the building to its site was of paramount importance, and his houses tended to be low, horizontal structures in natural materials. The influence of his Usonian houses, designed from 1936, can be seen in the work of Peter Muller, Neville Gruzman and Bruce Rickard, the latter commenting on their 'scale, the use of space, the warmth and mellow look from natural materials'.

In his book *Australia's Home*, Robin Boyd compares these two schools of thought, and expresses with clarity what they have in common. '...Both believed simplicity to be the omnipotent law of all design. Both rejected the idea of composing the façades of a building to preconceived rules. Both accepted spatial composition as the expressive field of architecture. Both believed that the building's function was the only basis for planning and that it should (and would automatically if permitted) be expressed in the building's form. Both believed that no material should be twisted into unnatural forms or asked to perform an unsuitable task.'

Despite these philosophical similarities, the resulting buildings could not have been more different. Seidler pulled no punches. 'Does not this [organic] architecture seem rather weak, subservient and not very proud of itself?' he said. Battle lines were drawn, particularly in Sydney, with architects such as Neville Gruzman rising repeatedly to the debate.

In an email exchange with Peter Muller, I asked him if he was aware of Seidler's quote at the time. Although he did not recall it, it didn't surprise him, and he clarified his view on the matter. 'Seidler was pushing for International architecture which abnegated all concerns to preserve local diversity. The climatic, the geographic, cultural and spiritual integrity, and deeper meanings for ornament were regarded as some kind of superstition. So-called organic architecture was regarded as "romantic" and intuitive rather than intelligent, and no match for what the Brave New World had to offer with its high-tech, machine-driven materials. Today, of course, with concerns for global warming, fossil fuels and so on, emphasis shifts once again, and the use of natural and sustainable materials in an intelligent and sensible way to reduce energy overloads is considered admirable and strong minded. Pride comes before a fall, subservience to Truth is a blessing, and the weak shall inherit the earth.'

From the early Fifties, there was a movement in Sydney (a collection of individual architects, but sometimes called a 'school' because of like-minded attributes) towards houses that embraced the Wrightian principles. These were often built on difficult sites, predominantly in bushland settings on Sydney's North Shore. Architectural historian Jennifer Taylor makes the point that there was an 'intentional understatement'. The goal was to integrate the building with the site with as little disruption as possible. In 1955, Peter Muller built a house for himself at Whale Beach that accommodated existing trees and rocks, and his palette of building materials reflected the colours of the landscape. In an era where the English country garden was still popular, it was considered 'alternative' to appreciate native plants and bushland settings.

Taking the bush setting to the ultimate of integration is the Glass House (1957) by Ruth and Bill Lucas, in Sydney's Castlecrag. This glass pavilion illustrates the idea of 'barely there' structures, and shows how Bill Lucas felt the frame was of crucial importance and 'everything that goes on after that destroys the original structure'. Built for his family, and constructed with economy in mind, the house utilises standardised sections of steel, timber and glass.

OUTSIDE INFLUENCES

Travel was crucial for this generation of architects. Often their degrees were practical, with little emphasis on contemporary buildings and current ideas. Exposure to other cultures and significant buildings in Europe and the United States was influential, as were the architectural journals of the day. George Henderson, who worked for 'regional modernists' Hayes and Scott, in Brisbane, and later for Seidler, recalls the copies of international magazines coming into the office. Pages were torn out and filed under the various architects of interest: Alvar Aalto, Marcel Breuer, Mies van der Rohe and so on, each with their own file to be pored over.

Also significant was the role of émigrés as teachers and architects. Hayes and Scott, for example, were influenced by Dr Karl Langer, from Vienna, whose 1944 booklet, *Sub-tropical Housing*, advocated, among other things, long, shallow floor plans which allowed maximum penetration of natural light. Langer also developed the first sun chart for Brisbane, a copy of which every architectural practice had, and which was continually used at Hayes and Scott in their quest for optimum orientation.

Architects themselves brought a European sensibility to Australia. 1957, for instance, was the year that Danish architect Jørn Utzon's design for the Sydney Opera House was picked, the story goes, from a pile of rejected entries by the American architect Eero Saarinen. Among local architects, Seidler's philosophy was shaped by the direct teachings of Gropius and Breuer; Taglietti came from postwar Italy, where he was taught by Carlo Mollino and Pier Luigi Nervi; Iwanoff came from Bulgaria, and Buhrich from Germany via Holland and London.

Architects who travelled were often able to find an inspirational source that resonated with their natural inclination. For Neville Gruzman, some of whose houses were inspired by Wright, the major influence was Japanese architecture. Many attributes of the aesthetic and building techniques have been adopted for use in Australian domestic architecture: the tradition of post and beam construction; extensive use of wood and the exposure of the structural elements; sliding screens for flexible floor plans; changes in internal levels; framed garden views and the linking of internal and external space.

THE LEGACY OF THE PERIOD

From the Fifties onwards, the kitchen slowly infiltrated the dining and living space. Often small yet ingeniously fitted out, it could be tucked behind partial walls or banks of storage cabinets, as in the Buhrich House. The open-plan kitchen/living/dining room (with access to a courtyard or 'outdoor room') that every house renovation aspires to today can find its antecedents in the relaxing of divisions pioneered by the forward-thinking architects featured in these pages.

Few architects (except perhaps Neville Gruzman and Guilford Bell, who both had a penchant for the glamorous effect of multiple mirrors) prefigured the rise of the bathroom as such an important room, or rooms, in the house.

What has altered drastically is the scale of homes. While the postwar restriction of 134 m^2 was undeniably small, the average new house is now around 230 m^2 with 600 m^2 not unheard-of. Design-wise, few domestic buildings in this present culture share the Sydney School's desire for modesty and lack of pretension. As Neil Clerehan pointed out, 'We never imagined there would be a trend for Neo-Historicism. We thought we were forging a brand new way forward.'

THE NEW RURAL

Like many great works of art, the Sydney Opera House was ahead of its time, and while Utzon's personality inspired a number of Australian architects, the built form did not produce a corresponding aesthetic. For Richard Leplastrier, it was Utzon's lack of prejudice, his sensitivity to nature and his openness to new ideas that he appreciated. By the time the Sydney Opera House opened in 1973, Leplastrier and Glenn Murcutt were beginning work on their ground-breaking projects – the Palm House on Sydney's Northern Beaches and the Kempsey House, in rural New South Wales. A little later, Daryl Jackson was developing a very different type of vernacular for his homestead, the Jackson House in Shoreham, Victoria.

SOCIAL PROGRESS

Victorian architect Kevin Borland was defined by his social conscience. 'Borland always understood the basic premise of design is about social exchange. He had a very strong socialist mindset,' says Daryl Jackson, who collaborated with him on the award-winning Harold Holt Swimming Centre (1969). His philosophy brought Borland a particular genre of work, from houses to larger scale projects such as Clyde Cameron College, Wodonga (1975–77), a union training facility for tradespeople. Bernard Brown explains in Doug Evans' *Kevin Borland, Architecture from the Heart*, how Bob Hawke, then union leader, persuaded prime minister Gough Whitlam to green light the project with the words, 'I've got a mate who's an architect and he is just the bloke for this little job.' Architect Norman Day describes it as representing 'a vision of an Australian architecture – the rural, the working-class, self-sufficient Aussie...There are other Borlands – suburban, urbane, refined and tailored – but this building is the best architectural measure of a rough, likeable mateship that he built.' Architect Kai Chen notes, 'He was talking about community long before it was fashionable.'

Also in Melbourne, Graeme Gunn (2011 Australian Institute of Architects AIA Gold Medal winner) was designing public buildings, such as the Plumbers and Gasfitters Union Building (1970), in the Brutalist style, but also experimenting with cluster housing, most notably in Winter Park, Doncaster (1970–75). Seeking to emulate the success of Sydney's Pettit & Sevitt in the project home market, Gunn developed, for Victorian company Merchant Builders, five different house types, clustering them around courtyards, with the whole site integrated with landscaping and parklands. In Sydney, in a more urban context, Ancher Mortlock Murray and Woolley developed town houses in Cremorne with planning devices such as shared garaging and a swimming pool to foster community spirit.

SUBURBIA CELEBRATED

A contrast to Glenn Murcutt's rural modernism was the philosophy of Victorian architectural practice Edmond & Corrigan, established in the Seventies, with Maggie Edmond and Peter Corrigan as its principals. Corrigan made clear his views. 'I have always been an unabashed fan of the suburbs...I see them as a source of fabulous energy', and of greater cultural importance than the bush, in which he felt uncomfortable. Their 1988–89 Athan House in Monbulk is archetypal, showcasing their preoccupation with colour, abstraction and fractured form, with bridges, balconies and decks imparting a whimsical spirit.

A CULTURE OF LEARNING

As a longstanding professor at RMIT, Corrigan's teaching influenced students from the Seventies, including such players and practices as Ashton Raggatt McDougall, Lyons, Norman Day, Wood Marsh and Ivan Rijavec. This passing on of architectural philosophies to the next generation is strong in Australia, and examples abound in this book. Leplastrier, taught by Lloyd Rees and influenced by Utzon, inspired Peter Stutchbury who now, along with Murcutt, Brit Andresen and Leplastrier, gives masterclasses to students. Gabriel Poole learnt from the great Queensland modernist Robin Gibson and, in time, Poole was mentor to Kerry and Lindsay Clare. Brit Andresen, at the University of Queensland, taught Brian Donovan and Timothy Hill, and Kai Chen sought out Kevin Borland as a mentor, while Kerstin Thompson worked in the offices of Robinson Chen before setting up on her own.

CONCRETE FORMS

Parallel to the theatrical inventiveness of Edmond & Corrigan ran another genre in which sculptural form took precedence. Concrete was used in innovative ways by Harry Seidler, whose early concrete buildings were geometric in form, becoming increasingly curvaceous (the Berman House, 1996–99) as concrete technology improved. The material began to find full expression with the dramatic abstractions of the Canberra-based Enrico Taglietti. His McKeown House (1965) began to push the boundaries of the material; 30 years later, his award-winning Sea Residence (1996) in Lilli Pilli, NSW, shows his passion for the plasticity of form had not waned.

Three significant houses featured in this book are Barrie Marshall's Phillip Island House (1983–90), Robinson Chen's Hildebrand House (1988–90) and Wood Marsh's Gottlieb House (1990–94), which all exploit monumentality and mass with very different results.

THE LIGHT FANTASTIC

These sculpturally dense houses are a far cry from the increasingly lightweight, open buildings being designed in Queensland to accommodate the subtropical climate and embrace the land. In 1951, Robin Boyd commented of the Mornington Peninsula that, 'this was holiday land, it was holiday time for architecture. The overanxious architect has been left in the city. Here the plans were simple and free. Buildings were able to discard their clothes, they went naked and unashamed and seemed to enjoy the sunshine.'

This, remarks Peter Hyatt in his book *Local Heroes*, could also be said of the Sunshine Coast. His book examines the work of three architectural firms – John Mainwaring, Kerry and Lindsay Clare and Gabriel Poole – all committed to a sensitive response to the land and climate, a desire to avoid the gratuitously fashionable, and to work with local trades and craftspeople. New technologies were found and exploited to advantage with Poole's quadropod system, allowing building to take place on steep sites formerly considered unworkable.

INNER-CITY REVIVAL

To date, the projects outlined here have been rural, coastal and suburban. In the Seventies, the sensibility around inner-city living began to change as conservation movements within residential areas, and within the profession, began to spring up. During the Sixties building boom, little regard had been given to the value of nineteenth-century buildings, many of which were lost in the wave of enthusiasm for the new.

As gentrification took place in inner-city suburbs, the requirement for architectural services grew. The Osborne House in Melbourne's South Yarra was a fine example of the maintenance of a nineteenth-century façade while architect Neil Clerehan created a modernist clean sweep of the interior, skilfully incorporating an art gallery and living space. Peter Stronach's work for Allen Jack + Cottier on the Victoria Street Apartments in Sydney's Potts Point showcases how 1897 terraces could maintain their exterior character while concealing open-plan living with white walls. 'The main work on the terraces was completed in 1980 and the absence of a rigid, conservationist approach denotes changes in the attitude towards the intrusion of new work in old buildings,' wrote Jennifer Taylor. This has become the solution for many to inner-city family living. The 'opening up' of the terrace and the semi has probably brought more work to architects and builders than the individual house in recent years.

Elegant white spaces such as those by Engelen Moore defined much of what it was to be cutting-edge in Nineties Sydney. Their Price O'Reilly House (1995) in Redfern was engineered to be as much photo studio as it was a home, with the modernist aesthetic married with the functionality of a full-height stacking door system allowing easy access for equipment and furniture.

The notion of New York–style loft living and of adapting commercial spaces for domestic use started to gain currency, and with it came a change in the social make-up of the inner city. Daniel Droga (owner of Durbach Block's Droga Apartment) moved into Sydney's Surry Hills in the early Nineties and recalls not even being able to buy a carton of milk locally at the time.

WHEN A HOUSE FITS

This book deals with residential projects and, as such, only tells part of the story of Australian architecture. Many architects featured have produced office blocks, university buildings, cultural centres, churches, embassies, hotels and government buildings. Yet, there is merit in the exploration of the house, as it distils architectural concepts into something we can all relate to. Richard Leplastrier talks of the 'fit' of a house with its client, and describes a house as an 'outer garment for their lives'. What strikes me about all these houses is that the fit is exceptional. Of course, it is not so unusual when the architects are their own client, as in a number of houses here, and can drive their own agenda unimpeded.

What guarantees a great architectural house? Gabriel Poole said that 'good clients get good houses'. I met and interviewed the clients and, although all very different people, they shared certain traits – a generosity of spirit, open-mindedness and a trust in the architect and process. While this book celebrates the work of the architects, it also pays tribute to the role of the enlightened client, without whom the outcomes would have been very different.

There is much to be learnt from looking back and, hopefully, the examples contained in this book, and others like them, will be around to inspire and inform new generations of architects. Sadly, as Professor Philip Goad pointed out, many of the light-structured Fifties buildings on valuable sites have already been demolished.

In Alan Bennett's *Untold Stories*, he describes the demolition of his alma mater, Leeds Modern School. It reminds him of what Brendan Gill from *The New Yorker* called the 'Gordon Curve', after architect Douglas Gordon.

'This posits that building is at its maximum moment of approbation when it is brand new, that it goes steadily downhill and at 70 reaches its nadir. If you can get a building past that sticky moment, then the curve begins to go up again very rapidly until at 100 it is back where it was in year one. A 100-year-old building is much more likely to be saved than a 70-year-old one.'

Many of these houses are approaching the dangerous age. Let's hope, with the help of sympathetic owners and bodies such as Sydney Living Museums, Docomomo and the Robin Boyd Foundation, they make it to their centenary.

THE R

HARRY SEIDLER

OSE SEIDLER HOUSE

1950

At a time when Australia was struggling to find a national architectural style, along came this brash young man with American training and a European sensibility, who built a relentlessly modern house in the International Style in the heart of suburban bushland.

PREVIOUS PAGE The exterior mural was designed and painted by Seidler himself. The colours are repeated in the interior to link the two spaces, such as the yellow in the door, above.

OPPOSITE Set amongst the bushland of a conservative northern Sydney suburb is the house architect Harry Seidler designed for his parents.

The house that Harry Seidler designed and built for his parents in Wahroonga, on Sydney's North Shore, was completed in 1950. It launched his career, defined the decade and caused a stir. Not only did it excite the architectural establishment, but it also attracted public interest in a way that domestic architecture rarely did. Visiting the perfectly preserved house more than 50 years later, it still feels daringly modern, so it's easy to imagine the curious public who came all those years ago to gawp at the house that Harry built.

Harry Seidler was born in 1923 in Vienna, where he lived with his well-to-do parents, Max and Rose, in an apartment remodelled by avant-garde architect Fritz Reichl. With the Nazi occupation of Austria in 1938, Seidler followed his brother Marcell to England, and was taken as a refugee to live with two ladies in Cambridge, where he attended school for 18 months. He was then interned, in Liverpool and the Isle of Man, before being transported to Canada. After his release in 1941, he gained a first class honours degree from the University of Manitoba before winning a scholarship to Harvard Graduate Design School.

The period at Harvard was to be a defining experience for him. Walter Gropius, founder of the Bauhaus movement, and Marcel Breuer, a teacher and practitioner of the Bauhaus principles of design, ran the postgraduate course. Later, Seidler worked as Breuer's chief assistant in his architectural practice in New York, studied design with Josef Albers (a former Bauhaus teacher) in the short-lived, but highly influential Black Mountain College, North Carolina, and spent a summer with flamboyant modernist Oscar Niemeyer in Brazil. All combined to ensure that, by the time Seidler moved to Australia at the behest of his parents, he had experienced an amazing exposure to the world's most influential architects and teachers. At 25, his architectural mindset was confident, complete and ready to be exercised.

'Rose Seidler House may look like a young architect's house for his parents, but really it is built manifesto, representing all the Modernist principles of Australia's most famous modern architect...As an attention getter the house remains unbeaten. A homage to Seidler's former New York employer Marcel Breuer, this house – with its TV-screen frontality, open pinwheel plan and elevated trapdoor entry – perches on the grassy site like an arrival from space.' This remarkably astute quote from Elizabeth Farrelly's article in *The Sydney Morning Herald* in 2005 sums up the house as a statement of intent.

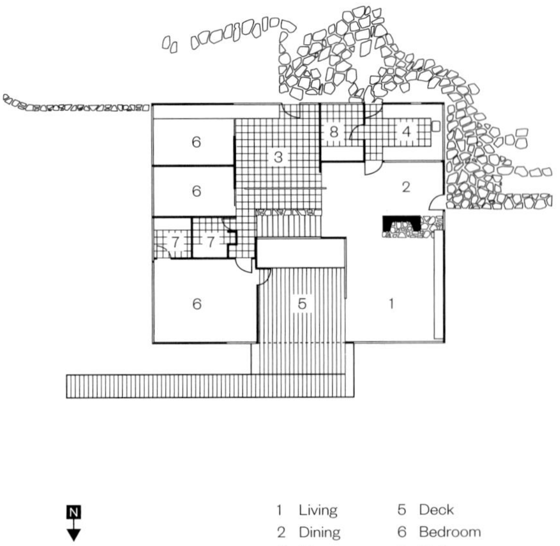

1 Living
2 Dining
3 Playroom
4 Kitchen
5 Deck
6 Bedroom
7 Bathroom
8 Laundry

At a time when Australia was struggling to find a national architectural style, along came this brash young man with American training and a European sensibility, who built a relentlessly modern house in the International Style in the heart of suburban bushland. While the design came about with apparent ease, the construction was fraught with difficulty. There were problems finding a builder to undertake such a project, but with the help of well-established architect Sydney Ancher, Seidler appointed Bret Lake. In the postwar period, materials were not easy to come by and there are stories of Seidler driving around building sites, picking up a few bricks here, a few bricks there.

Even the siting of the house was considered unusual. In an era where the front door inevitably faced the street, the Rose Seidler House is positioned in the centre of the block, with trees providing privacy and floor-to-ceiling windows opening up the house to bushland views.

Such was the influence of Breuer that the house conforms to his binuclear layout, with one arm containing the public areas – the living room, dining room and the kitchen – and the other, the private ones – the bedrooms and bathrooms. Connecting the two internally is the playroom and, externally, a courtyard. Because there are few internal walls, and glass replaces external ones, there is a tremendous sense of openness. For flexibility, a dividing curtain 'wall' can be pulled across to segregate the living area from the playroom. Today, we are accustomed to this flow of one living space to another, but in the Fifties it must have seemed highly unconventional. A design factor the newspapers of the day picked up on was its elevation. Traditionally, houses were solid and grounded while this seems to float, supported by spindly legs and sporting a strange projection to one side – a ramp.

This house has endured stylistically because of the conviction with which it was planned both inside and out. Take the colour scheme. 'People who live complicated lives (and most of us seem to) cannot be comfortable in a highly colourful interior,' said Seidler in 1954. Here, bold colour, neutrals and earthy shades are held in perfect balance, with the external mural setting the tone. Painted by Seidler himself, it recalls artists Miró and Calder, whom Seidler later collected, and captures all the colours used in the interior. There are cool greys on the walls, mid-greys in the carpet and deep brown upholstery on the sofa. The curtains, which provide walls of colour when drawn, are bright orange, electric blue and dark brown.

The furniture was bought, along with the light fittings, in New York before he left, knowing that he wouldn't get what he wanted in Sydney. DCM dining chairs, designed in 1946 by Charles and Ray Eames, were the result of wartime exploration into the potential of moulded ply. Combined with a chromed steel structure and exposed rubber shock-mounts, the look is industrial rather than domestic. The Eero Saarinen Womb chair (1948) and Grasshopper chair (1947) have a sculptural quality that provides a counterpoint to the linear design of the living room. The Ferrari-Hardoy Butterfly chair in eye-popping yellow is placed beside the mural where it looks like a 3D extension of the work's black outline and infill of solid primary colour. The built-in furniture was designed by Seidler, and made by another Viennese immigrant, craftsman Paul Kafka. The cantilevered wall cabinet is a particularly contemporary execution, with its combination of black polished glass and matt painted wood suspended on an Atlantic grey painted wall.

The fireplace and balustrade in rough-hewn sandstone are the only points in the interior where a sense of the randomness of nature intrudes, reflecting the exterior walls and the organic environment within which the house sits.

With the scarcity of materials in this period, necessity proved the mother of invention. Seidler used galvanised piping for the handrail, and explored the possibilities of other new materials.

OPPOSITE The cantilevered cabinet, which spans the rear wall of the living space, was made by Paul Kafka, a fellow émigré from Vienna. The mix of timber, finished in matt black paint, and the reflective qualities of black glass is highly effective.

ABOVE The dining table, also by Kafka, is surrounded by plywood DCM chairs, designed in 1946 by the influential American industrial designers Charles and Ray Eames.

The asphalt tiles in the playroom, while deemed less successful because of their lack of durability, have achieved a rich patina over time. Seidler's experimental thinking was particularly successful in the kitchen. It was the last word in kitchen design in its day, with *House & Garden* and *Home Beautiful* magazines wowing their readers with the cutting-edge, labour-saving devices, wipe-clean industrial stainless steel benchtops and coloured glass-fronted cabinetry. Not even the convention of handles was observed – simple, circular cut-out shapes in the glass were enough. A Dishlex dishwasher, Crosley Shelvador fridge of grand American proportions, Kenwood Chef Mixmaster and Bendix front-loading washing machine ensured this 'machine for living' had all the necessary cogs in place.

While the bedrooms are small, they are well-equipped and reflect more intensely the colour scheme of the rest of the house. By extending the door cavities to ceiling height, and using sliding doors, the entrance to the rooms feels generous, and the outlook onto nature from every room keeps them light and airy. In the master bedroom, a deep brown feature wall with flexible wall-mounted light, orange curtain, grey fake-fur bed throw and a simple black desk by Paul Kafka combine comfort, sensory pleasure and functionality.

In 1952, the Rose Seidler House was awarded the highest architectural accolade in Australia, the Sulman Medal. The significance is not to be underestimated, with the establishment seeking a style to call its own for so long. Seidler's view, according to writer Donald Leslie Johnson, was that his architecture achieved 'not only a total response to Australia but in complete sympathy, created out of the needs of Australia (society), the site (environment) and that it was logical (rational) and therefore suitable'.

While that may be open to debate, what is incontrovertible is that this house was visionary. So many of its concepts are now commonplace, from the importance of aspect and siting, open-plan living and the integrated kitchen to the painted feature wall, the cantilevered cabinet and insistence on well-designed furniture.

This, Harry Seidler's first commission in Australia, was as confident a statement as a young architect could make to establish his credentials, and laid the foundations for his career as one of the country's most eminent and enduring architects.

THIS PAGE A floor-to-ceiling curtain 'wall' sweeps across and can either extend the living area or create privacy between the living area and playroom.

OPPOSITE Seidler directly imported furniture from the US, such as the Saarinen Womb Chair, Knoll Model 70. Artworks by Josef Albers sit on top of the cantilevered wall cabinet.

T

PETER MULLER

E AUDETTE HOUSE

1953

Grounded and low-lying in the landscape, connected to nature and making the most of winter sun, while minimising summer heat, the house is created in materials that hark back to a more rustic age.

As an architect, Peter Muller has always run his own race. His innate affinity with nature and music has shaped his philosophical outlook and created a mindset that is as subtle as it is strong. This house, in Sydney's Castlecrag, is the first he designed as a qualified architect. As an early example of his work – he was only 24 at the time – it encapsulates many of the preoccupations and ideas that have endured throughout his long career.

Fundamentally, his architecture is known for an organic, romantic quality which works in harmony with its setting and exploits the inherent beauty of natural materials. He is particularly drawn to materials that are modified and enhanced by the passage of time – wood that weathers, stone that melds into the landscape, or copper that gains the patina of age. While the Audette House is the start of an architectural journey for Muller, it is also a highly significant house in the development of a distinctive regional Australian style.

Born in 1927, Muller grew up in the Adelaide suburb of Leabrook, where he recalls a semi-rural upbringing. A preference for the countryside over cities is something that has never left him and this longstanding connection to, and love, of nature was fostered by his mother, a keen gardener. He was also clear from an early age of the profession he would join. 'When I was three years old, my mother says I wanted to be an artichoke when I grew up.'

Muller describes the School of Architecture at Adelaide University as more like a technical college. With a hefty dose of plumbing, carpentry and surveying on the curriculum, it lacked any contemporary context for architecture. So while Muller applauds the sound training in the practical aspects and technical knowledge of building he gained, he also admits that '...the consciousness of world architecture did not extend beyond the Greek orders'.

Muller was a quick and clever student, managing to complete a degree in both engineering and architecture in a record four years. In 1949, he moved to Sydney, took a stepping-stone job at Hennessy and Hennessy architects and set about applying to American universities for a place on a master's degree course. Primarily, he wanted to travel, and in 1950 was one of six postgraduate students to receive Fulbright Scholarships funded by The United States Educational Foundation. The University of Pennsylvania could accept him immediately (Yale and Harvard had one- to two-year waiting lists), and with his first class passage fully paid for, he set off.

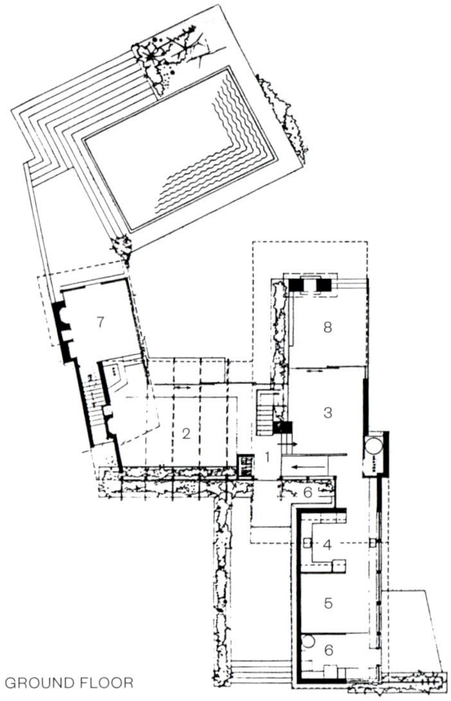

GROUND FLOOR

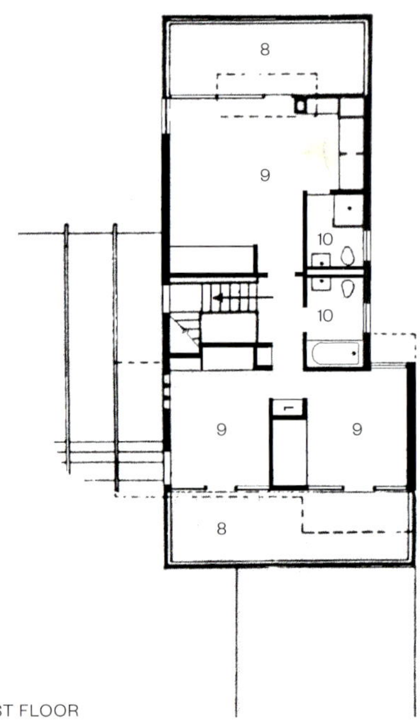

FIRST FLOOR

N

1 Entry
2 Living
3 Dining
4 Kitchen
5 Breakfast
6 Utility
7 Study
8 Terrace
9 Bedroom
10 Bathroom

BELOW LEFT While the interior has been considerably refurbished, the original exposed timber beams create a graphic statement. Their connection with the external timbers link interior and exterior visually by leading the eye from one space to the other.

BELOW RIGHT The 'snotted brickwork' was an attempt by Muller to breathe some life and create some texture in the wire-cut bricks his client purchased without his knowledge.

While studying in the States, he made no attempt to visit the buildings of the great practising architects of the day. 'I never visited a Frank Lloyd Wright building. I never visited a Marcel Breuer building,' he says. 'I just went skiing instead.' In an encounter at the Harvard School of Architecture, the Bauhaus architect Walter Gropius quizzed him about Australia. Muller can remember him talking about architecture; he says it went in one ear and out the other.

A European trip followed – Denmark, Sweden, England, Italy, France and Switzerland – where his memories are of the food, the people, the countryside. In Paris, he did pay a visit to one modernist icon. 'I had a look at one of Le Corbusier's buildings and decided I never wanted to see another as long as I lived...I was so shattered and disappointed, I found it so ugly and so bad in detail and so scungy...I never related to his philosophical or social views of architecture,' he says. Muller may not have had a firm handle yet on his own philosophy, but he certainly had a highly developed sense of what it was not.

On his return to Australia in 1952, two significant things happened. Taking a job at Fowell, Mansfield & Maclurcan to make ends meet, he met a young draughtsman called Adrian Snodgrass, who was to become a lifelong friend. In Snodgrass he had met someone of like mind who could stretch Muller's natural field of interest. For example, he introduced Muller to the extensive works of Frank Lloyd Wright. Where Muller had reacted so negatively to the work of Le Corbusier, with Wright the connection was instant. The simplicity of materials, the love of nature and the harmonious relationship of a building to its site – Wright's principles resonated with Muller's natural leanings.

The second significant event was a commission that would launch his career and oblige Muller to develop his architectural philosophy and translate it into the three-dimensional. Mr Hauslabe owned the Ford car concession in Australia, and was chairman of the Fulbright Scholarship Committee. His stepson, Bob Audette, had bought a north-facing block of land with Middle Harbour views in Castlecrag and wanted to build a family home. Mr Hauslabe's thoughts turned to the intelligent young architect the Fulbright Scholarship had sent to the US a couple of years earlier, and reasoned that his Stateside sojourn would have taught him a thing or two about building an American Colonial house. Peter Muller was the man for the job.

Muller tells of laying out the plans on the bed of his tiny Kings Cross apartment and setting up a model he had made himself so that Bob Audette and his wife could walk around it. When they arrived, Muller excused himself to get cigarettes and left them to view the model and plans alone without undue persuasion. While it was nothing like the original commission of a Colonial house, on Muller's return they agreed to build it, on the condition that it passed the CSIRO's sun orientation tests. It succeeded on all counts.

The model reveals the architect's original intent. The main wall was to be of rustic stone used in conjunction with Australian hardwood, treated only with linseed oil so that it weathered to a soft silvery grey. The combination of honest, unadorned materials was to ensure the house, set among angophoras, blended into the landscape. In this postwar period, access to building materials was still extremely limited, and Muller admits to bitter disappointment when Audette seized the opportunity to purchase cheap, awful red bricks in lieu of sandstone for the façade. 'It was my first house, so in hindsight I should have been more demanding,' he says.

To create texture in the brickwork, Muller came up with some innovative solutions. When laying the bricks, mortar was allowed to ooze out, which gave the wall a rustic appearance. As well as this technique, which came to be known as 'snotted brickwork', random bricks were raised and slices of terrazzo were inserted. These elements gave Muller something of the organic feel lost by the failure to use stone, yet still delivered the form he intended.

Although the land had no houses on either side, Muller experienced difficulties with its siting. A freeway was planned to run along the northern, water side of the block and prevented him siting the house as far forward as he would have liked. Hence, the Audette House has a strong street presence, unlike the 'hidden' siting of many of his subsequent houses. It is, however, not a mere façade – its three-dimensional quality is one of its defining aspects. While it is grounded and integrated into the site, with the garage disappearing under the living area, it also has a dynamism and strength created by the bold use of horizontal planes floating above the rows of windows.

Muller's plan was radical for the early Fifties. Most houses presented a flat façade to the street with the important rooms – the living room and master bedroom – at the front. Taking their cue from British housing, the rear of these houses incorporated the service areas – kitchen and laundry – with little or no thought given to orientation, siting or access to outdoor space. Muller turned all this thinking on its head. What is now commonplace was then revolutionary.

There are three zones at ground level – the living/study area, the dining area and covered terrace, and the kitchen/breakfast and utility area. They are held together by the first floor bedroom/bathroom level, which sits predominantly over the dining/terrace area but also links the other two zones.

There is a satisfying sense of forms echoing one another, of repetition and symmetry within the context of a limited palette of materials. Muller has always had an emotional and intellectual connection with music, particularly that of Bach, and this appreciation has given his work a distinctive rhythm.

The interior has since been altered, but the essence of the plan has been retained. The open-plan living area connects through floor-to-ceiling doors, originally in timber, to a lawn terrace and pool beyond. Again, the Audette House was a departure from the prevailing arrangement of space, which tended to be boxy, compartmentalised rooms with little relationship to outside. Timbers running through the living area were extended beyond the glass to join their exterior counterpart and lead the eye from one space to the other. The U-shaped courtyard, pool and Middle Harbour views created a compelling vista.

Three years earlier, Harry Seidler had completed the Rose Seidler House – an uncompromising residence in the International Style which quickly became accepted as the defining form of modern architectural thinking. What Muller offered in the Audette House was an alternative, an opposing architectural standpoint. Grounded and low-lying in the landscape, connected to nature and making the most of winter sun, while minimising summer heat, the house is created in materials that hark back to a more rustic age. Yet, the use of these materials was far from traditional. They were fashioned to create a fully formed, dynamic aesthetic which enabled a contemporary way of living. It is easy to see the significance of this house and to understand why many architects drove along Edinburgh Road to view first-hand the work of this audacious young architect.

The Audette House is undoubtedly in line with Frank Lloyd Wright's philosophies. Many of Wright's architectural pillars are also those of Muller and he does admit to leaning too heavily on Wright for solutions to problems, rather than for the generation of ideas.

Interestingly, only two years later, Muller's own house, on an awkward site at Sydney's Whale Beach, had moved further from obvious Wrightian devices to take his fast developing philosophies to a new level. The integration of house and landscape allowed for trees to be incorporated into the living area and for rock formations to be preserved. 'I was living in the site as well as the house,' says Muller. It is this house that architectural historians see as his coming of age as an architect, and it is, to this day, Muller's favourite house, but the Audette House is where the journey began, and for that it is worth celebrating.

OPPOSITE The house has many strong, graphic angles. Garden beds were integrated into the original design, such as this one which runs along the windows facing the street.

ROY GROUNDS

TH

E GROUNDS HOUSE

1954

The plan of the Grounds House takes geometry to an extreme, and involves two primary forms – a square enclosing a central, circular courtyard. To the street, it presents an impassive façade of immaculate proportion.

PREVIOUS PAGE The exterior of Roy Grounds' house is an exercise in simplicity. One side of a perfect square faces the street, an oversized door sits centrally and the high-set windows let in light while ensuring privacy.

OPPOSITE All the cabinetry has been carefully reconstructed in accordance with the original drawings. A cupboard in limed Victorian ash divides the entrance from the bedroom area.

THIS PAGE The circular courtyard set within an external square illustrates Grounds' preoccupation with geometry. Thirty-two window or door openings onto the courtyard reinforce the connection between the two spaces. Black bamboo acts as a shield from the sun, as do the internal bamboo blinds.

Sir Roy Grounds was a distinguished and controversial figure in the Melbourne architectural scene. He had a caustic wit, at times at his colleagues' expense. He once said of his associate Frederick Romberg, 'Freddy's the grain of sand that irritates me to produce a pearl.' From architectural concept to realisation, Grounds was a perfectionist, believing in the power of a single idea, masterfully executed. This award-winning house, built for his wife and family, is a prime example of his preoccupations at the time, and is viewed as a precursor to his best-known public building, the National Gallery of Victoria.

Even before the Second World War, Grounds established a reputation for avant-garde thinking. He had travelled to London in the late Twenties with his college friend, and later partner, Geoffrey Mewton. From there, they moved to New York where they both worked in architectural firms: Grounds in a practice specialising in Collegiate Gothic, while Mewton, at the other end of the spectrum, worked on skyscrapers. Grounds then moved briefly to Hollywood to join his wife, Virginia Marr, and turned his hand to designing film sets for MGM and making furniture in the Bauhaus style for LA's design cognoscenti.

He observed the work of significant American architects practising at the time, such as Richard Neutra, Frank Lloyd Wright and the lesser known William Wurster, who was an exponent of the Bay Area Modern Style. This style emphasised the use of locally found materials with a continuity of indoor and outdoor space through the use of window walls.

In 1932, with his wife and young son, Marr, he moved back to Melbourne where he designed his first house, known as The Ship, at Ranelagh, Mt Eliza. It had asbestos cement siding, with rope handrails and a porthole window lending a nautical air to its seaside setting. The Ship and Mewton's Stooke House attracted attention for their functionalist style; in 1935, the RVIA (Royal Victorian Institute of Architects) recognised them as notable examples of inter-war domestic architecture. High praise for architects barely 30 years old.

A series of houses designed in this period – the first Henty House, Portland Lodge in Frankston (1933–4), Lyncroft in Shoreham (1934), Fairbairn House in Toorak (1936) and Ramsay House in Mt Eliza (1937) – all show the influence of Wurster. Whether they fulfil Wurster's criterion that a house 'should be an unlaboured thing, that looks as inevitable as something that comes out of the frying pan just right, like an omelette in France', remains to be seen. These are

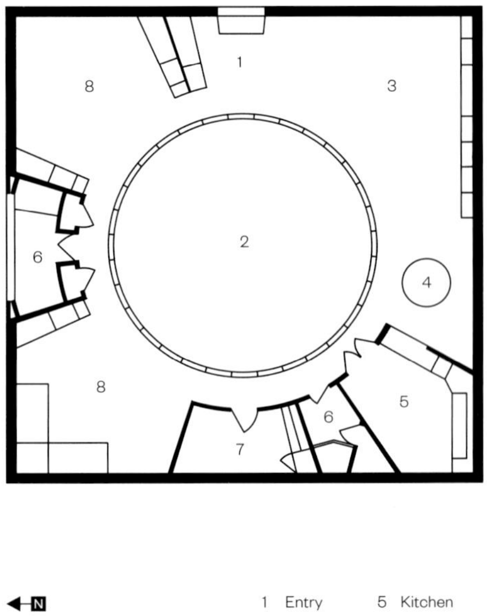

1 Entry
2 Courtyard
3 Living
4 Dining
5 Kitchen
6 Bathroom
7 Guestroom
8 Bedroom

THIS PAGE A cork-tiled wall divides the kitchen from the dining area, with a hatch allowing for easy access between the two rooms. The US company Expanko, from which Grounds originally sourced the tiles, provided imperial measure tiles for the restoration of the wall. The black slate table (ingeniously engineered to heat up) is surrounded by four MR10 chairs by Mies van der Rohe positioned at the four points of the compass.

important buildings, with Robin Boyd describing the living room/kitchen area of the Ramsay House as 'the most important room of the century'.

In 1937, Grounds and his second wife, Betty, spent a year in France but, with the outbreak of war imminent, they returned to Melbourne, where they moved into the Ramsay House. During the early years of the war, Grounds was sought out for a new type of commission – apartment blocks – which were to cement his reputation as one of Melbourne's most prominent architects. With a shifting demographic, there was an increasing demand for one- and two-person apartments. Grounds undertook Clendon (1939–40), Clendon Corner (1940), Moonbria (1941) and Quamby (1941) – all of which stand to this day. Here, he explored the potential of continuous space, undertaking thoughtful detailing, including retractable ironing boards, fold-up beds and writing desks. The Grounds House in Hill Street is a projection of the line of development he first employed in the design of Quamby flats, also in Toorak. There, the walls form a gently curving arc, radiused from a point some distance from the flats.

Grounds joined the RAAF as a flight lieutenant during the war, and was involved in the construction of airfields and defence buildings. After a brief period of farming postwar, he was appointed senior lecturer at the University of Melbourne in 1948 and was involved in structuring the curriculum. He was a powerful influence on many of his students. Don Fulton, in particular, remembers that 'Roy said a building should have "one simple, strong idea"', a dictum which Fulton followed in his subsequent, award-winning works. Grounds appointed both Frederick Romberg and Robin Boyd as lecturers and, in 1953, they formed the famous partnership Grounds Romberg & Boyd.

Robin Boyd described Melbourne in the 1950s as 'Australia's cradle of modernity', and it was certainly a period of intense experimentation for architects such as Peter McIntyre, Kevin Borland and Boyd himself. Shape and colour, technology and materials, combined with a certain theatricality of construction, all conspired to challenge the establishment. Grounds' use of geometric shapes in plan-form is evident in the designs of the triangular (Leyser) house in Kew (1951) and the round (Henty) house in Frankston (1952). The circular Henty House II was considered such an unusual building that those driving past it on the Nepean Highway referred to it as 'the flying saucer'.

Early proposals for Hill Street featured three-storey apartments set behind the house. However, the Grounds House, which won the partnership of Grounds Romberg & Boyd the RVIA Architecture Award in 1954, is sited close to the street and was ultimately accompanied by a series of small two-storey townhouses staggered behind it, following the slope of the land.

The plan of the Grounds House takes geometry to an extreme, and involves two primary forms – a square enclosing a central, circular courtyard. To the street, it presents an impassive façade of immaculate proportion. The roof is cantilevered with up-sloping eaves, and seems to float above the high windows set just below it. It is easy to see the influence this house seemingly had on Grounds' design for the National Gallery of Victoria (1961–68).

A large front door has Grounds' signature door knocker, and a Japanese maple stands to one side of the slate forecourt. The house is the perfect marriage of forcefulness and elegance, comparable to oriental architecture, where nothing is given away at street level, but also to Palladian architecture, in which proportion is paramount.

Entering the house, one is immediately invited into the seemingly large, open living area. Thirty-two full-height windows that form the circular courtyard wall admit an abundance of light. Each area of the house opens into the courtyard through glass doors. The space is continuous with few interior walls. Those that do exist are clad in vertical ribs of Victorian ash, and frame only the kitchen, bathrooms and children's room. The precision of the design ensures that all joinery, mullions and fitments are set out on radial lines from the courtyard's centre. Bedrooms are closed off by sliding doors, finger-pulled from radial slots, with the edge of the door cleverly disguised among the other ash ribs.

The house has not always been in the immaculate condition shown here. For many years, it was neglected, unloved and its basic design somewhat abused. Fortunately, it was bought in 2003 and painstakingly restored by cardiologist Dr Martin Hiscock. Through original drawings found in the State Library of Victoria, he discovered that architect Don Fulton, as Grounds' assistant, had prepared the 1953 plans. He contacted Fulton, who advised him throughout the restoration. Hiscock sourced original materials and skilled tradespeople, and also adopted a hands-on approach to the project himself. He carried out the painstaking tasks of stripping the ash mullions and doors of overly heavy liming, laying cork floors and installing aluminium acoustic ceilings in both bathrooms. 'I was determined to restore the house back to its original intention because I think it should never have been allowed to have lost it,' says Hiscock. 'Too often we see architecturally important buildings "improved"...and the whole potency of the original and enduring design is lost.'

Under Hiscock's eagle eye, joinery was expertly reinstated by David Burke, using limed solid timber. Bathroom mosaic tiles matching the originals were found and individually hand-laid in brick pattern according to Grounds' design. A large disc of black slate used for the dining table (the original had been removed from the house) was located in Genoa, Italy, and imported, not once, but twice, due to damage en route. Following Grounds' design, electrical cable is connected to heat the table in winter. Cork tiles of imperial dimensions from the original company, Expanko, have been used to re-tile the dining room wall with its 'secret doors', and the kitchen restored with the addition of modern appliances, underbench fridges and the return of the cork floor.

The hand-beaten and rivetted copper flue in the living room has not been replaced, although as with everything to do with the restoration project, Hiscock has tracked it down. It used to smoke; one night, during a party at the house, an unfortunate student was given the task of sitting on the roof to fan the smoke and try to increase the draw of the fire!

Heating was originally achieved with Pyrotenax cables laid in the concrete slab, but these had been interrupted over time. Reverse cycle air conditioners, hidden in the living room cupboards, now cope with temperature fluctuations. As architect and writer Neil Clerehan once remarked, the house is a 'fascinatingly detailed treatment of climate and human scale'.

As the courtyard is visible from every room, the use of materials and plants contribute significantly to the ambience of the house. The original Silurian mudstone pavers in the central courtyard had been replaced with bluestone offcuts from the National Gallery open spaces. Hiscock resited the bamboo planting from the south to the north to help screen the living area from the sun. In addition, he removed an unsightly canvas awning and fitted bamboo matchstick blinds to the insides of the windows. On top of that, Hiscock commissioned Don Fulton's son, Simon, to restore the paving to the forecourt.

The use of materials such as Victorian ash, cork, slate and lightly bagged brick recalls the comment of Jennifer Taylor, who said of Grounds' work, 'He combined rationalism and economical planning with a love of warm, natural materials.' There is a Scandinavian feeling redolent of Alvar Aalto's approach to interiors. Hiscock has returned the aesthetic values of the house with due regard to heritage principles. When visiting, Lady Betty Grounds exclaimed, 'Why, it looks just like new.' Having restored the lustre to this architectural 'pearl', Hiscock reflects, 'This house makes you wonder why we live the way we do, surrounded by four walls covered in Dulux. I prefer to be looking into a garden all the time, thanks; there's a lot to be said for inward looking.'

PREVIOUS PAGE The living area has been furnished with design classics in keeping with the era. A pair of Barcelona chairs by Mies van der Rohe, with a matching coffee table, sit opposite a Florence Knoll sofa. The zebra skin rug is a recent addition. Cabinetry in the original design has been reinstated along the wall.

OPPOSITE The bedroom is one of the areas with a sliding door for privacy. The treatment of the timbers, from the very fine ribs of ash to the timber-clad ceiling and the limed Victorian ash cabinetry, is redolent of a Scandinavian aesthetic.

THE

PETER McINTYRE

BUTTERFLY HOUSE

1955

'You must remember that the postwar nation felt as if it had been let out of a bleak grey prison, so we just splashed colour everywhere, without really comprehending the significance of what we were doing.'

PETER McINTYRE

PREVIOUS PAGE The land on which Peter McIntyre built his experimental house in 1955 overlooks the Yarra River, Melbourne.

THIS PAGE McIntyre's original drawing emphasises the bold geometry of the structural design by the use of block colour in primary shades.

OPPOSITE The entrance to the house is via a set of stone steps, the rough hewn quality of which contrasts with the precision of the building.

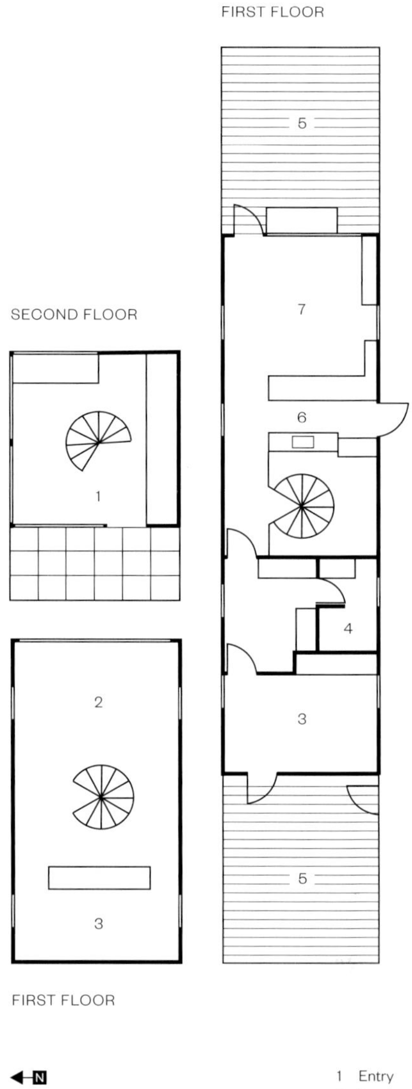

1 Entry
2 Study
3 Bedroom
4 Bathroom
5 Deck
6 Kitchen
7 Living/dining

'This piece of land has dominated my life,' says architect Peter McIntyre. And when you hear the story, it is true – it has not only dominated his life, but shaped his career. The land in question is 1.6 beautiful hectares right on the Yarra River in the Melbourne suburb of Kew. Here, in 1955, he built the highly experimental Butterfly House...but before the house came the land.

McIntyre came from a family of architects. His father started a practice in 1921, with McIntyre's uncle joining him in 1930. From the age of seven, Peter McIntyre was running errands and, at 13, was doing advanced drawings. By the time his father enrolled him in architecture, at 16 (overriding McIntyre's desire to study medicine), he was something of an old hand. Sent out in the spring of 1947 by his father's office to survey a piece of land for a potential client, he spotted the land directly below, which ran beside the river. He slid down on his backside – access was impossible any other way – and was immediately enchanted. 'I had been born in Kew and had grown up swimming in the river,' he says. 'I was absolutely in love with the river, it was everything, and this was absolutely the most fantastic piece of land.'

He asked a real estate agent to find out who it belonged to and approached the owners with all the confidence of a 19 year old without a penny in his pocket!

The land was a leftover part of the Buchan family's subdivision of the Finhaven homestead, a mansion that had been demolished, with parcels of land sold off to create Finhaven Court. This piece of inaccessible land was made even less desirable because the bottom part was subject to flooding, and government plans from the 1930s existed for a boulevard from the city out along the river. John Buchan, the executor of the estate, was prepared to sell for £100 but needed the agreement of his brothers and sisters. In the meantime, McIntyre would visit the site, and one weekend while surveying it, a man from a neighbouring house asked him what he was doing. They had tea, and McIntyre talked about his passion for the land and explained that he was buying it. At the next meeting, John Buchan revealed that the neighbour had offered £2000 for it, having previously offered only £10. McIntyre recounted their conversation, and again it went back to the family for discussion. In the end, they agreed to sell it to McIntyre for £400 with a period of six months to pay. He signed a contract on the spot.

When he showed the land to his father, he forbade him to buy it and so McIntyre approached his mentor and friend Robin Boyd. 'Of course, Boyd fell in love with it himself. At the time he was running *The Age* Small Homes Service and gave me well-paid work doing amendments to working drawings and perspectives of new houses. I worked night and day, didn't attend lectures and eventually wore myself out and had to go to bed, sick. My parents found out and my father agreed to pay off the balance, making me work the amount off in his office. I had the land but couldn't do anything with it.'

That was all to change with the winning of one of the most prestigious commissions in Melbourne at that time – the Olympic Swimming Stadium – and the land played a role here, too. Graduating students in that postwar period seized the opportunity to travel to Europe, Canada and, if they could, the US. All McIntyre's year went off on the grand tour, but as he was still paying for the land, he couldn't go. It did mean, however, that he, along with ex-serviceman Kevin Borland, John Murphy and John's wife, Phyllis, entered the competition for the Olympic pool. 'It was in my final year when my lecturer Norman Mussen introduced me to prestressed concrete construction and how counterbalancing forces could make economic sense,' says McIntyre.

On the judging panel were fans of their proposed scheme: Robin Boyd, who defended the aesthetics of their plan, and Professor Francis, in charge of engineering at Melbourne University, who confirmed that it was viable. The scheme utilised high tensile steel post-tension under the guidance of the very experienced structural engineer Bill Irwin. McIntyre is the first to admit the concerns of the architectural establishment around this young team. 'They did indeed query if we were old and experienced enough to do a structure like that, to pioneer that type of construction and to guarantee that the whole thing would stand up.' So many dimensions were a given – pool size and seat size – that new thinking was essential to deliver a workable building while significantly reducing the tonnage of steel required in a time of material shortages. 'Melbourne City Council refused a building permit and we had to go to Sydney to the Building Research Station to have the structure assessed and provide building permits. We had to fight all the way.'

While this commission kick-started McIntyre's career as a young gun of the Melbourne architectural scene, it also provided funds to build a house on the land in Kew. Working in the offices in St Kilda at that time was a final-year architecture student, Dione Cohen. She helped with the drawings for the house, and one day asked McIntyre who was going to live in it. His response was to ask her to accompany him to Fawkner Park, behind the office, where he said, 'Why don't we live in it together?' At their 50th wedding anniversary, they went back to the same park bench to 'plan the next 50 years'.

The house itself is extraordinary and experimental. Putting to use many of the things learnt from the Olympic Swimming Stadium experience, and using the same engineer, Bill Irwin, the house is described by McIntyre as an 'A-frame double cantilevered truss. Cantilevered in one direction and then balancing that cantilever with the other direction. Essentially putting one force against another.'

The site was difficult to access and, in order to build effectively, explains McIntyre, 'there was no structural member of the cantilever truss any larger than three inches [7.5 cm]. We were able to fabricate it on the ground in small sections, bring it up by hand, lay it on the side of the hill, bolt it together then stand it up and roll it out.' The steel frame was filled in with Stramit, a material made of compressed straw, and the surface painted with polyurethane paint in shades of red, yellow and white. 'You must remember that the postwar nation felt as if it had been let out of a bleak grey prison, so we just splashed colour everywhere, without really comprehending the significance of what

PREVIOUS PAGE Cantilevering out 12 metres, and 3 metres above ground level, the decks illustrate the combination of lightness and strength that define the building's construction.

OPPOSITE The spiral staircase, against the strong wall colours and ceiling timbers, brings to mind a Russian Constructivist painting.

we were doing.' What the vibrant colour and unusual shape did was attract lots of attention. The day they moved in, a feature appeared in *The Herald* newspaper, and by Saturday morning hundreds of people were coming down the driveway to have a look.

Finished in December when the foliage protected the house, it was a different story come autumn. Suddenly, it was exposed and highly visible from the tram that passed over Victoria Bridge. People would rush to the tram windows to speculate on what sort of a building it was.

Radical from the exterior, it did, however, prove to be a difficult house to live in. McIntyre is the first to admit its shortcomings. 'Most of the top room was glass to let in the northern sun and boy, did it do that. It also let the cold in as the glass froze – it was like living under a refrigerator. I had to reduce the size of the skylights, insulate the floor and in the early Sixties we clad the outside in hardwood. It was a gradual process of overcoming the inexperience.'

It is important to remember that McIntyre was only 26 when he started designing this, his fourth house. He was also a bachelor with no idea that the house would eventually become home to himself, his wife and four children.

The A-frame construction houses two levels of living space which pivot around a spiral staircase, and allow for generous decks at either side. The rooms are small, but the setting among the treetops is always evident. The triangular form recurs in windows, giving a faceted appearance to interior spaces and, in its highly coloured original state, it is easy to see why the house was compared to a Paul Klee butterfly.

The interior sports glossy red cabinetry in the kitchen and bathroom (which originally had two bathtubs) and bold yellow walls echoing the colour schemes of Charles and Ray Eames. In fact, the house was furnished with the classic Eames lounge chair and ottoman alongside Australian designer Clement Meadmore's metal and string stools, and Contour chairs by Grant Featherston.

As McIntyre learnt, the difficulty of being at the cutting edge of design was a worrying lack of commissions. He designed a house in Ivanhoe in 1953 for Hans and Pam Snelleman, who lived there for more than 50 years and loved what McIntyre had done for them. But, by 1960 he had no work, so travelled overseas. 'I realised after winning the pool and doing experimental things, that I really had tickets on myself. I thought it was everyone else's fault that I didn't have work. Travelling made me realise what a small fish I was. I had to go away in order to see it. To see how inexperienced I was.'

When he returned, it was with the resolve to change direction and learn more about the building trade. In the following decade, he created an extremely large, successful practice that won many prestigious awards.

This house has survived because it was on land that Peter McIntyre has never left. Other houses, all within the McIntyre family, now share the site, but the A-frame house is testimony to a time of optimism and spirit of experimental thought. In his book *Australia's Home*, Robin Boyd sums up the house with a wonderful description. 'The home of architects Peter and Dione McIntyre on a precipitous bank of the Yarra...symbolised the spirit of the new Melbourne house in the mid-1950s...Form and colour raised the spirits of the converted and deliberately jarred the unconverted into recognition that war was declared on conservatism.'

THIS PAGE Originally designed in 1960 by Charles and Ray Eames for the Time-Life Building lobbies, the chair was put into general production by Herman Miller a year later.

OPPOSITE The kitchen, open to the dining area, uses the same bold colour palette for cupboard doors and inside of the shelving. A Clement Meadmore Cord bar stool sits by the breakfast bar.

RUSSELL JACK

THE JACK HOUSE

1957

This house is modest and functional, it is human and nurturing, and provided warmth and shelter to Jack and his family for 50 years.

PREVIOUS PAGE The decorative wooden panelling at the end of the broad verandah illustrates the appeal the Japanese aesthetic held for Jack.

THIS PAGE Timber-clad walls in red mahogany impart a rich character to the interior spaces. Classic furniture choices mix with ceramics and wallhangings to create a warm, humanising atmosphere.

OPPOSITE The Jack House faces away from the street and onto the bush. It was designed with such sensitivity to the site that little by way of vegetation had to be moved to accommodate the building.

While watching her seven-year-old grandson playing with his building blocks, Russell Jack's grandmother commented, 'That boy will be an architect.' She was spot on. 'I never wanted to do anything else. Not so much from the design perspective, I just always loved building things,' he says. 'I went to carpentry classes and closed in the back verandah to make myself a bedroom when I was 14.' He received a sound education at Scotch College in Melbourne and Knox Grammar in Sydney and, at 18, enlisted in the RAAF. He acknowledges he went from the rather rarefied atmosphere of an upper North Shore boys' school into the cut and thrust of the forces, but managed to stay true to his calling with correspondence courses in several architectural subjects.

In 1946, Jack enrolled at Sydney Technical College, and his time there was important to his career on several counts. 'The course was certainly practical, and the academic side erudite. One academic tutor, Harry Foskett, was quite brilliant and inspired everybody.' Jack worked simultaneously in the offices of Rudder, Littlemore & Rudder, gaining practical, hands-on experience. Most importantly, at STC, he met and struck up a great friendship with John Allen, with whom he was later to go into partnership. Together they formed what was to become one of Australia's most significant architectural firms, Allen Jack + Cottier, which has been responsible for a range of high-profile projects in Australia and overseas. (Keith Cottier became a principal in 1965.)

But the story of this house is the very opposite of international building contracts and multimillion dollar commissions. This home is modest and functional, it is human and nurturing, and provided warmth and shelter to Jack and his family for 50 years.

In 1952, Jack won the Byera Hadley Travelling Scholarship; the topic for his studies was related to human expression in contemporary architecture. At this time, the opposing ideologies of Le Corbusier (the white modernist box) and Frank Lloyd Wright (an organic connection to the site) were the prevailing architectural influences. In London, Jack caught the tail end of the Festival of Britain, where he was pleased to see that modernism and decoration could get along perfectly well. He worked for Tripe & Wakeham before returning to Sydney in 1954 with Pamela, his future wife. In 1956, he set up the partnership with John Allen, and built the Jack House. When it won the prestigious Sulman Award in 1957, it gave the firm's reputation for innovative work a great boost.

1 Entry
2 Bedroom
3 Living
4 Dining
5 Kitchen
6 Terrace (now enclosed)
7 Study
8 Bedroom/laundry
9 Deck
10 Court
11 Carport and toolroom
12 Store

THIS PAGE The approach to the house is through an arch in a wall and along a timber walkway to the front door. 'The expression of the structure is important. It is there for all to see,' says Jack. The exposed post and beam framing and the unpainted woodwork speak to the honesty of the building, which is part of its enduring appeal.

'This land was the last undeveloped block on the street. They just couldn't sell it because of the steepness of the site and the creek running diagonally through it,' says Jack. While the current siting of the house seems the inevitable choice, the first plan was very different. 'The original house Pamela and I designed was steel framed and ran down the western boundary, elevated above the ground with the other wing running east-west. It went to tender, but was too expensive and had to be abandoned. In despair, sitting in a restaurant one evening, thinking what to do, the idea just materialised on the back of an envelope. My wife said we should think about timber framing and so we did,' recalls Jack. 'I don't think the other design would have had the same human feeling that this has.'

In the Fifties, some councils made attempts to govern aesthetics, and occasionally flat-roofed houses failed to get planning permission. Then there was the division between 'brick and tile' areas, deemed to be more upmarket, and less salubrious areas, where fibro and weatherboard were still acceptable. The Jacks were fortunate. While the other side of the road was 'brick and tile', theirs fell into the less rigorously policed category, and so the council had no issue with either the design of the building or the materials used to achieve it.

Interestingly, it is easy to miss the Jack House as you drive by. It doesn't declare itself obviously as part of the streetscape but, rather, is oriented away from the road and towards the bush. According to Jack, 'the prevailing style was for little brick boxes with the important rooms – the living room and the main bedroom – at the front irrespective of aspect or privacy. The accepted thinking on living style was very different from our own. We had to convince lots of our clients that it was the right thing to do. We believed passionately that it was, and having built this house, they could see what we were talking about.'

What you do see, set back from the road, is a wall with decorative, bagged and painted brickwork. This wall is one of the things that makes Jack's quiet independence of thought apparent. The International School, no doubt, would have designed a precise, unadorned white wall of immaculate proportion, while the typical Sydney School architect would have left the bricks self-finished, as the kiln had produced them. Jack did neither, and the result adds immense texture and interest to a large surface area. The wall is surrounded by a slim band of windows on both sides and along the top under the eaves. This visually lightens the density of the wall, especially at dusk when lights are on inside.

The other contentious decision was the arch opening in the brickwork that forms the entrance to the house. At the time it was considered reactionary by Keith Cottier, amongst others. Modernity demanded right angles, but Jack defends its appropriateness. 'The logical, natural opening in a brick wall is an arch,' he says. And there is not only one; a second, small-scale arch sits next to the main one, acting as a passage for the stream to run from one side of the wall to the other.

The driving force behind his thinking, he says, 'was that the building had to work – it had to be functional'. It has a simple L-shaped plan; turn left from the front door and you are in the family spaces – the dining room, living room, kitchen and study. Turn right and you are in the bathroom and bedroom wing.

'It was an economical house, there is nothing extravagant about it,' says Jack. 'In the early days, our clients didn't have a great deal of money, either, and this house could grow and expand.'

Internal walls were non-structural to allow flexibility in the future. Indeed, the house developed with time and a growing family. A verandah between the main living area and the study was closed in and two bedrooms added, with an exterior wall of grey, beautifully weathered timber forming the interior wall of the main bedroom area.

OPPOSITE The tiled area was originally an external space but, as the needs of the family grew, it was enclosed to create another room.

OPPOSITE The wallpapered wall divides the dining area from the kitchen.

THIS PAGE The kitchen is a good example of the economy in Jack's approach, with simple joinery and an open shelf for crockery and kitchenware.

While the purse strings were tight, the ideas were expansive. 'The other thing we tried to do was make it as psychologically big as possible – the free-flowing plan and the floor-to-ceiling glass meant the rooms were never boxes. There is privacy to the street and the rooms themselves are open to the bush,' says Jack.

The space is continuous with no connecting doors, but is still broken up into specific rooms. 'I like to be able to live in different spaces, not one huge space. Initially, there was no door on the study – until the children came along.' Ever practical, Jack remarked of the dining room, 'It is only used for an hour a day so it makes sense to use it as a thoroughfare.'

Linking the indoor and outdoor spaces was also integral to the scheme. The house was carefully sited, facing north, with minimal vegetation disturbed to accommodate it. The roof and floor planes extend beyond the glass line to increase the sense of space and create unity, while the same materials were used inside and out. As Frank Lloyd Wright, Jack's hero as a student, wisely said, 'I knew well that no house should ever be put on a hill or on anything. Belonging to it. Hill and house should live together each the happier for the other.' This applies very directly to the Jack House and its surrounds.

But it is not so much Wrightian principles that inform the design itself, but rather a mix of influences, from Japanese traditional houses to Alvar Aalto and, closer to home, one of the pioneers of Australian modernism, Sydney Ancher. Ancher's beautifully open house in Neutral Bay, and Bill Lucas' Glass House in Castlecrag were both finalists in the Sulman Award the year the Jack House won.

'The expression of the structure is important. It is there for all to see,' says Jack. The exposed post and beam framing and the unpainted woodwork speak of the honesty of the building and also create its enduring appeal. The non-standard windows are generous and proportionally pleasing and allow the outside in.

It is a robust house that has weathered the years well; it is unfussy but, unlike many of his contemporaries, Jack does not shy away from pattern. One of the appealing aspects of this house is the original wallpaper in the study and dining room. Jack is unable to recall whether it was he or Pamela who chose it, but it serves to emphasise the fact that 'Pamela and I were so much of the one mind that, with any disagreement about what to do in the house, the compromise was always better than what either had originally wanted.'

The publicity in the wake of the Sulman Award created a groundswell of public interest and the Jacks often found people peering in from the courtyard. Their neighbour jovially suggested he set up a lemonade stall for the thirsty onlookers. They were not all fans, and one woman wrote to the press saying that to give an award to a house that looked like 'a series of hen coops on sticks' was a disgrace.

Yet the house attracted clients of like mind. Artist Tony Tuckson and his wife, Margaret, commissioned a house in the early Sixties and, as Jack says, 'They didn't so much choose an architect as a house.' Margaret Tuckson looked at two of Jack's houses and knew he was the man for the job. She was there for around 50 years, so her instincts were right, and she described it as 'a truly wonderful house'. It is modest and unassuming, on a battleaxe block, and you need to be invited to know it is there at all. She tells of a visiting curator, a young man who, after an hour there, declared that he loved it more than any house he had been in. But then, it is partly because house and owner are so in tune with one another.

In her book *An Australian Identity: Houses for Sydney 1953–63*, Jennifer Taylor discusses the work of Russell Jack as creating 'easy and elegant' environments. She qualifies 'easy' as an ability to accept demands put upon it and requiring little maintenance. 'Elegant' equates with restrained, human and compatible and the result of the use of natural materials. There is no greater accolade for an architect whose primary aim is that 'it works superbly'.

THIS PAGE While considered reactionary by some, Jack found the arch entirely suitable. It was the logical, truthful way to form an opening in a masonry wall, since it needed no overhead support.

OPPOSITE The wall that faces the street is surrounded by a strip of glass to lighten its appearance. The bricks have been arranged in a repeating pattern to create decorative interest in what would otherwise have been a large plain surface.

THE WA

ROBIN BOYD

LSH STREET HOUSE

1958

It is not hard to see why visiting Japanese architecture students in the late Sixties identified strongly with the building's aesthetic and why an appreciation of Boyd's work developed in Japan.

PREVIOUS PAGE The courtyard was Boyd's solution to creating a private outdoor space on a narrow block in a suburban subdivision setting.

THIS PAGE From the street, there are only glimpses of the house, situated behind an enormous pine tree that was on the land when the Boyds bought it in 1957.

OPPOSITE Boyd's appreciation of the Japanese aesthetic is evident from the entrance to the house. The timber steps are open treads and have a measured, proportionally pleasing quality.

OPPOSITE In addition to pieces of furniture by Grant Featherston and Clement Meadmore, Boyd designed his own furniture specifically for the house at Walsh Street, including the long, low sofa and complementary coffee table.

THIS PAGE The deck extends from the main living space to create an entertaining area overlooking the courtyard garden.

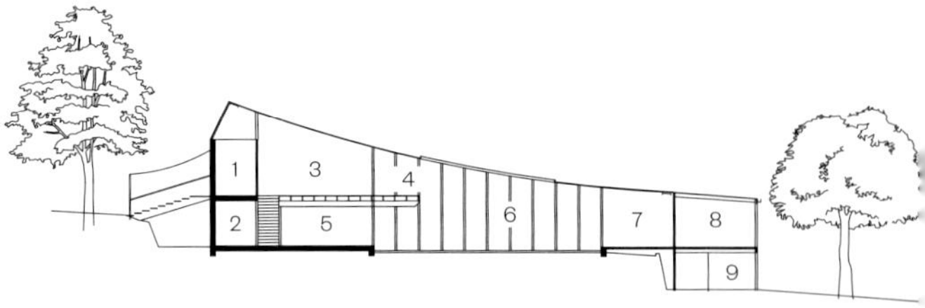

1 Entrance
2 Kitchen
3 Parents' bed-sitting room
4 Balcony
5 Family living room
6 Courtyard
7 Children's sitting room
8 Children's bedrooms
9 Carport

Not only was Robin Boyd a partner in one of Melbourne's leading postwar architectural firms, Grounds Romberg & Boyd (or Gromboyd, as it was wittily known), but he was also a highly respected architectural critic and social commentator. It is no surprise, then, given his facility with words, that he once described with great clarity what it is for an architect to be his own client. 'In his own home all his philosophy of building must surely blossom, if ever it is so. Here, he is both playwright and actor, composer and executant. What manner of architect he is will be laid bare for all the world to see...'

Examining Boyd's Walsh Street residence illustrates many of the traits that define one of Australia's most influential architects of the period. In 1957, Boyd and his wife, Patricia, had just returned from a year-long trip to the US. As a visiting professor to the Massachusetts Institute of Technology (MIT), Boyd reconnected with Bauhaus movement founder Walter Gropius, whom he had written about in 1953, and met other luminaries of American architecture such as Eero Saarinen, Mies van der Rohe and Frank Lloyd Wright. (It is worth noting that Boyd's erudite writing on Gropius' work ensured an ongoing friendship, and Gropius was to champion Boyd in years to come.) When Boyd attended an American Institute of Architects (AIA) convention, he noted that all the influential architects spoke with a European accent, confirming the significance of émigrés on the US architectural landscape in the 1950s.

Returning to Melbourne from the States, the Boyds were keen to move to a more central location than their house at Camberwell. Patricia saw an advertisement for land for sale in the upmarket suburb of South Yarra. The owner, Mrs Bishop, anxious about rising land taxes, was keen to subdivide her property and sell the long, narrow block that was originally the rose garden. Boyd, no stranger to awkward sites, saw the land, bought it on the spot and designed this, the second house he had built for himself and his family.

An early proponent of modernism, he saw the technical developments in materials and engineering as the way forward. It was with a great sense of optimism that he talked about the ability to 'make great open spaces without visible means of support, to throw out parts in cantilever and to open up entire walls to the outdoors through sheets of glass'.

Boyd was also grounded in a belief that well-designed, functional housing was for all, and a decade earlier had devoted years to the development and

operation of the Small Homes Service, run by the Royal Victorian Institute of Architects in conjunction with *The Age* newspaper. Opening postwar in 1947, with Boyd as director, the service offered 40 different house plans for sale at £5 each. An astonishing 1000 were sold, mostly to young couples, in the first nine days, and by 1951 the service was providing plans for more than 10 percent of all new housing in Victoria.

From 1948, Boyd wrote weekly articles for *The Age*, which increased his public profile. Recruited as a lecturer by Brian Lewis, professor of architecture at the University of Melbourne, Boyd was immersed in architecture in all its facets – practising it, teaching it and writing about it. In 1952, he published his second influential book, *Australia's Home*.

Boyd's work was primarily residential and it is said that he yearned for those large-scale commissions that gave broad recognition to an architect's career. In 1953, when he was on the jury to select a design for Melbourne's Olympic pool, he championed his friends and contemporaries Kevin Borland, Peter McIntyre and John and Phyllis Murphy in their submission. Genuinely thrilled at the successful outcome of such a bold, modernist scheme, it did cause Boyd, understandably, to question whether his role was always to be that of persuader on behalf of others rather than take centre stage himself.

As an architect, Boyd was a subtle practitioner. Writer Peter Blake commented that his houses were often 'almost invisible from the outside: it was the quality of the space inside that counted, not some heroic architectural gestures towards an impressionable world'. In Boyd's Walsh Street House, there is little sense from the street of what lies beyond. A wall with high windows set behind a pine (that Boyd was at pains to retain from the original garden) is the only visible clue. The house is set back from the street, and wide, open jarrah steps, tapering as they rise to the front door, are protected from the elements by a boldly striped canvas awning. This bridge-style entrance sets the tone for the rest of the house, which feels sensitive and considered, simply designed with a quiet integrity. It is not hard to see why visiting Japanese architecture students in the late Sixties identified strongly with the building's aesthetic and why an appreciation of Boyd's work developed in Japan. A red gate and tea-tree fence were added later to stop local dogs using the forecourt as a toilet stop.

Boyd's original plan was for a three-storey house but, having spent one noisy school holidays at home with the children, he radically revised the scheme. In his own words, 'The device adopted was to divide the house in two by a garden square, 40 feet [12 metres] deep, two-storey parents' block at the front, single storey children's block at the back. Tall glass walls, partly obscure, partly hooded, were erected on each side of the garden to protect it from wind and most of the rain, but not sun.'

Boyd's contemporary, architect Peter McIntyre, commented on his 'sheer inventiveness' and his ability as a designer to come up with fresh solutions every time. Walsh Street's construction can only be described as ingeniously simple. A wall two storeys high at the street side and a lower wall near the rear of the block, where the old rose garden finished at a retaining wall, were connected by woven steel cables, slung between the two. Onto these cables were laid timber boards, butted against one another and held in place with nails pierced through the cables, and bent flush underneath. This innovative tension roof structure was protected externally by a bituminous layer which became molten on the day of pouring. Boyd's practical solution was to add slim timber battens at random to prevent the roof bitumen from seeping through any oversized gaps.

In 1947, Boyd had used builder John Murphy to construct his first home in Camberwell, and he was called on again for Walsh Street. Boyd left drawings sketchy enough that the council wouldn't ask too many questions, enabling him to push the boundaries of how a home should look and function.

The layout is far from conventional, and must have seemed even more so at the time. It was, however, perfect for the lifestyle of the Boyd family. From the entrance, a long thin dressing room and bathroom lies to the left. Daylight pours in from the row of west-facing windows sitting under the eaves, creating a source of light for both the bathroom and main living area beyond. Separating these two rooms is a partial wall which stops at the base of the windows. A door in the timber wall leads to the main living area. As with their previous house, Patricia and Robin used this room as a bedroom by night and living space by day – something their friends found highly amusing.

The furnishings are spare. There's a bed which becomes a generous daybed with fitted cover and cushions; twin Featherston two-seater sofas with button backs, which moved with them from their previous home in Camberwell; timber bookshelves, flanking both sides of the room, and a cork-topped coffee table designed by Boyd running parallel to a long, low sofa.

Art played a big part in the Boyds' lives. Robin Boyd came from a line of distinguished writers and artists, so a variety of artworks decorated the walls. In the dining area, 'Winter Triumphant' by Robin's father, Penleigh Boyd, originally hung above the table, while a portrait of Boyd's mother by E. Phillips Fox was placed at the top of the stairs. Work by Arthur Boyd, John Brack, Don Laycock, Asher Bilu, Kevin Connor and Tony Woods added to the artistic ambience of the space.

The colour palette, chosen by Patricia Boyd with interior designer Marion Hall Best, is warm and recessive. The internal rear wall was clad in jarrah boards and left unstained, while the bagged brick has been painted a mottled grey. The hit of colour comes from the deep red carpet. The entire breadth of the living area opens to the deck. 'It is a platform independently supported, emphasising that the whole space enclosed here is one, and in it conventional segregations are neither necessary nor desirable,' explained Boyd.

Active in the cultural life of the city, the Boyds were very sociable, and Patricia was a celebrated cook. The living room and deck were the main entertaining areas and, on one occasion Boyd, standing below, was alarmed to see the flex in the joists and ushered all but 12 guests back inside. Apparently, feeling that structural engineers were somewhat overzealous in their specifications, he was in the habit of reducing their recommendations.

The corresponding room below the living area is the family/dining/kitchen area. A wall of windows facing the garden illustrates Boyd's great sense of proportion. The raw timber beams, treated only with a light grey stain, owe a debt to the Japanese vernacular he admired, while the exposure of the structural elements emphasises the honesty of the building's construction. The limed timber kitchen is discreetly placed at the back of this space, separated from the main living/dining area by the open-tread staircase and a built-in cabinet in limed mountain ash. The cabinet, facing into the room, was designed to house audio speakers and, radically for the period, a TV set.

While the structure for the adults, family living and entertaining provided the hub of the house, at the opposite side of the block, a single storey building was given over to the children's quarters. It later became known by the children as the 'other side', and at mealtimes they were called from their homework by a short ring on the telephone extension. The children's zone comprised two dedicated bedrooms, a guest room, bathroom and a sitting room/study facing out to the courtyard. The rooms, with the same bagged walls painted warm mottled grey and timber partitions, are simply furnished with built-in desks and neat single beds. Robin's son, Penleigh Boyd, recalls a degree of freedom in having their own end of the house. 'We had our own access through the rear lane, a TV room and study space and a view into the marvellous courtyard. We even had a secret basement which was used for storage. Robin also had a passion for cars and we were one of the first

OPPOSITE The bathroom/dressing room is positioned between the wall that faces the street and the three-quarter height wall that divides it from the living room. It is a long slim space naturally lit by the bank of high windows under the eaves.

THIS PAGE The study area in the children's zone featured the same bagged brick walls and simple functional furniture as used elsewhere. As Penleigh Boyd recalls, there was an enviable degree of freedom in having their own end of the house.

families in Melbourne to own a Citroën Goddess. People looked at it as though it was a spaceship. So, all in all, we were a thoroughly modern family.'

Between the two areas of the house lies a garden. As Boyd said, 'One of the principal objectives in planning was to create a private indoor-outdoor environment despite the narrowness of the allotment and the congested surroundings of an inner suburb.' These days, we talk of the courtyard as an outdoor room and an extension of our living space as if it's something new, but Boyd had thoroughly embraced the concept in 1958.

The plan for Walsh Street inspired Mary and Grant Featherston to commission Boyd to design their house a decade later. The Featherston House is a tour de force with its completely integrated indoor garden, floating platforms and translucent fibreglass roof.

Boyd's ingenuity, illustrated by the Walsh Street House, is an example of his ability to think laterally, to be aesthetically inventive and to solve problems of difficult sites. The James House in Kew (1956) is semi-underground; the Lloyd House in Brighton (1959) is fan-shaped to work around a pear tree; while the Richardson House in Toorak (1953) was designed as a bridge over a dry creek bed. He produced an enormous range of housing in his career and embraced the possibilities of new methods of construction to realise his concepts.

His writings on architecture and society challenged and shaped popular opinion, and his work *The Australian Ugliness* (1960) pulled no punches in its attack on certain aspects of popular taste. He wasn't afraid to take Australia to task, especially in its increasing Americanisation, and endeavoured to make the country strive for its own, distinctive cultural identity.

His reputation as a writer grew when, at the recommendation of Walter Gropius, a New York publisher commissioned Boyd to write a short biography of Japanese architect Kenzo Tange. Tange's comment, 'I could not help admiring you for your deep understanding and correct criticism on Japanese culture as well as my own work', goes some way to show Boyd's sensitivity and ability to tune in to the work of another architect in another culture.

Boyd may have felt disappointed that his career did not embrace large-scale commissions, but in many ways he played an even more significant role in the development of Australian architecture. He acted as the gatekeeper for aesthetic standards and played a crucial intermediary role, through his writing, between the profession and the public. As Joseph Burke said of Boyd after his untimely death in 1971 at the age of 52, he was 'the artistic conscience of his country, in the future of which he passionately believed'.

The Walsh Street House is the property of the Robin Boyd Foundation. The Foundation was established by the National Trust of Australia (Victoria).

THE

McGLASHAN AND

GRIMWADE HOUSE

VERIST 1960

Part of what was radical about this house was the flexibility it offered, and with it, a genuinely new way of responding to life and nature. Moving through it, one is well aware of the weather and what is happening outside.

PREVIOUS PAGE The north-facing terrace adjoins both the living area, to the left, and the flyscreened breezeway. Terracotta tiles inside and out, and the sliding doors from the living room, blur the lines between the two spaces.

THIS PAGE The flyscreened area is essentially a deep enclosed verandah which features a limestone wall, internally and externally.

OPPOSITE The entrance to the Grimwade House illustrates the mix of materials used throughout: glass, timber, limestone and terracotta tile.

OPPOSITE The main living area features David McGlashan-designed furniture. The walls are clad in cedar, which is the perfect backdrop for a collection of Aboriginal and Oceanic artefacts.

OVERLEAF The enclosed courtyard, protected from southerly winds, is an ideal area for outdoor entertaining. The house was designed to accommodate extended family during the holidays; a generous table, sited under a casuarina, is a perfect spot to gather.

This is the only house in the book credited as the work of two architects – David McGlashan and Neil Everist. It serves to highlight the particular working relationship of this Melbourne/Geelong-based partnership. They met while studying architecture at the University of Melbourne and formed the architectural firm McGlashan and Everist in 1955. Initially, McGlashan worked out of a room in his parents' house in Melbourne, while Everist set up in small premises in Geelong, Victoria's largest provincial city, to the south of Melbourne. While they had very different personalities, and worked from two offices, they set up a system of operating that ensured the work of the architectural practice had but one distinctive voice.

Neil Everist explains, 'We developed a series of planning processes and standard details. This meant that the architectural language of buildings emanating from either the Melbourne or the Geelong offices would be indistinguishable, but only one partner would engage with the client.' Ease of communication wasn't what it is today, and a combination of sketches sent by train and endless telephone calls meant that the 'best solution' was always the outcome. 'If one of us wanted to alter an approach to a design, change a detail, or overcome a problem, the process was to develop the "best solution"...David always said that if we had any real doubts about a solution, we were probably wrong and should start again,' recalls Everist. The system clearly suited them as they worked in this fashion for over 40 years, initially on housing and, later, mainly designing educational buildings, until their retirement in the late 1990s.

As young architects – in the right place at the right time – McGlashan and Everist gained commissions for several holiday houses. A product of peace and prosperity, the holiday house brought with it a certain freedom – a freedom to explore different ways of living and to push the conventional boundaries of what a house should be and how it should function.

In her essay for the exhibition catalogue *Living in Landscape: Heide and Houses by McGlashan and Everist*, Judith Trimble makes note of the connection both architects had as boys to the land, the beach, the light and the water, enhancing their feeling for and 'empathy with the natural environment'. Combined with this fundamental response to sense of place is an understanding of prevailing global trends in modernist architecture and an ambition to create a local response.

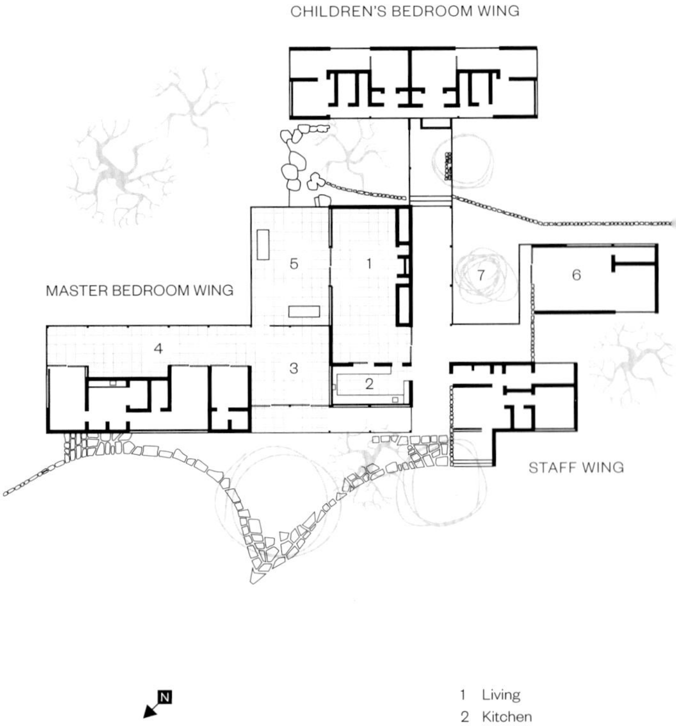

1 Living
2 Kitchen
3 Breezeway
4 Screened porch
5 Terrace
6 Rumpus
7 Court

In 1959, McGlashan had his first trip to the US, where he saw the buildings of some of the greats of American architecture – Frank Lloyd Wright, Richard Neutra and Marcel Breuer. Particularly inspiring to McGlashan was the work of Edward Larrabee Barnes and his Platform Houses, which were carefully integrated into the landscape and used pavilions to create a mix of connected indoor and outdoor spaces. Not long after returning home, McGlashan cancelled all the firm's subscriptions to overseas architectural magazines. They wanted to create an Australian approach and didn't want to be unduly influenced by what they saw happening at an international level.

The commission that was to change the course of their careers came from the Grimwade family, who owned a large block of land and an old boarding house in Rye, a coastal town outside Melbourne. Mr Grimwade wanted a house that could combine a permanent retirement residence for himself and his wife with a holiday house for his four daughters and their families. The main house needed to operate independently when guests were not staying, but have adequate space readily available to accommodate large numbers to sleep, eat and relax. Ideally, it would cater for a degree of separation between adults and children. The needs of their client and McGlashan and Everist's architectural preoccupations could not have been more closely aligned, as the unconventional requirements of the house allowed for, even required, a lateral approach to its planning and design.

Siting was a particular skill of McGlashan's, and such was his ability that he was often asked to site buildings other than his own work. In this case, the resulting plan includes a number of pavilions, each sensitively sited, and juxtaposed in such a way as to allow courtyards and outdoor spaces to be integrated into the design. The main house forms an L-shape. To the left of the entrance is the master bedroom wing, with four bedrooms and two bathrooms; to the right is the kitchen/living area. Accessed via both the living area and the entrance/breezeway is a north-east facing terrace positioned to maximise winter sun. The smaller pavilions consist of a children's bedroom wing, a rumpus room and staff quarters, between which is a large courtyard where a dining table sits under a casuarina tree.

While it is a large house, its mass is reduced by the modular approach, which McGlashan explained as the plan being 'taken apart', a deconstruction of sorts which allows the components to be arranged in a different pattern.

One of the most significant elements of the design is the treatment of the outdoor spaces. Terracotta tiles, used throughout the main house and terrace, have a unifying effect. As the walls facing onto the terrace are either glazed or flyscreened, each area, internal or external, is permanently visible from the other, and the sense of connection is obvious. The house turns its back to the south to ensure privacy and give protection from the southerly winds.

Also significant to the design is the extensive use of breezeways. The dramatic bedroom wing, which sits long and low on the land, is flyscreened but not glazed along the exterior wall to form an outdoor room. Moving throughout the house, one is well aware of the weather and what is happening outside. As Everist points out, space was seldom enclosed but, rather, 'movement is unrestricted and undefined through major spaces'. And part of what was radical about this house was the flexibility it offered, and with it, a genuinely new way of responding to life and nature.

On a warm evening, a family dinner can be held in the courtyard, with pre-dinner drinks on the terrace. On a cold winter's night, there is no need to stray far from the kitchen, the sliding doors open for easy access. The human scale of the design allowed for what McGlashan described as 'nearby spaces', and it is easy to understand how so many different activities, across the generations, could be taking place simultaneously in the house.

The house references Japanese architecture in several ways and, indeed, before designing the Grimwade House, McGlashan was given a book on the Katsura Imperial Villa, a Japanese country house and garden, with a variety of interlocking spaces. Echoes of Japanese architecture are seen in the simple measured quality of the spaces in the Grimwade House; the sliding doors and screens which allow spaces to change and adjust according to the weather or the needs of family life; the connection of the indoor and outdoor spaces; the lightness of the structure and the connection to the site.

So, too, does the restricted palette of materials. The floors, as mentioned, are terracotta tile, the walls are clad in western red cedar and the ceiling is a cream coloured Vermiculite, to help with the acoustics of a predominantly tiled space. Limestone, quarried on the site, is used for external, and one internal, walls. The house is constructed of honest, natural, warm and unadorned materials.

Adding to the sense of a whole, seamless space is the furniture. When interviewed by Eric Hunter for the TV programme *This Day Tonight* after the completion of Heide II in 1967, McGlashan described furniture he had designed there as 'an organic part of the architectural structure of the house – simple and complete. It fits in, in all respects.' Initially, the Grimwade House had only one freestanding piece that he had designed – a large glass mosaic coffee table. He had also designed the low outdoor benches, fixed in place on the terrace. Over the years, other pieces were added and the sense of a complete vision was established. Rectangular shapes form tables and bench seating. Steel frames are topped with materials already used in the house, such as terracotta tiles for table tops and slim cushion pads on the benches. The McGlashan-designed sofas, originally for Heide II, are based on the same rectangular steel shape, the back and arms formed by wooden planks and the webbed frames filled with large comfortable cushions.

While the design of the house is deceptively simple, there is an extraordinary level of thoughtful detailing. For example, a small leather pull handle in a cedar-clad wall is the only giveaway that a generous drinks cupboard lies behind – complete with a small sink, ample cupboards and a shelved wall backed with glass mosaics. The fireplace has integrated storage for logs, and the original mesh curtain fireguard. A large sliding door separates the kitchen from the dining area, and a connecting cutlery drawer can slide either way. However, McGlashan, in particular, didn't like mantelpieces and the Grimwades had an impressive collection of shells they liked to display. The compromise was what came to be known as 'the shell box', a long trough sunk into the tiles at the far end of the living area to house the collection.

Through a family connection, the Grimwade House came to the attention of John and Sunday Reed, who wanted a holiday house designed for a plot of land they owned on the beach at Aspendale, a Melbourne suburb on Port Phillip Bay. The Reeds were art collectors and the kind of unconventional clients who allow young architects to show the extent of their ability. As Everist says, 'The brief was exciting, imaginative and individual, and the site, virtually on the beach, was unique.' They also had another request – that it be finished in 34 working days.

'The Reed's [sic] enthusiastically responded to the developed bathing box concept, and loved the boardwalk and detached wings floating and embracing the sandy dune...this was the trial run and the first base. I was blessed to have clients who would commission my dreams,' wrote McGlashan.

Two glass pavilions – one for living, one for sleeping, connected by a covered walkway – were completed by the Christmas holidays, 1961. This commission was, Everist feels, something of a testing ground for their next, much more significant project – Heide II at Bulleen, which was awarded the

bronze medal of the Victorian Chapter of the RAIA in 1968 'for outstanding architecture'. This has become the firm's most famous domestic residence; the design of a gallery space to be lived in. Everist does, however, note that in this instance the design relationship was very much forged between the Reeds, particularly Sunday, and David McGlashan. With the brief requiring a romantic building with a sense of mystery, the space and natural light appropriate to a gallery, and the ability of the house to sit in the garden as though itself a sculpture, the commission was a challenge. The outcome, however, was an iconic building that answered every request.

As Professor Philip Goad notes, 'In choosing McGlashan and Everist to design Heide II the Reeds were commissioning a work of art. The Reeds regularly commissioned from emerging young artists. Which is what McGlashan and Everist were.'

McGlashan's view that houses are the 'background for people and the things they have with them' may have a simplistic ring to it. Examining the Grimwade House, which won the Victorian Architecture Medal in 1963, it is clear that McGlashan and Everist, working through their process of 'best solution', explored the potential of their projects from the macro (siting, spatial relationships and materials) down to the micro (how the kitchen drawer operates). Once a building was finished, the level of consideration was such that it became a truly complete space providing functionality, visual pleasure and a connection to nature. And, as architects, having done their job well, it did indeed, as McGlashan said, become the background, the context for living and for living well.

PREVIOUS PAGE There are certain vistas where the influence of Japanese architecture is evident. The measured proportions of the windows, the low, fixed seating (also in terracotta tile) and the view to the small pond, surrounded by rocks, impart sensitivity to a Japanese aesthetic.

OPPOSITE, LEFT The fireplace is set into the wall, flush with the cedar panelling that sits above it.

OPPOSITE, RIGHT The kitchen was originally designed in white laminate, but was renovated much later using Tasmanian oak and terracotta tiles, which brought it more in keeping with the materials used in the rest of the house.

THIS PAGE The bedroom wing sits long and low on the land, creating privacy for the north-facing courtyard.

ENRICO TAGLIETTI

THE DINGLE HOUSE

1965

'There is a concept I'd always been attached to: the principle that to be a modern architect, one has to sever oneself totally from the past and ask questions as though nothing existed before. Canberra was the ideal place.'

ENRICO TAGLIETTI

PREVIOUS PAGE Taglietti's design for the Dingle House had to accommodate the cross-sloping nature of the land. Set back from the street amongst established trees for maximum privacy, it is the strong use of horizontals that define this building.

THIS PAGE As a means of breaking up the visual solidity of the wall, Taglietti uses his signature void, in this case a half hexagon, seemingly cut out of the brickwork.

OPPOSITE The generous timber deck runs the entire length of the house and is protected by the deep overhang of the roof.

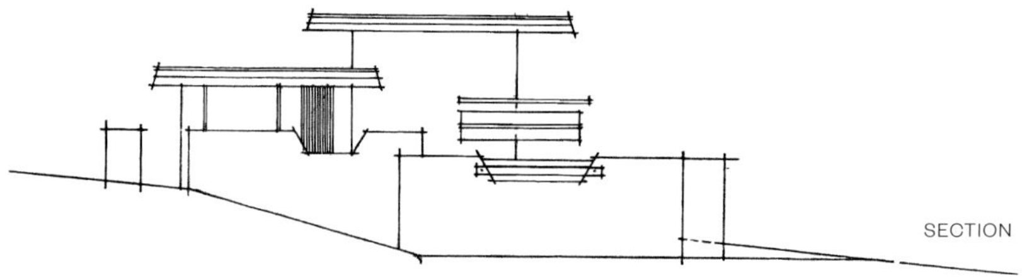
SECTION

Italian-born architect Enrico Taglietti and Australia's barely formed capital city, Canberra, found one another in 1955. It was a marriage of person and place that has remained almost unbroken ever since and, as with the best marriages, the influence of one upon the other has been mutually beneficial.

Born in Milan in 1926, Taglietti spent his formative years with his family in Asmara in Eritrea. Moving back to Italy in 1948, he took up architecture at Milan Polytechnic. During this period, he was exposed to the teaching and thinking of Italy's leading architectural intelligentsia. Carlo Mollino, he recalls, 'probably influenced me in relation to Baroque form', which Taglietti qualifies as an intention to 'create *meraviglia*, to amaze the visitor'; Gio Ponti he remembers as being 'so fresh in his approach, so naïve that he had enormous value as a teacher'. Artist Lucio Fontana, whose slicing of the canvas indicated a personality more about action than words, became a close friend. Add to the mix the teaching of Marco Zanuso, Bruno Zevi and Pier Luigi Nervi, and Taglietti's few years in Milan enabled the formation of his enduring philosophy of an organic approach to architecture. In 1954, he attended the Le Corbusier summer school in Marseilles and directed the foreign entries at the Tenth Triennale in Milan, which brought him into contact with Aalto, Niemeyer and Buckminster Fuller among others. All in all, his contacts in the early Fifties are a roll call of the postwar avant-garde architectural set both in Italy and abroad.

The photographs of the Milan apartment he shared with his wife, Franca, reveal a home that is the epitome of modern style. Chairs by Mollino and a table by Carlo de Carli are accompanied by Taglietti's own designs of a large honeycomb bookshelf comprising a series of stacked hexagons in blue, yellow and black, and a crafted, sculptural coffee table which owes a debt to Finnish designer Tapio Wirkkala. The apartment not only had style, it had panache.

An opportunity that arose in 1955 was to change the course of Taglietti's life. David Jones, the Australian department store chain, was to host an exhibition in Sydney of Italian architecture, furniture and fashion, and wanted an Italian architect to design it. They first approached Gio Ponti, but it was Taglietti who ended up with the commission. 'My wife and I thought of it as a second honeymoon,' he recalls. The exhibition was a great success, as was Taglietti's relationship with Sir Charles Lloyd Jones, who put him on a retainer. His scheduled stay of six weeks turned into six months. During this time he

OPPOSITE View from the raised living room towards the dining area shows how the two spaces relate. The timber-clad section of wall is broken by the clerestory windows which admit light from the west.

OVERLEAF, LEFT PAGE This was originally a study area at the rear of the living room, separated from the staircase by a low blade wall.

OVERLEAF, RIGHT PAGE The open-plan living space is divided by a painted brick fireplace. A large cavity in the structure is a storage area for wood.

was sent to Canberra to find a site for a new Italian Embassy, and from that moment on it was to that city he was drawn.

In 1955, Canberra had a population of only 40,000, and its appeal to this architect from the old world was the very new-worldliness it offered. 'There is an old concept I'd always been attached to: the principle that to be a modern architect, one has to sever oneself totally from the past and ask questions as though nothing existed before. Canberra was the ideal place.'

Taglietti is a great lover of the written word and his published work is littered with poems and literary references. The similarity between Canberra, a city without history, and Zobeide, a fictional city in Italo Calvino's novel *Invisible Cities*, was not lost on him. He felt he had found a place untouched by 'ugliness or history'. He embraced the empty spaces and the silence. Socially, however, it was far from silent and Taglietti commented that 'a young fellow arriving from Italy could mix without any problem with the atomic energy scholar, a Nobel laureate and with a Prime Minister' (Sir Mark Oliphant, Sir John Carew Eccles and Sir Robert Menzies, respectively). Taglietti wasn't just any young architect. He would have presented as sophisticated and debonair, well-read and well-connected; a man to whom aesthetics were grounded in an understanding of site, environment, aspect, client and economics. However attractive his attributes and his Italian qualifications, he wasn't permitted to register with the local architectural body and it was through the Department of the Interior in Canberra rather than the Board of Architects that he initially received permission to practice. It's interesting that half a century later, he was awarded Australia's most prestigious architecture prize, the RAIA Gold Medal 2007.

His instinctive response to Canberra and its people was rewarded by dozens of commissions over the years, ranging from houses to embassies, libraries, schools, conference centres and a cinema complex. His many commissions from the National Capital Development Commission include the Australian War Memorial Repository in 1978. He was there at the beginning of Canberra's major growth spurt and shaped the urban landscape of this growing city.

The house shown here is from his early period, and illustrates in a domestic setting many of the preoccupations that were applied in larger, more dramatic scale, in his public works. His approach was always consistent. In his own words, he describes the process of creation: 'First, I develop a brief, speaking with the client, and together with the client I create the basic area requirements...I then transform this floor plan in a volumetric mass and put it in context with the environment and the block of land. At this point, I forget the requirements for a moment and consider only the volume. Then I play with the volume. If I cut here, if I add there, I might overhang there. What is the most suitable volume to the particularity of the site, to the orientation, to the environment and finally to the agreed brief.' To realise these volumes, his favourite material was concrete for 'its plasticity, its ability to make any shapes or volume and still stand up'.

It is obvious that many of these ideas are at play in the Dingle House. The site was not an easy one – a steep cross-sloping block – but had the appeal of facing north at the rear and overlooking the pleasing panorama of the Federal Golf Course. The house is set back from the road, and the façade designed to maximise privacy. No windows face onto the street and even the entrance is tucked discreetly behind a walled garden area. The half-hexagon cut-out in the bagged brick garden wall is signature Taglietti. What is visible from the street makes a strong statement, and Taglietti's philosophy is at work here. He talks of the 'plane of the earth' which follows the land; the 'vertical plane' is subject to gravitational forces, and this he tries to break visually by use of strong shadow or, in other instances, windows that are not quite vertical. The third and, to his mind, 'freest' of the planes is the 'roof plane', and throughout his career Taglietti's roof lines, which have, in his words, 'the greatest possibility for shaping an architectural space', are a signature of his work.

Here, in the Dingle House, it is the various horizontal roof planes which define the exterior space. A public building Taglietti was working on in the same period, the Associated Chamber of Manufacturers Conference Centre, employs the same timber fascia with angled edges and overlapping roof lines to cap the main structure. While the fascia are finer in this domestic setting, they are more complex in their arrangement and impart a strong sense of form. They offset the solidity of the vertical planes and create a certain dynamism through the exaggerated timber horizontals. Originally, the house was bagged brick, painted white, with redwood timber used to create a strong contrast. This illustrates something of the sculptural, graphic qualities to which Taglietti was naturally inclined.

The house is not large, but the arrangement of the space is a clear interpretation of the needs of the client. In response to the site, the design solution is an ingenious three-way, split-level plan. The entrance is via a walled garden and leads directly into the dining room and kitchen level. These two rooms are connected by a large serving hatch in the wall dividing them and an open corridor which runs straight from the front door to the rear of this platform, where the master bedroom and bathroom are located.

The living area, with study at the north end, runs the length of the house, and is accessed by a small set of stairs at each end of the entry-level corridor. Stairs at the far end of the corridor lead down to a children's bedroom, guest bedroom and bathroom.

The living space benefits from a high ceiling with clerestory windows running the western length of the room. Hence privacy is maintained, but light is admitted. This extra height is clad in redwood timber which adds warmth to the space. Also connecting the split-level living spaces, by spanning the lower and upper level, is a brick column, bagged and painted, which forms the fireplace. Located centrally in the living room, it also features an open area for wood storage. The overall effect is of a continuous, interconnected space, yet each with a specific function. The dining area is visible from the living area, while the kitchen is connected to both the living and dining areas. The generous deck, which faces north towards the garden and golf course, and wraps around the building to the east, is accessed directly via floor-to-ceiling glass doors from the living area. The play of intersecting volumes creates an open and fluid scheme that makes the most of the site and the available space, and clearly connects inside with out.

Decoratively, the spaces are simple. The long, slim windows and timber cladding give a measured, linear feel to the house. The colour scheme of white painted walls and wood detailing is rather like the original exterior, showing the visible connection between the two. The kitchen and bedroom cupboards reflect this aesthetic. White melamine faced and with a deep wood trim, they are designed without the interruption of handles.

As Andrew Metcalf points out in his book *Canberra Houses*, the Dingle House is an example of 'Taglietti's dual theme of sheltering privacy externally and spatial finery internally'. Creating an almost fortress-like façade to the street was taken to new levels in the Paterson House (1968) and the Evan House (1971) where the life of the house, complete with internal courtyards, took place inside the enclosure. While the Dingle House is less extreme, it illustrates many of Taglietti's architectural ideas – the play of volumes, the sense of unfolding internal spaces, the freedom expressed by the roof line and the ability to work with the site to find the optimum outcome.

THIS PAGE The Cord chair, designed in 1952 by Clement Meadmore, was made from mild steel rods, welded together and painted black to form the frame. Taglietti knew Meadmore and commissioned him to create panels for a motel project he was working on.

OPPOSITE The design for the kitchen cabinets requires no handles and became something of a Taglietti trademark. He favoured this treatment for wardrobes both in this house and others of a later period.

THE ROSEN

NEVILLE GRUZMAN

BURG/HILLS HOUSE

1966

Gruzman was a pioneer of new technologies, and much of the effectiveness of this house comes from the manner in which he manipulates space through the use of materials.

PREVIOUS PAGE Neville Gruzman's perfectly sited house, at the end of a cul-de-sac, has dramatic views over a gorge. Privacy was created by Gruzman's landscaping – a series of man-made hills on the approach to the house to screen it from view.

THIS PAGE The bookshelf and wall cabinet are situated where the kitchen once was. The original cantilevered cabinet was in stainless steel and illustrates Gruzman's forward thinking in his early adoption of the open-plan, one-wall kitchen.

OPPOSITE Gruzman was interested in new technologies, and this pavilion in glass, timber and concrete illustrates some of his preoccupations. The house originally comprised a bedroom and bathroom mezzanine at entrance level and a large open-plan living area of double height, as shown, on the lower level.

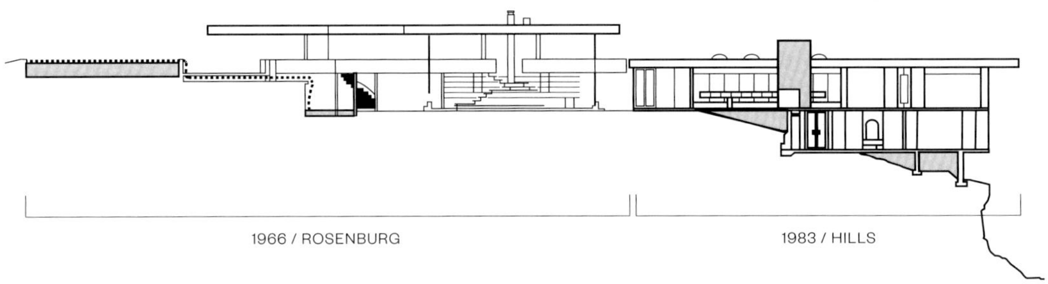

'I really dislike Gruzman because he is the most aggravating, demanding, sometimes impossible person I have ever known – nothing is ever done well enough to satisfy him – he is concerned for reaching for the stars...the result is that he has given me two heart attacks, caused me to have a quadruple bypass and in the end will be the death of me.'

It was with these words that Neville Gruzman himself opened his talk (Gruzman on Gruzman) to the members of the Royal Australian Institute of Architects (RAIA). It was his way of acknowledging his reputation for being difficult to deal with; his way of letting them know that he knew.

This lecture, conducted in the third person, explained something of his past. 'Gruzman grew up in the Depression – as a result, he had a depressed personality – he will never throw anything away.' Poignantly, the stresses of the Depression are said to have killed his father, a Jewish immigrant, who, with Gruzman's mother, ran a pub in the Sydney suburb of Matraville. 'Gruzman's widowed mother set out to bring up her three sons on a tiny income, ensuring that they got love, affection and a good education,' he told his audience. He was later to acknowledge the lack of a male role model, and felt fortunate to have a series of significant influences which helped to fill this gap.

Neville and his brother Laurence converted to Anglicanism and went to Sydney Boys High School. Subsequently, his time at the University of Sydney was a mixed bag. 'I was a lousy student and I struggled through third year,' Gruzman once said. The acting dean went so far as to tell him he would never make it as an architect. With a typical spirit of defiance he thought, 'I'll show the bastard.' And then, what Gruzman describes as a miracle happened in the form of the Hungarian lecturer, cartoonist and architect George Molnar, who had arrived in Sydney fresh from the modern movement in Europe.

Until then, the study of architectural history had concluded at the end of the nineteenth century. Before Molnar's teaching, there had been no mention of the work of Le Corbusier or Mies van der Rohe. Molnar's Point Piper flat became a place for discussion, debate and the drinking of red wine. 'Molnar would settle in a chair he designed himself – set himself up like a little god – and espouse architectural philosophy,' Gruzman recalled. His eyes were further opened by his friend and contemporary, Bruce Rickard, who introduced him to the work of American architect Frank Lloyd Wright.

As a student, Gruzman also found pleasure in attending the freehand drawing classes of eminent artist Lloyd Rees. The tide in Gruzman's relationship with architecture was turning, and another piece of good fortune was to come his way. An aunt was creating a subdivision of waterfront land at Rose Bay, and part of the condition of sale was that her nephew, the architecture student, was to design the house. He later admitted this was rather daring on her part. The resulting house, influenced by Le Corbusier, was such a success that the builder asked him to design a house for himself next door. Suddenly the student, who graduated in 1952 and was expected not to make it as an architect, had two waterfront homes to his name by his fourth year of study.

An epiphany of sorts occurred in Sydney's The Craftsman Bookshop in 1955. He came across a book published the same year called *Architectural Beauty in Japan*, picturing the Ryōan-ji rock garden in Kyoto. So deeply felt was his reaction to what he saw that he promptly abandoned his practice and, at the Japanese government's invitation, moved to Japan for four-and-a-half months of study. The Ryōan-ji rock garden didn't disappoint. The effect of its beauty was 'transporting', and he saw clearly that 'architecture is more than putting together space and material; there are heights that we as creators can reach'. He praised the Katsura Imperial Villa for its spatial qualities, particularly the relationship of inner and outer space, and level of detailing.

Once he returned to Australia, Japanese architecture had an enormous impact on his work – the use of materials, the level of craftsmanship and the intellectual rigour all shaped Gruzman's sensibility. He went so far as to announce that, post-Japan, he was a 'born-again architect'.

Working on Sydney's North Shore in the 1950s and 1960s, he produced a number of houses that reflected his natural flamboyance. There's a theory that, because his style was hard to pigeonhole and he didn't adhere consistently to any particular school of architecture, he has received less recognition than he deserves. Gruzman himself was of the opinion that his buildings had no obvious signature, that each project was answered with its own set of architectural solutions dictated by the site and needs of the client.

Indeed, a snapshot of three houses built around the same time show his diversity. The Salz House, in Rose Street, Mosman (1960), uses unadorned clinker brick in a strict linear design recalling the work of Frank Lloyd Wright; the Holland House in Middle Cove (1961) is a modernist cantilevered structure, predominantly built in glass and timber, and is restrained and geometric; while the Chadwick House in Forestville (1961–64) is an organic, cave-like dwelling constructed of a series of interlocking hexagons using bush stone. Bruce Rickard, however, points to their similarities. 'They all have a beautiful spatial flow, the living areas all face north and they are exquisitely detailed.' Whatever the style, these buildings all have the panache of their creator; as Peter Watts, former director of the Historic Houses Trust (now Sydney Living Museums), said of the houses, they are 'one-off major gestures, very Hollywood glamour'.

Two aspects of Gruzman's architectural philosophy are outlined in *Australian Style*, a book written by Babette Hayes and April Hersey in 1970. The first is to do with siting for maximum sunlight. 'Even in the brief winter months the admission of the winter sun can do more than merely supplement other forms of heating...its sense of warmth can be developed by the architect when he encourages it to push deeply into the space to paint the interior with its pale golden light.' The second addresses privacy, and he talks of 'that increasingly elusive quality of privacy, now almost lost to us, privacy visually and privacy audibly'.

The issue of privacy would have received a thorough exploration for Gruzman while designing the Rosenburg/Hills House on Sydney's upper

PREVIOUS PAGE The remarkable sculptural fireplace and stairway is the centrepiece of the room. Its gravity-defying structure illustrates something of the bravado that characterises Gruzman's architecture. This view is from the lower level of the dining area, through the stairs to the living space and out to the bush.

OPPOSITE The elegantly proportioned floor-to-ceilling glass doors open onto the north-east facing, cantilevered concrete platform.

OVERLEAF Gruzman was sensitive to 'privacy audibly', and the inclusion of a waterfall within the grounds creates a completely secluded environment where nature can be seen and heard.

North Shore. His bachelor client, Sam Rosenburg, was a practising naturist and wanted to be able to 'wander around his house nude', said Gruzman. Not something, one suspects, the rather conservative suburb of North Turramurra would approve of. Rosenburg had read a *Sydney Morning Herald* article by Gruzman on architectural education, and commissioned him to build his home on that basis alone.

The large site sits at the end of a cul-de-sac, overlooking a gorge. Gruzman, who had also studied landscape architecture, created a sense of arrival by designing impressive semi-circular walls at the entrance from the street and a long driveway curving down to the house. He built a series of hills which screen the approach to the house, and created a dramatic waterfall, the sound of which fills the air. This planned environment formed the perfect context for the house.

Gruzman was very attuned to the land he built on, and the setting for the Rosenburg/Hills House is incredibly dramatic; perfect for an architect whose work is described by Professor Philip Goad as 'theatrical and performative'. Overlooking this majestic bushland view, the house itself seems to settle with a light touch on the land. Constructed of glass, timber and concrete, it echoes rather than mimics a Japanese aesthetic. It also, as Goad points out, 'brought together two iconic twentieth-century houses (Wright's Fallingwater, and Mies van der Rohe's Farnsworth House) to create the ultimate diagram of abstract shelter in the landscape'.

Gruzman was a pioneer of new technologies, and much of the effectiveness of this house comes from the manner in which he manipulates space through the use of materials. Walls of glass are intersected by a roof line which butts into the interior; double-height pillars give a monumental sense, and the central sculptural fireplace, integrated into the staircase, is engineered to appear to defy gravity. It is a house without a bad angle, inside or out; it is highly photogenic.

The front door is imposing for a house that is more like a large-scale pavilion. At entrance level is a bathroom and bedroom open to the amazing view. Downstairs is a large dining and living area. Three sides are glass, and the rear wall, which is solid, originally supported a cantilevered stainless steel bench which constituted the kitchen. Today, the one-wall kitchen, open to a larger room, is commonplace, but in 1966 it was a radical way of approaching the lifestyle requirements of his client. It recalls one of Molnar's cartoons for *The Sydney Morning Herald*, showing two rather hoity-toity ladies with the caption, 'We don't eat in the kitchen, we cook in the dining room.'

It was Gruzman's view that 'outside spaces are often rightly regarded as extensions of inside spaces', and the concrete platform that extends from the living area faces north, guaranteeing daylong sunlight. The linking of indoor and outdoor space is strengthened by the use of concrete in both areas – a material that Gruzman felt was organic and connected readily to the landscape.

When designed in 1966, it had a bold interior created by the famous Australian decorator, Marion Hall Best. The carpets were bright red, the sofas ponyskin, the mullions were painted dark crimson, and Marcel Breuer Cessna cantilevered chairs sat around the Eames Aluminium Group dining table. This avant-garde approach was also matched by Gruzman touches – a square, glass-faced pillar that housed the plumbing for the bathroom was originally painted various colours by Leonard Hessing to create, in Gruzman's words, 'a vertical sculpture'. This was a seriously cool, designer bachelor pad set among the gum trees.

The original owner only lived in the house for a few years before his death, and it fell into rather unsympathetic hands. Many of the attributes that made it great were either covered or corrupted. Besser blocks and beaten copper panels were a crude attempt to create privacy, and although the new owners sought Gruzman's advice, he didn't take up the challenge.

Thankfully, the next owners, Michael and Kerrie Hills, who bought in the early Eighties, appreciated the good bones beneath the vulgar add-ons. Not only did they set about restoring it but, with the needs of their growing family in mind, contacted Gruzman with a view to a substantial addition. Gruzman came to 'interview' the Hills in their rather conservative house in Sydney's Beecroft and agreed to take on the project. Later, at a pre-arranged meeting at the Turramurra house, he was more than an hour late. Upset by the neglect he was aware it had suffered over the years, he had forgotten its exact location and got lost.

Space had been left on the site for an addition and, in 1983, it was built, complete with a truly spectacular bathroom. As John Haskell in his article on Gruzman for *Art & Australia* points out, 'The house therefore combines Gruzman's work over almost 20 years and again shows his remarkable consistency of style.'

Part of the reason Gruzman produced such successful houses is attributed to his ability to connect with his clients, to take on not only their practical living demands but also their personal traits and attitudes, and mould them into a very personal building. The Hills had a long and pleasurable relationship with Gruzman. 'He was always generous with his time and would discuss the most minute details with us, sometimes over hours,' says Michael Hills. He acknowledges frustrations, but senses that Gruzman, having regretted compromising in the past, didn't want to do it anymore. In his quest for perfection, cost was never an issue. As Kerrie Hills astutely points out, 'Neville needed patrons, not clients.' But the Hills credit Gruzman with opening their eyes to a different way of seeing things. 'He was opinionated, but always spent the time to talk it through,' says Michael Hills. 'He was widely read and extremely knowledgeable. He got us young and made us part of the process.'

In Gruzman's own Darling Point home, glamour played a central role. The bathroom alone speaks volumes. A completely mirrored space, it allows for endless, faceted reflections – leading more than one journalist to draw the analogy between it and the multi-faceted nature of Gruzman's personality. As well as an architect, he was for many years the very vocal Mayor of Woollahra, in Sydney's eastern suburbs, and a dedicated university lecturer, giving generously of his time to students, beyond the call of duty.

Conversely, he was a highly successful litigant and, in almost 50 years, had taken 30 cases to court. This is only matched by the staggering number of times the accident-prone Gruzman was admitted to Sydney's St Vincent's Hospital – 40 times in 30 years.

Over the years, the written word became increasingly important to him and, holding fast to the view that 'architects have a responsibility to the built and natural environment', not much escaped his eagle eye. The standards he set for himself he also expected of others, and more than once was reprimanded by the RAIA for the public criticism of the work of fellow architects.

His personal life appears highly charged and passionate, and yet in his work he found inspiration in the principles of Japanese architecture, striving to create serene buildings that harmonise with their surroundings. As Professor Philip Goad said, 'His work, like his personality, was chimerical, brilliant, outspoken and assertive. You could not divorce the two.' Through a lack of compromise comes a reputation for being difficult. Through lack of compromise also come great buildings.

THE

BRUCE RICKARD

MARSHALL HOUSE

1967

Bruce Rickard's approach to architecture is human in both its scale and its sensitivity. It is essentially life affirming, optimistic and makes a meaningful connection with nature.

PREVIOUS PAGE Set on a battleaxe block amongst angophoras, the Bruce Rickard house sits into the hillside. Built in sandstock brick and timber, it blends seamlessly with the landscape.

THIS PAGE At the south side of the living room is a deck surrounded by trees on two sides and facing the Spit Bridge on the other. The shiplapped western red cedar balustrade gives a sense of enclosure and echoes the timber treatment internally.

OPPOSITE The bedrooms, which Rickard describes as 'cabin-like', retain a feeling of spaciousness as they all open onto the lower deck.

OPPOSITE A Hans Wegner CH24 sits in front of built-in kitchen units and shelving. Fluorescent lighting is discreetly hidden under the top strip of wood to illuminate the work surfaces.

OVERLEAF, LEFT PAGE By using the same sandstock bricks for the internal and external walls, and continuing the treatment of the western red cedar ceiling to the underside of the eaves, the sense of continuous space is emphasised. The courtyard faces north to capture as much sunlight as possible.

OVERLEAF, RIGHT PAGE The galley kitchen has a stainless steel bench on one side (just visible to the left) and a row of cupboards on the other. Simply and inexpensively designed, it has endured more than 50 years of use without addition or amendment.

I have to come clean and confess that I am a fan of Bruce Rickard's work in general and this house in particular. For a number of years it has been home to my family, and so my experience of Rickard's architecture is a very personal one. I can still recall when a colleague showed me snaps of the Marshall House, which was for sale for the first time since it was built in 1967. Its special qualities were immediately evident, and I have to say, still are.

Born in 1929, Rickard studied architecture at Sydney Technical College in the evenings while working during the day for celebrated architect Sydney Ancher. In 1954, he travelled to the UK where he studied landscape architecture at University College London, and in 1956 received a fellowship to study at the University of Pennsylvania, Philadelphia. In Europe and America, Rickard had the opportunity to see the work of many of the great modernists of the day, such as Le Corbusier and Mies van der Rohe, but it was the houses of Frank Lloyd Wright that he 'found staggering'. He admired the way they responded to the site, the flowing spaces and the warm feeling, 'like the inside of a rum barrel'. He saw a lot of Wright's work during his time there, and was convinced that architecturally this was the way forward. Coming home to Australia in 1959, he was free to adapt Wrightian principles to the local climate and culture, and create from it his own distinctive signature style.

Bruce Rickard was 36 and already had 26 domestic residences under his belt when Penny and Greg Marshall approached him on the recommendation of their friend Richard Leplastrier, an architecture student at the time.

By this time, Rickard had already worked through many of the principles that have endured throughout his long career. The house he built in 1961 in Kokoda Avenue, Wahroonga, for his own family and architectural practice, was something of a model for the Marshall House. There's the strong emphasis on living spaces – indoor and out – and the flow between the two; the choice of natural, organic materials, and the desire to add warmth with as much winter sun as possible through sensitive siting. Both projects tackled the difficulties of building on a battleaxe block. Rickard, surprisingly, expresses a preference for this narrow type of block as it 'allows you [the architect] to extend your wings'.

Articulating the philosophy that has informed his architecture throughout his working life, Rickard, in 1994, described buildings 'that allow and encourage people in their everyday life to enjoy and partake of the pleasant sensations

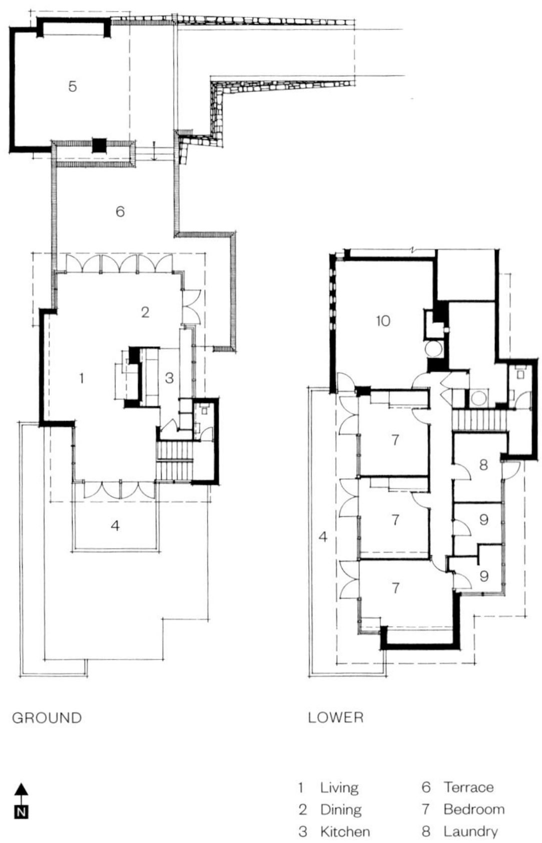

1 Living
2 Dining
3 Kitchen
4 Deck
5 Carport
6 Terrace
7 Bedroom
8 Laundry
9 Bathroom
10 Study

emanating from climate and the natural and built environment, such as the wellbeing felt from sun in winter and shade in summer; the delight of seeing trees, plants and the sky'. Before I read this, I implicitly knew it to be true. There are those moments in life which one doesn't often appreciate are the result of someone else's consideration – the ability to read the Saturday paper in winter in a patch of sunlight; coming up the stairs each morning to a knockout view framed by trees; taking a coffee in a sun-dappled courtyard. Rickard's approach to architecture is human in both its scale and sensitivity. It is essentially life affirming, optimistic and makes a meaningful connection with nature.

The Marshall House was built on a rather restrictive block – down a steep driveway with a sewer line running through the west of it. For this reason the top of the block was chosen, which also had the advantage of securing better views. The house is a typical example of Rickard's ability to extend the living space by blurring the line between inside and out. 'One of the design problems was where to put the front door,' says Rickard. 'The terrace, facing north, was the best spot for the outdoor living area but as it also had a view, a front door would have blocked all that out.' In the end, the idea of a conventional front door was abandoned and, instead, a bank of glass and timber doors, all opening outwards to the courtyard, serve to give the house a broad and welcoming aspect. On the south side, a deck captures the view across the Spit Bridge and beyond.

The main living space is one large room flanked by the two outdoor spaces. As with some of Rickard's other buildings, it pivots around the central core of a fireplace on one side and galley kitchen on the other. The fireplace is generous and open, with a hob for a tray to its left, used as a seat by both us and the Marshalls. The kitchen is a simple design of great ingenuity. Not only has it endured more than 50 years of use with immense durability, but its stylistic devices are still the source of admiration. A stainless steel bench runs the length of it, behind which is a recessed cupboard housing everything from recipe books to condiments. Three extra chopping boards, or pot stands, slide out from under the benchtops and long thin timber shelves are perfect for having everyday cooking ingredients to hand.

The cupboards are all in laminated timber with brass D-handles. The style has lasted because it is simple. It was also economical. The Marshalls would be the first to admit that the house had to be built within a strict budget and they entrusted the project entirely to Rickard without much interference, enabling the architect's vision to remain intact.

The living area faces west and, while the view is compelling, Rickard chose to build a solid wall along its length to absorb the heat of the afternoon sun. The view is revealed by a large window to the left of this wall, and glass doors lead out onto the deck. What works so well about this design is its ability to adapt to seasonal change. In summer, the doors can be opened up, extending the living areas out onto the deck and courtyard. In winter, the house closes down, the solid wall creating a sense of protection against the elements, while the centrally placed fireplace provides a source of heat and comfort.

The lower floor houses three bedrooms and a workroom, originally used for carpentry projects, but now a study. The bedrooms, as Rickard says, are like 'ship's cabins', but all have double-glass doors onto the west-facing deck to allay any sense of being closed in. Everything is built in, so the only additional items required are a bed and chair. The rooms have laminated timber built-in cupboards, a simple desk and a shelf that sits over the bedhead, and houses two light bulbs. The bedrooms are a pleasing mix of brick, cedar panelling and white-painted plasterboard. Both bathrooms (one ensuite) are small and serviceable but far from the luxury of today's bathroom requirements, and have had the original bronze/brown glass mosaics replaced with sturdier slate tiles.

Much of the house's warmth comes from the choice of materials. The construction material is predominantly recycled sandstock bricks sourced from Paddington houses demolished when the Eastern Suburbs railway was being built. They are undeniably bricks of character. Small explosions of impurities in the clay add bursts of grey to the soft sand base colour. Bricks are used both externally and internally and are left unadorned. The brick is combined with shiplapped western red cedar chosen for its richness and depth, and used for all windows and doors. This timber was even used for the living room ceiling, and the choice of wide boards running the length of the space creates a linear pattern that elongates the room.

One of the fundamental, but often neglected, aspects of a home is the choice of lighting. I have grown up with a central ceiling light and a lamp. Here, the lighting plan is ingenious but, in keeping with the house, modest. In the bedrooms, the main switch turns on recessed lights above the wardrobe doors. Upstairs, set into the red cedar ceiling, are six recessed lights 20 cm square; discreetly hidden behind a timber strip in the kitchen are long fluorescent tubes, and built into the shelving that runs the length of the living area are lights behind specially constructed shades in linen-covered Perspex. The combination of different lights allows for infinite variety and the ability to 'close down' certain areas at night to create a feeling of intimacy while eating, reading or just watching TV.

As for the landscaping, Penny Marshall tells how it was Rickard who introduced her to native plants. He had studied landscape design, and in Pennsylvania had been impressed by an exhibition of the work of Burle Marx, who used natives. Returning home, Rickard found it hard to find Australian natives – nurseries had few, and officials for public planning favoured British plants. Around Lake Burley Griffin, for example, they wanted weeping willows, not river red gums.

The Marshalls opted to plant natives and the house is now surrounded by huge angophoras and native flowering plants, which in turn attract birds. The setting is complete. After 33 years, the Marshalls sold their house to us and commissioned Rickard to design a second house for them. Looking through his lifelong list of projects it is interesting just how many clients have come back for a second house...and then there are those who have simply never left.

PREVIOUS PAGE Rickard places great emphasis on the connection between indoor and outdoor spaces. Hence floor-to-ceiling timber-framed doors open up to allow the integration of the two. The Heart chairs and table by Danish furniture designer Hans Wegner continue the feeling of wood and warmth.

THIS PAGE The bedrooms have a shelf with hidden reading lights above the bed. The considerate detailing reduces the need for too much extraneous decoration.

OPPOSITE Each bedroom has a built-in desk. In the master bedroom, the wide western red cedar boards are visually extended by the mirror on the rear wall.

TH

HUGH BUHRICH

BUHRICH HOUSE II

1972

The dominant feature is the incredible wave ceiling which gives an organic, expressionist feel to the room. Cedar boards were steamed to make them pliable, and then Buhrich nailed each one into place.

PREVIOUS PAGE The Buhrich House II sits beside the water at Sydney's Sugarloaf Point and is approached from the road through low-lying bush. The unique blend of its design elements is immediately evident: the wave roof line, the organic use of concrete and the panel of threaded timber all create the façade of this extraordinary house.

THIS PAGE Outside the floor-to-ceiling windows in the living room is a narrow balcony made of planks, purely for the purpose of cleaning the windows. Access from this space to the floor below is via a daringly constructed external staircase.

OPPOSITE Behind the timber textured wall is a concrete panel which appears to float in its glass surround. The wave roof line and ceiling add to the sensuous quality of the house.

OPPOSITE The wave ceiling came about while working through a strict set of building height regulations. In Buhrich's own words: 'It was just a practical response: I decided to push the ceiling up between the trusses.'

OVERLEAF The dining table is positioned on a raised area with the kitchen adjacent, accessed to the right of the table behind the bank of cabinets. The wallhanging is a piece of carpet customised by Buhrich to soften the appearance of the suspended concrete panel behind it.

There are some houses that just stay with you. They capture your imagination the first time you see them and they live in the back of your mind forever.

In the Nineties, I was a devotee of British *Elle Decoration*, edited by the inspiring Ilse Crawford. Each month would deliver a mix of British and overseas stories that satisfied my growing appreciation of architecture and interiors. One memorable issue, in 1998, showcased the Buhrich House II in Sydney's Castlecrag. Architecturally, there was a lot to absorb: the undulating wave roof line, the fire-engine red bathroom and the awe-inspiring setting. When I pictured this book on Australian modernist architecture in my mind's eye, this was one of the houses that defined it.

It was, therefore, with a sense of excitement and curiosity that I made my way along Castlecrag's Edinburgh Road in search of number 375. The road is wide and impressive and has a range of architecturally interesting houses, such as Peter Muller's Audette House and a number of fine examples of Walter Burley Griffin's work. At one stage, the road narrows to a lane and I think I have run out of numbers when, at the very end, at the very tip of Sugarloaf Point, there are some stone steps cutting through a low bush garden. And there, as described by architect Peter Myers, sits 'easily the best modern house in Australia'.

Architect Hugh Buhrich's path to this, his final destination, had been far from straightforward. Born in Hamburg in 1911, he had a difficult and disadvantaged childhood, made no easier by the suicide of his father on returning from the Russian front after the First World War. Buhrich is on record as being rather disparaging about the quality of his education, describing the Munich architectural school he attended as 'not very good' and completing his degree at 'a really shocking university'. On a more positive note, he worked in Berlin for Hans Poelzig, a prestigious architect with an enormous breadth of work, from the Poelzig Building at the Goethe University (1931) to large-scale set designs for film, including the 1925 production of *The Golem*. Fortuitously, also studying under Poelzig was Buhrich's wife-to-be, Eva. The circumstances leading up to the war pushed the couple around Europe – to Holland and then briefly to London where they were married, finally arriving on Australian shores in 1939. After a short-lived, shared architectural appointment in Canberra, war broke out and Buhrich joined the army. His son Neil recalls his father's time as a

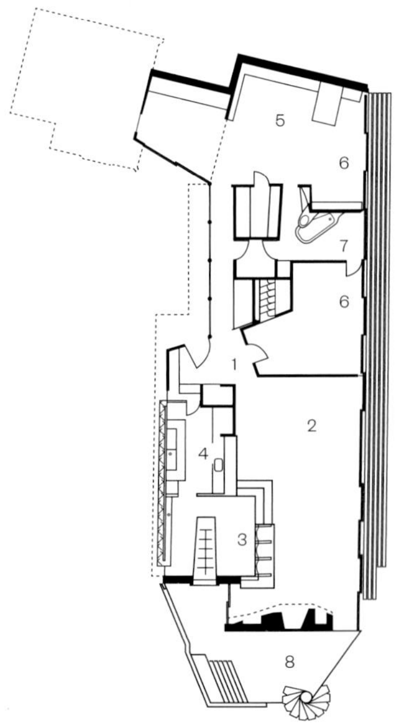

N

1 Entry
2 Living
3 Dining
4 Kitchen
5 Study
6 Bedroom
7 Bathroom
8 Deck

private in the Citizen Military Force (1942–45). Not trusted with real weaponry and trained with a wooden gun, he did, during games of chess and soccer, make lifelong contacts with fellow émigrés, who later provided the lion's share of his architectural commissions. Educated central Europeans, many Jewish, went on to become successful, and turned to their architect friend when any kind of building was required.

After the war, Eva embarked on a long writing and editing career that included architectural criticism, under her own name and several male pseudonyms, for *House & Garden* magazine. Eventually, she wrote a column for *The Sydney Morning Herald*. Her writing work provided financial support, and her outgoing personality enabled the couple to have an interesting social life that included artists Robert Klippel and Francis Lymburner. The Buhrichs also hosted discussion groups attended by immigrants intent on continuing the cultural life they had left behind in Europe.

What must have been a great disappointment to Buhrich was the refusal of the Board of Architects to recognise his qualifications and, in doing so, deny him the right to practise officially as an architect. 'The Buhrichs must have been somewhat nonplussed by the refusal, especially as the equivalent body in the UK, the RIBA, had clearly recognised them as a talented couple, and helped support them financially to make the trip to Australia,' comments Peter Myers. For many years, Buhrich worked under the title of 'planning consultant' and much of his work was restricted to alterations and interiors. Neil Buhrich recalls his father sitting for the exams and while he passed on the technical specifications part of the test, it was the design component that caused his rejection. His ideas were perhaps too radical for the conservative mindset of the Board of Architects in the 1950s. In 1971, it gave him the acknowledgement that would have been so useful earlier in his working life. As a result, apart from a few synagogues, small business premises and car parks, there are no major public works to speak of.

He did, however, design around 20 domestic projects, many of which are now altered beyond recognition or demolished, but it is the house he built for himself, and pretty much by himself, between 1968 and 1972, that has become the enduring testimony to Buhrich's creative genius. This 'intensely personal' project took four years to complete because most of the work – the hand cutting of sandstone, steaming and shaping of cedar for the ceiling, and designing specific pieces of furniture – was undertaken by himself and his assistant, Bill Chambers. There is a strong sense of a complete vision both externally and internally.

The house was built as an extension to an old Walter Burley Griffin structure which had been used as a fisherman's cottage and was bought with money received as reparations from Germany. Set on a difficult site with an incredible view, Buhrich's house settles into the landscape with a lightness that is both subtle and unassuming for such a remarkable building.

Buhrich was 57 when he designed this house, so it was to some degree the culmination of his ideas and influences. He had been a long-time admirer of the work of Ernst Plischke, an Austrian émigré who, like Buhrich, had fled Europe. He set up a practice in New Zealand and was also refused registration with the local architectural body, but was fortunate with his patronage and built some interesting houses. Thoroughly steeped in European culture, Plischke considered 'the aim to be to achieve a synthesis of the conception of space and sculptural quality. Each of these two components must be evolved out of the function and the construction of a building.' Although Buhrich was much more plain speaking and would not have chosen these words to express his vision, this philosophy is embodied in the Buhrich House II.

The last interview Hugh Buhrich gave before he died was with architectural critic Elizabeth Farrelly, for *Architecture Australia*. In it, he explained in plain and practical terms how many of the sculptural elements, particularly the roof and ceiling, came about, and, indeed, they were the result of 'function and construction'. But there is too much ingenuity and beauty for one to be the mere result of another. The main living space is large and open, 10 metres by 7 metres. One wall of glass faces north-east, to the impressive view across Middle Harbour. The interior palette is natural – a mix of smooth black slate flooring, silver ash veneer for cupboards, hand-cut local sandstone for the wall that houses the fireplace, cedar boards for the ceiling, and concrete for the wall. There is nothing particularly special in this combination in itself; it is how it is used that makes it extraordinary.

The dominant feature is the incredible wave ceiling which gives an organic, expressionist feel to the room. Cedar boards were steamed to make them pliable, and then Buhrich nailed each one into place. They have stood the test of time remarkably well. Facing the bush is a 'floating' concrete wall inset with slim steel columns to provide support. The concrete wall is partially obscured inside by a carpet customised by Buhrich with a dark red wave pattern running through it – a subtle echo of the ceiling above.

Years of designing furniture for clients enabled Buhrich to integrate most of the furniture needs of the house into the overall plan. Very few extra items were needed, and so the interior retains a completely resolved feel. The dining table sits on the slightly raised back platform of the living area. Its simple structure of a metal bar with acrylic ribs supporting the smoked glass top gives the appearance of being barely there. Where the table meets the rough sandstone wall, there is a picture window, precisely the same width, which serves to extend the eye-line along the table's surface to the bush outside.

The kitchen, accessed by the raised dining area, is compact but open to the larger living space. A bank of 15 press-open cupboards in silver ash veneer provides the divide between the kitchen and living space in a functional but sculptural way. More sculptural than functional, however, is the external staircase. Precast in concrete, it extends from a narrow deck outside the living area to the level below. Neil Buhrich points to his father's dislike of bureaucracy and there is something rather rebellious about this precarious twisting, turning, open-to-the elements staircase.

One of the most remarkable aspects of this already remarkable house is the bathroom. Nothing quite prepares you for it. Lulled by warm, organic shapes and natural tones, the fire-engine red room in seamless fibreglass takes you completely by surprise. Again, Elizabeth Farrelly's article quotes Buhrich's practical view of its genesis. He had been boat building in fibreglass and was familiar with its properties. He didn't like fussy bathrooms but did like occasional strong colour. He presents it casually, as though there was no other conceivable outcome for this set of parameters. With a large, uncurtained window to the view, nature is part of the decor and this combination of the highly man-made within a natural context somehow makes it all the more effective.

Buhrich has described this house as his 'most intensely personal' project, and it hopefully would have gratified him to learn that, in March 2006, it was named 'Building of the Decade' for the 1970s by a panel of RAIA judges. The architect refused registration all those years ago had designed a building which not only garnered much international acclaim (French critic Françoise Fromonot described it 'a truly radical building'), but has now been embraced as one of Australia's most defining domestic residences.

OPPOSITE The compact kitchen with its simple bank of built-in cupboards is enhanced by the beauty of the wave ceiling and the natural light it allows into the room.

OVERLEAF, LEFT PAGE The bright red fibreglass bathroom is something of a tour de force in a house of natural toned materials. The floor-to-ceiling windows ensure that the view of the trees and water creates a natural element in this extraordinary man-made space.

OVERLEAF, RIGHT PAGE Wood panelling creates a corner for a double bed; the door leads directly to the bathroom.

THE L

IAN McKAY

BSTER BAY HOUSE

1972

The intention was to create a building that sat lightly upon the land. As a result, many of the descriptions of the house liken it to a tent, a nest or even a giant seabird.

PREVIOUS PAGE Blending into the silvery greys of the surrounding bush setting is the holiday house commissioned by celebrated Australian photographer David Moore.

THIS PAGE The entrance to the house is via a timber walkway, and the door itself is protected by a canvas hood which, over time, has become as lichen-covered as the surrounding rocks.

OPPOSITE Ian McKay acknowledges the dual influences of Australian vernacular and Japanese architecture. Hence, the ability to mix a corrugated material for the roof with the sliding timber screens that divide the living area from the deck.

OPPOSITE The series of triangular windows running from ground level to the top of the children's sleeping area is a defining aspect of the house. They form part of the intricate design of the joinery and, facing north, allow light in all day.

OVERLEAF The entire structure of the building is exposed internally, and it is this honesty and lack of embellishment that appealed to David Moore. Ian McKay points out the need for precision in design and documentation. 'Every single thing was there...every decision was made. Otherwise it simply wouldn't have fitted.'

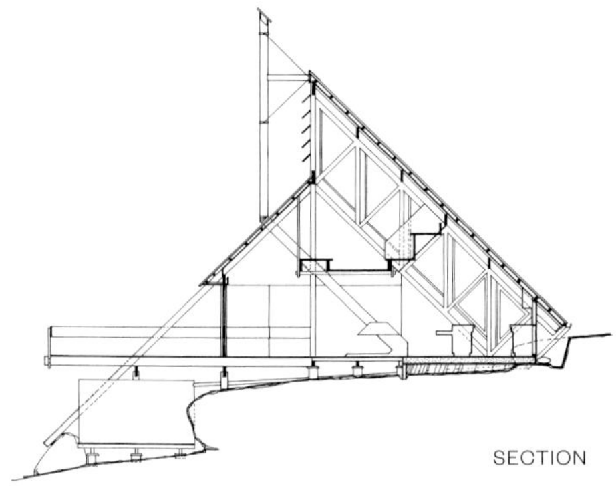

SECTION

'The house is a small cathedral of timber that caresses the trees' is the poetic description given by photographer David Moore of his Ian McKay-designed holiday house. On the New South Wales Central Coast, McKay describes the land it stands on as 'one of the most beautiful sites I have ever approached'. Set high above the bay, on the edge of Bouddi National Park and overlooking Brisbane Water, it is a tangle of mature angophoras and, in Moore's words, 'lichen-covered rocks as big as houses'. Moore had acquired it in 1968 and, recently divorced, wanted a weekender within reasonable striking distance of Sydney. He was a camping and bushwalking enthusiast, but with four children in tow, a house provided a slightly more permanent version of tented accommodation. Regarding his role as essentially custodial, Moore had a great deal of respect for the land, and the intention was to create a building that sat lightly upon it. As a result, many of the descriptions of the house liken it to a tent, a nest or even a giant seabird.

The siting of the house was immediately evident to architect and client alike, who agreed to place the building on a rock shelf, with the deck cantilevered off to the west and 'embracing an enormous Sydney red gum'. The house would command 180-degree views from its perch high on the rock. McKay's vision was for a recessive house that blended tonally with the surrounding environment, but its precise execution was a more difficult matter. David Moore was one of Australia's most celebrated photographers and, as such, highly visual. His father was the renowned architect John D. Moore and his brother Tony Moore was also an architect. Moore himself had undertaken many architectural commissions, and so understood the profession extremely well. With all those connections, Moore could have chosen anyone but, on reflection, McKay believes the Leppington Boys' Home, a project he did in conjunction with Philip Cox for the Presbyterian Church, may provide the answer.

'Moore had photographed the Leppington job and it was as much a springboard for this house as anything. It was very spare and had some innovative social thinking about it. It had an authenticity, simplicity and a modesty that David would have appreciated.'

Moore was, says McKay, 'an exacting client. My first design...he just sent me away. You always knew where you were with David,' he says philosophically.

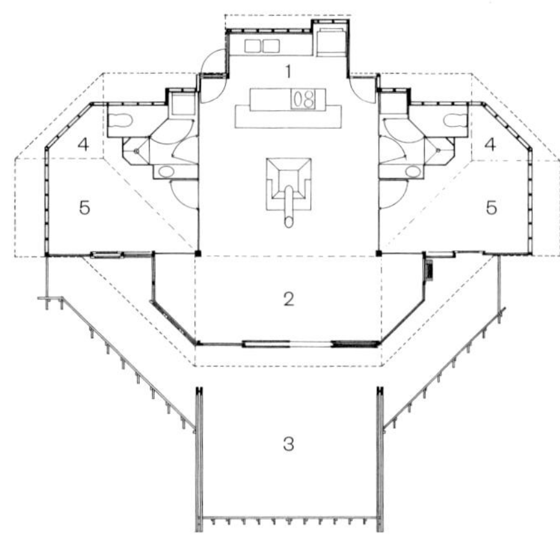

1 Kitchen
2 Living
3 Deck
4 Bathroom
5 Bedroom

LFB 603

The second fared little better. 'I knew they weren't quite right myself, but the third one, he knew it was absolutely right.

'Poised on the rock, as he suggested, embracing the angophora trees, spaces flowing up and around, snug bedrooms, views from the pillow, open living spaces in and out – I think I met his asking.'

Indeed, to satisfy this list of simple, life-affirming requests, a great deal of ingenuity has been applied. The house is essentially symmetrical, designed around a large open-plan living/dining/kitchen area, extending out to the west-facing deck. On each side of this space are small double bedrooms with views out to the bush and sky. A functional shower room sits beside each bedroom. Above this area is the kids' bunk room accessed by a ladder, which in itself creates a sense of adventure.

Six bunk beds (the floor and the supports for the beds are part of the structure) fit into the space, which is open to the living area below. This ensures the children could be involved with what was happening in the main living area. Lisa Moore, David's daughter, remembers lying in bed, eavesdropping on the post-dinner conversations of the adults.

There is a communal sense about the space, achieved not only through spatial considerations, but also through the spareness and simplicity of the design. As well as the clear influence of Japanese architecture, McKay also acknowledges something of the early Australian tradition in his approach. The house lacks any extraneous embellishment, giving it a sense of honesty which goes some way to explaining how it has managed to stand the test of time. Architectural writer Philip Drew has even gone so far as to call it 'a thoroughly modern masterpiece'.

Designed in 1969, the house wasn't completed until 1972, partly due to the nature of its construction. The site's beauty was matched only by its difficulty. Initially, access was via a fire trail which only extended to the base of the site. No wonder Central Coast builders shied away from such an arduous project. But, in the end, Moore found his man – Peter Velling. McKay explains, 'He was an ex-shipwright and did everything himself from beginning to end. It took him an awfully long time as he had to carry all the materials up by hand. He was very interested in the project, otherwise he couldn't have sustained it. It was a labour of love. The only time he had assistance was to lift the truss. That was an amazing day. The posts were up, tied back to angophoras or rocks and we all hauled it up and he climbed up the truss and bolted it in place.'

Lisa Moore remembers feeling that 'we all knew that new ground was being broken; this wasn't any "ordinary" holiday house, it was an adventure'.

The house is built in tallow wood, oregon and 3/16 plywood for ceilings and walls. Its ability to sit lightly on the land comes both from the precision of its design and a certain 'thinness' of execution. 'Adrian Boss, one of the finest delineators I have ever employed, did the documentation for me,' says McKay. 'Every single thing was there, every junction, every decision was made. Otherwise it simply wouldn't have fitted.' In fact, everything needed to fit because nothing is covered up. The structural workings of the building are undisguised and on display, and are the very elements that give the space its visual interest. Any patterning in this spare interior comes from the lines of the beams themselves and the shafts of sunlight that filter through the slatted Japanese-style sliding doors onto the deck.

The asbestos roofing material, Super-Six AC, was chosen for its robustness and longevity, but also for aesthetic reasons. While McKay now admits it was a mistake to use it, the hope was that it would weather and become like rock, allowing the building to recede into the landscape. And, indeed, the grey lichen-covered sheets have taken on the appearance of the surrounding bush.

As for the budget, there was never really any discussion, says McKay. 'It was a holiday house and there was nothing lavish about it. That is what I like about it. Every structural piece does two or three jobs.' In fact, the costs have been recorded as totalling $27,524.

It requires little in the way of furniture to feel complete. A generous dining table and benches, some portable director's chairs, low beds and fitted lights are all that is needed. Photographer Anthony Browell observed the atmosphere well. 'Despite this formal symmetry, the house seems very casual, the sort of house where discarded bathers, undies and toppled dominoes don't wreck the feel of the place.'

For Moore, the surrounding area of 'The Bay' was a source of inspiration. 'I found new meaning to life and photography in the early 1970s. The rocks and the trees, the beaches and the ocean gradually spoke to me and I learned to love them,' he said. One of his most beautiful portraits is 'The Impossible Tree', an angophora sited on the land, with a myriad twists and turns to its branches.

As it turned out, McKay was to spend more time than most architects do in houses they have designed for clients. He married David Moore's first wife, Jenny, and so many a weekend was spent in the house with his stepchildren.

After 20 years, the inspiration Moore had taken from 'The Bay' began to wear thin, and he considered selling the house. His children, in particular Lisa and Michael, were extremely keen to keep it in the family. It was a big part of their lives and they didn't want to let it go. 'The original vision is still there, it hasn't been altered and I am very, very grateful for that,' says McKay. 'A good house can only come out of enjoyment and this was a wonderful experience from beginning to end. Best of all, it was a venue for some very happy times, with happy people in a happy place.'

The day in the Easter holidays when my family and I visited Lisa Moore and her husband and children at the Lobster Bay House was a special one. We parked on the road and climbed the 45-degree slope to the base of the site. From there we huffed and puffed our way up the rock steps to the house itself. It has a quality that makes you feel instantly relaxed. It's to do with the lack of interior decoration, except for some weathered rubber thongs found by Moore on local beaches, and nailed directly to the wood itself; the open aspect of the living areas; the climb to the bunk bed area and the direct connection to nature, all of which conspire to create the ultimate holiday house.

We had lunch, a glass of wine and walked up the stone steps (that Moore had painstakingly placed to look as though nature herself had laid them there) to Top Rock. The view did not disappoint. As we left, my son asked, 'Are those people old friends?' I explained that this was the first time we had met. McKay would, no doubt, be pleased that the house continues the spirit of 'happy times, with happy people'.

RICHARD LEPLASTR

THE PALM HOUSE

ER 1973–1975

'Leplastrier has a deeply rooted minimalistic approach to his work. He makes no unnecessary moves. Less is always more. He believes in simplified spaces that give room for things to happen and nature to enter.'

GUNNEL ADLERCREUTZ

Judge in the International Spirit of Nature Wood Architecture Award, 2004

PREVIOUS PAGE The sleeping pavilion, as seen through the palms, shows the fine timber work and canvas panel sitting below the roof of corrugated copper.

THIS PAGE The guiding principle of the garden, designed around a grove of ancient palms, was to look at what was already growing there, and work with large leaves close to the house and smaller leaves further away to give the illusion of space.

OPPOSITE The entrance is low and dimly lit, in contrast to the height and openness of the living space beyond. The woven timber panel to the right allows filtered light through, and serves to delay, momentarily, the visual experience of the space to come.

Richard Leplastrier's Palm House has been called an upside-down boat in the middle of paradise; a garden shed; a splendid curiosity; the most impractical house in Australia; the most beautiful house in Australia. Impracticality, like beauty, is in the eye of the beholder; its owner appreciates the latter and does not acknowledge the former. From the start, he says, he experienced 'excitement at what I had rather than looking for lack in the building'.

When Leplastrier first visited the site, he says, 'we were sitting with him in the garden, amongst the palms, and he looked at the trees and said, "You have got your house, here is the canopy." It was very much his first response – that the house was already there, and from that point us working together was something of a foregone conclusion.' Even before the drawings were done, Leplastrier had the scheme in his head. 'He knew to insert the house between the trees on the southern boundary, to enclose the garden with a wall and, while the house should be as frail as possible, there would be a strong sense of floor and wall. The roof should be – if breathtaking is too extreme a word – at least it should defy the rules of frailty,' explains the owner.

Nature and the outdoor life have long been pleasures of Leplastrier. 'He told me his earliest childhood memory was driving with his family towards the Blue Mountains and seeing the change in the horizon as the mountains rose up around Penrith,' says the owner. His father's job with Caltex Oil Company meant the family moved many times while Leplastrier was growing up. His formative years, from nine to 14, were spent in Hobart. 'We lived in a little house looking right down Storm Bay. I had my own dinghy and Dad had a sailing boat. I used to catch fish and sell them to local pubs. I even had a rifle and would shoot rabbits.' While this life gave him a love of nature, Leplastrier points out that his parents were conventional. 'Mum was a nice middle-class North Shore girl, and as a family there were no pretensions to the arts, music or reading.' Those influences were to come later and with great significance.

Studying architecture at the University of Sydney brought him into contact with his first real mentor, drawing teacher Lloyd Rees, who was to become a lifelong friend. 'Wednesday was art day and he would take us out to look at the city,' says Leplastrier. 'He loved landscape and had a passion for architecture.'

After university he worked with architect Don Gazzard and followed the Opera House construction with interest. 'These shells were slowly growing,

THIS PAGE Leplastrier's drawing of the Palm House scheme.

OPPOSITE The living/dining area is simply furnished with a daybed at one end and a table by Jeffrey Broadfield at its centre. The retractable roof opens to the palms and the sky beyond.

increment by increment, and when a friend of mine got a job with Utzon, I thought, if he can, I can.' He remembers, late one evening, writing on a piece of old butter paper with a 6B pencil, 'Dear Mr Utzon, I have been out (of university) for a couple of years. I just admire your work so much. I hardly know anything. I would love to work for you.' Many years later, architect Peter Myers was looking through Utzon's correspondence in the Mitchell Library in Sydney and found Leplastrier's letter. He noticed that it was smudged across the bottom in such a way as to indicate that Utzon had rubbed his finger over the words to check that Leplastrier had used a really good quality 6B pencil.

Fortune was on his side in other respects. Both Utzon and Leplastrier lived in Bayview, on Sydney's Northern Beaches, where Leplastrier was building his first house for the Halford family. Utzon saw it and liked it very much. Leplastrier had also spotted Utzon examining his little sailing boat – a moth – but was too shy to introduce himself. When Leplastrier got the call to go to the Opera House there was no interview – he was employed by Utzon's right-hand man Mogens Prip-Buus on the spot. 'When we were confronted with all those amazing problems, there was never a sense that we couldn't do it, because we had Utzon on our side,' says Leplastrier.

He saw in Utzon 'a man utterly without prejudice – meaning before judgment – he approached everything without prejudice.' Leplastrier also witnessed the process of simplification that Utzon went through when designing a house for himself at Bayview. 'It took five years and five drawers of drawings. It had an incredible impact on me,' he says.

The next phase of his learning took him to Japan where he studied under Professor Tomoya Masuda, an architect and philosopher. Here Leplastrier learnt an appreciation both of the clear floor plan from which a building grows and the importance of the origin of things. When Masuda visited the Palm House as a work in progress, he knew the origin of the design. 'Ah, you have discovered the palm tree,' he said. The owner also recalls how Masuda had come from Peter Muller's house at Whale Beach and commented that, while Muller's house was built to view the sea, this one was built to hear it.

After study, Leplastrier worked with architect Kenzo Tange. Still only 26 years old, he taught English in a girls' high school for two hours before working a 10- to 12-hour day in the architectural practice. He then returned to his tiny tearoom in a temple. 'It was in that room I learnt about scale and harbour,' he says. While he worked with some of the greatest architectural minds in Japan, he had to come to terms philosophically with the Japanese trait of indirectness. 'It was a small office – maybe 15 people – and problems were discussed around and around. I was young and a bit brash and they were very patient with me. They sought harmony, not conflict.'

After a year of this intense, measured existence, he bought a motorbike, fitted it with long-range tanks, packed a small bag of spare parts and some sketchbooks and set off. His eight-month overland trip eventually took him to London, where he worked in an architectural practice for a year.

In his time away, Leplastrier had been exposed to great minds and great works of enormous cultural diversity. After returning to Australia in 1970, it took him five years, he says, 'to steel myself against our abrasive cultural qualities. I was unbelievably sensitive and Australia seemed so blunt.' What gave him emotional sustenance was a growing understanding of nature in general, and the significance of the Australian landscape in particular. 'I came to Lovett Bay to live in 1971/72, to the original old cottage. I took a sledgehammer to all the internal, and most of the external, walls and worked, as I have always done, engaging the landscape.'

The Palm House, one of his first commissions after his return to Australia, also had a hand in helping him to settle back into the country. 'I poured myself

OPPOSITE This corridor, open to the garden on the left, shows the 'service spine' in rammed earth on the right, housing the electricals and plumbing, and hence the kitchen and bathroom.

THIS PAGE The entrance echoes the aesthetic of Japan, illustrated by the sensitive placement of the stone steps and the simplicity of the sliding timber door set in the rammed earth (pisé) wall.

into the place by way of reconciliation,' he recalls. The client was introduced to Leplastrier through his friend Mary Andrews (ex-wife of designer Gordon Andrews) and all he knew about him was that he had returned from Japan, had worked with Utzon, was a sailor and very much of the earth. Before working with Leplastrier, the owner took a look at the house he had designed for the Halford family in Bayview. 'It was an extraordinarily beautiful house – quite a revelation. Japan was everywhere and, as I hadn't been to Japan at that stage, it was the closest thing I had seen.'

He recalls Leplastrier standing in winter, in his greatcoat, at his drawing board discussing the 'tyranny of comfort', as he worked on details. 'Richard was very persuasive. If he felt I wasn't seeing something, he would do a mock-up. To show me a wall height he would put string between the trees and hang a piece of newspaper over it.'

Leplastrier's houses tend to be secluded in location and rarely publicised, and the Palm House is a case in point. Hidden from the street, 'the heart of this house is the garden, into which the house dissolves at its edges like a mirage', says Leplastrier. It challenges one's conception of a house. To many, there is an expectation of four solid walls, a roof – pitched or flat – window openings and a garden accessed via a door. Leplastrier's thinking is radical because he throws out those notions and creates a whole new vocabulary.

With its single rammed earth wall, canvas walls, and gallery roof that resembles, in Leplastrier's own words, 'a pair of upturned rowing sculls', it is so thoroughly integrated into the site that it has a timeless quality. The only nod to the decade of its creation is a white Joe Colombo table in the garden, bought by the owner in London before the house was finished.

All functionality is exquisitely expressed. The rammed earth wall retains the suggestion of the timber planks that formed it; the timber gulleys running the interior length of the house are fashioned in redwood factory offcuts with bands of laminated oregon and are, according to Leplastrier, like 'a musical instrument'. The canvas walls combine with the steel framing to evoke lightness and impermanence.

The entrance to the house recalls Japan. Irregular stones, as though placed by nature, lead to a sliding door and narrow entrance covered by vines. This space is low and intimate in scale and so the sense of awe, as one steps into the main living area, is enhanced by the contrast.

'I learnt from the Japanese about the structure of landscape and how a good work of architecture brings the landscape into being,' says Leplastrier. And when you enter this first room it is to the garden that you are immediately drawn.

The house's structure is simple in that the rammed earth wall becomes a 'service spine'. All electrics and plumbing run along it, as do the kitchen and timber-crafted bathroom with sliding privacy screens. The bedroom is on the garden side and, while modest in dimensions, is rendered uplifting with its arched windows infilled with canvas.

The subtext of the house is the balance of the organic and the measured. The proportion of the arch is pure geometry – a square and a half circle – and the regularity and repetition of the terrazzo tiles point to what Leplastrier recalls as 'the original structural system and module that gives an inner order – it goes beautifully with the garden as they counterbalance one another'. For the owner it is the rhythm set by these recurring lines in the construction module – the repetition from the floor planks to the ribs in the roof – that renders it 'too good to be accidental'.

When asked if it garnered praise from the architectural profession or brought potential clients, Leplastrier is philosophical. 'The house wasn't published anywhere, but occasionally possible clients came and fled. A wonderful man called Mr Christmas came to see us on the job when the Palm

THIS PAGE The Japanese-style bathtub sits behind a sliding screen. This exquisitely detailed room illustrates how boatbuilding skills have been incorporated into the building.

OPPOSITE The vaulted bedroom showcases the fine timber work and the use of canvas infills.

OVERLEAF, LEFT PAGE Leplastrier's inspiration for pleated canvas came from a rickshaw, and echoes the pattern of the cabbage tree fronds.

OVERLEAF, RIGHT PAGE A ceramic bowl by Anders Ousback sits in front of the richly textured pisé wall that runs through the house.

House was three-quarters finished. I could see the look on his face. We laughed and admitted we couldn't work together – it was the best test.'

The relationship with clients is at the heart of Leplastrier's practice. 'A good house is an outer garment for their lives, and if you don't have a good rapport with those people, and overlapping values by which you live, well, we are wasting each other's time.' The owner of the Palm House has, says Leplastrier, brought the house into flower, the ultimate compliment from the architect.

While gentle in manner, Leplastrier has little time for those who don't appreciate the things he holds dear. The owner of a house he had designed some years earlier took issue when the architect, requested to consult on an alteration, proposed a simply crafted study space with a slit window looking to the water. The client needed more storage space for his suits. 'Why don't you have half as many suits and have them twice as well made and leave the study as it is?' asked Leplastrier.

He is aware this has limited the number of commissions he has accepted over the years, but when the relationship works, the pleasure he gets from it justifies the process. For 'a cottage for Philip Searle and Barry Ross, production drawings were done, with brilliant builder Rolley Clarke, on the back of pieces of plywood. It was a lovely collaboration.'

He acknowledges there has to be a degree of faith. 'There are times when it is hard to understand why things have to be done a certain way, and the great client will trust the process.' Leplastrier also equates the size of the 'work in progress' file to the success of the job. A thin file is a good file and the Searle/Ross job was a mere centimetre thick.

When asked the size of the file on the Palm House, both architect and owner agree it was a 'no file' job. 'There wasn't much paperwork,' says the owner. 'That would have been a parallel universe.' What is not in doubt is that the house and its 'fit' with its owner is second to none. Leplastrier said in an architectural conference in 1993 that 'things only become truly beautiful with appreciative use'. If this is the case, the Palm House and its true beauty are beyond question. Leplastrier acknowledges that, when first inhabited, a house is not at its most beautiful, only becoming so when it has been used, with love. 'This is the one that has shown that resonance over time.'

It is also a house that would have been impossible to create without a client who had faith. While the owner says he was practical and had no sense that he was commissioning (which sounds too grand for his intentions) what is essentially a work of art, the truth is that without such an exceptional client the house could not have been built to the original design. Leplastrier recalls that he 'never pulled the pin on anything and said many times there should be no compromise. If we ran out of money we just held off for a while.'

Leplastrier's reputation for integrity has been recognised both locally and internationally. He has won Australia's highest architectural award – the RAIA Gold Medal (1999) – and, in 2004, the International Spirit of Nature Wood Architecture Award; other winners include Renzo Piano, Kengo Kuma and Peter Zumthor. In 2009, he received the Dreyer Foundation Prize of Honour for his commitment to sustainability, the first non-Dane to receive it.

Writing about the award in *The Australian* newspaper, Philip Drew pointed out, 'Leplastrier's quietly restrained approach and philosophy is more akin to the ideas of mid-nineteenth century American nature writer Henry David Thoreau who posed the question, "How much house is really necessary?"' I think it is a question that is answered by the Palm House.

When asked how he feels sitting in the house years later, Leplastrier says, 'I love to come here. I always have and it gives me the same pleasure now as always. But I doubt I would have the courage to do it now. We were both young and foolish, and we were both driven by beauty. And still are.'

T

GLENN MURCUTT

E KEMPSEY HOUSE

1974–1975/1980

'By mixing together Australia's vernacular style with the clean lines of modernism, he has created an architecture that is both true to place and unexpectedly rigorous, like a bow and arrow made of titanium.'

JIM LEWIS

The New York Times

PREVIOUS PAGE The offset of the two pavilions that comprise the Kempsey House is clearly shown from this south-eastern end of the house. The entry is via the covered verandah with direct access to the timber-lined living room.

THIS PAGE The Pressu, a lightweight armchair following the Bauhaus aesthetic, was designed by Yrjö Kukkapuro and imported from Finland by Murcutt.

OPPOSITE The large pivoting door from the north-western verandah to the bathroom and bedrooms appears to be part of the wall when closed.

OPPOSITE The living room imparts a sense of warmth and honesty through the use of timber-lined walls and ceiling. The furnishings and lighting are Nordic, illustrating Murcutt's life-long love of the work of such designers as Yrjö Kukkapuro, Alvar Aalto and Arne Jacobsen.

OVERLEAF Simplicity and symmetry are the hallmarks of the kitchen-dining space. The degree to which the design is completely open-plan was still new at the time. The banks of louvres, manufactured by Pillar Naco, form the northern and southern walls of each pavilion.

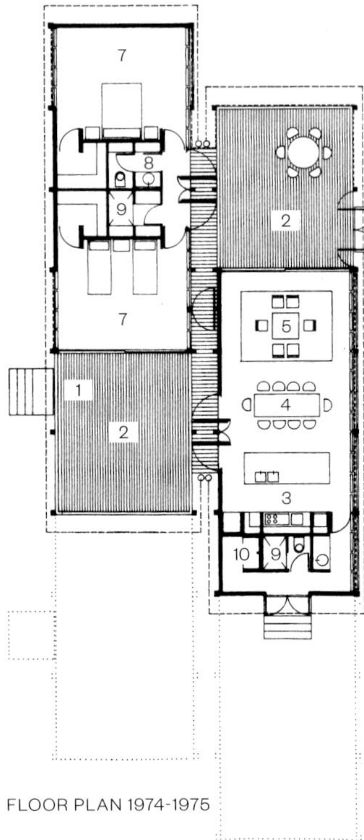

FLOOR PLAN 1974-1975

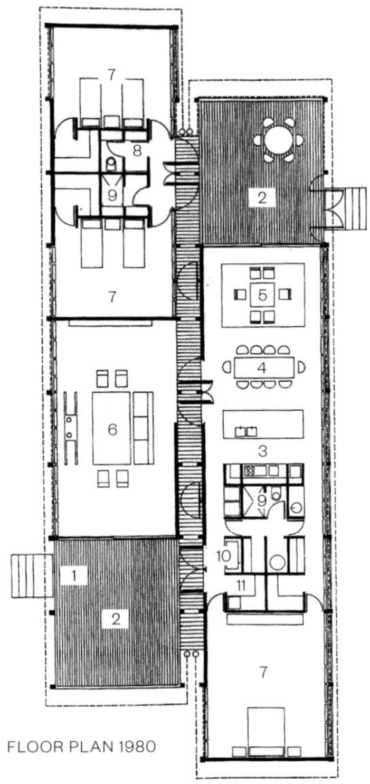

FLOOR PLAN 1980

N →

1 Entry steps
2 Deck
3 Kitchen
4 Dining
5 Living
6 Lounge
7 Bedroom
8 WC
9 Bathroom
10 Laundry
11 Store

Glenn Murcutt was already an award-winning architect prior to the Kempsey House, but there was something in the nature of the brief and the client, the remoteness of the site, and Murcutt's own life stage that propelled his work to a new level. No-one else could have designed the house at that time, as it represents so much that is core to his values and vision. He had studied Mies van der Rohe's classic, the Farnsworth House (1950), under the direction of his father. 'I had to read [the article in *Architectural Forum*] about five times to get all the answers right, and my father ended up by saying that it may well turn out to be the twentieth century's most incredible house,' says Murcutt.

He also talks of the strong influence exerted by some buildings on a farm his father owned. 'I said to my brother Gary that if we keep the farm, I know exactly how to design a building within the shed. It was about four metres wide and I said we can insert a kitchen and bathroom core, make a bedroom at one end, the living room at the other, it is all orientated the right way.'

While these are two primary influences, they form only part of the story. To understand the brilliance of the Kempsey House, aka the Marie Short House, it is necessary to know more of Murcutt the man – childhood, other influences that shaped him, and the resulting strength and clarity of his philosophy.

Murcutt's father, Arthur, born in 1899, left the Sydney slums of Surry Hills at 15 to go sheep shearing in Bourke. In 1920, he went pioneering through the villages of Watut and Upper Watut River in Papua New Guinea. Out from Wau, in the Surprise Creek area, cannibalism was still prevalent. Murcutt tells how his father, a boxer, would disarm a Kukukuku chief with a punch in the solar plexus and a faceful of pepper. He also describes how his father chummed around with Hollywood legend Errol Flynn before he was a star. The boat he financed and Arthur built was sabotaged because of the debts Flynn had run up with locals.

It was to a gold mine in the heart of Papua New Guinea that Arthur brought his wife Daphne Powys in 1934. Glenn was born in England, on the couple's way to the Berlin Olympics in 1936, but spent the first six years of his life in PNG.

'We lived in the region known as the Upper Watut on the junction with Surprise Creek, which was the home of the Kukukuku people,' says Murcutt. 'Their approach, sighted only by the snake-like movement of the grasses in the landscape, created great fear in the local miners. My father, while fearful also, knew how to handle them.'

ATLAS OF THE WORLD

He says, 'Our survival was related to observation, listening, seeing, smelling, touching'. This ensured his profound connection to nature, and he still appreciates the simple beauty and logical form of the conical huts of the Lower Highlands. Life revolved around swimming in the pool his father built by putting a concrete wall across a creek, and searching the kunai grass for the long red tail tied to mail dropped from a Gipsy Moth by way of a postal service.

Local villagers cared for him, his sister and brother, and when he came back to Australia in 1942, at the age of six, he spoke only Pidgin English. 'A helicopter was "Impelar Mixmaster bilong im God". It is an amazing language,' says Murcutt.

His father had invested in land, amassing more than 100 sites in Clontarf, in Sydney's north. The family moved to the seaside suburb of Manly where Murcutt marvelled at the number of cars and white people, while remaining terrified of the black habit-clad nuns from the nearby convent. School was challenging, especially when it came to the written word, and to this day he feels much more able to articulate ideas than write them down.

With proceeds from the mine, Arthur Murcutt bought a concrete brick maker and designed modern houses on sites he owned. In 1949, he opened a joinery factory run by an 'incredible Scottish craftsman called Bill Davidson' to prefabricate elements for his projects. By the time Murcutt was 18, he had laboured on building sites – mixed concrete and poured footings – crafted different sorts of windows and staircases in the joinery factory, and worked up drawings and photographed models of his father's designs to submit to council. If ever there were a practical training for an architect, this was it.

Arthur Murcutt subscribed to a number of American architectural journals, such as *Arts & Architecture*, and encouraged his son to read them until he understood the principles they described. 'My father introduced me to Gordon Drake's work in 1948 when I was 12, alongside Philip Johnson, Frank Lloyd Wright and Craig Ellwood and many others. All this was part of my childhood.'

The other traits Arthur Murcutt strove to engender in his five children were a musical mindset and mental toughness through sporting achievement. 'We lived in a three-storey house with seven pianos. It was like a conservatorium,' says Murcutt. 'The discipline of getting up at six in the morning – a half mile swim, come back for half an hour's piano practice, then walk to school.'

Architecture was the only career he considered, 'and while my father gave me all the encouragement, he gave me no financial assistance. He said, "Now that you have got into university, son, pay your own fees and get a job. You work in an office and you do studies in architecture half time. Furthermore, don't go for the money, go for the experience."

'He gave me some names – Peter Muller, Harry Seidler, Neville Gruzman and Bill Lucas. Neville took me on for nineteen and sixpence per week.' Not only did he assist Gruzman on a number of houses, including the Goodman House in Middle Cove and the Benjamin House in Longueville, but he was also exposed to the thinking of Bill and Ruth Lucas, who shared the office space, and whose Glass House (1957) in Castlecrag remains one of the groundbreaking designs of the era. 'Neville was as tough as nails,' says Murcutt, 'but he would take our university work and critique it, and he was a marvellous teacher for me.'

Another architect he acknowledges as influential was Russell Jack. 'He taught me to detail and to draw, and he had a very powerful affinity with, and respect for, the work of Frank Lloyd Wright. It was also the first generation to become interested in the Australian landscape and building.'

A three-year period in Europe followed an annual pattern of eight months of work and four months' travel. Of all places he visited, the country that was critical to his architectural development was Finland, through the work of Alvar Aalto. 'The use of concrete and timber, the white walls and the screening systems...it was a real turning point for me.'

Returning to Australia in the mid-Sixties, he took a job with one of Sydney's most prestigious practices, Ancher, Mortlock, Murray & Woolley, but by 1969 was ready to set up on his own. 'My father gave me this piece of advice: "Now that you are entering practice, you must remember to start off the way you would like to finish. And remember that for every compromise you knowingly make in your work, the result represents the quality of your next client." That is something I have lived by.'

He launched his practice in a recession and designed a house for his brother Douglas and wife Ruth, with his other brother Gary doing most of the building work. He had one other job, for his accountant, which became a lesson in the importance of quality products. The budget was radically reduced mid-project and, in an attempt to save money, Murcutt specified fittings he lived to regret. 'It taught me to save on the size of a building, never to save on products,' he says.

In 1969, he also undertook a bold renovation of his own house in Mosman, grafting a homage to Mies van der Rohe onto the back of a traditional semi. Internal walls dissolved to form open living spaces, and the floating platform extended the structure into the garden. Importantly, in 1972, it won an award. The RAIA Gray & Mulroney Award came with a round-the-world plane ticket. He used it, first, to travel to Los Angeles to meet an architect he had long admired – one of the self-proclaimed 'three blind Mies', Craig Ellwood. 'He was very generous and gave me access to the Daphne House and to a lot of other buildings,' says Murcutt. 'But when I broached the subject of climate control inside his buildings, he looked at me as though it was the silliest question he had ever been asked.' When Ellwood told him that they were air-conditioned, it was another turning point in Murcutt's career. 'I recognised several things – no overhangs means potential for leaking windows, you get good winter sun but unwanted summer sun, and no window openings, no eaves overhang, and a flat roof, poorly insulated, means you can't have that sort of building in my country.'

On the same trip, Murcutt also visited the highly influential Maison de Verre (1931) in Paris, by Pierre Chareau and Bernard Bijvoet. 'I was given absolute access to the house for hours and hours. I was struck by the skill of the metal fabricator, Dalbet, because he was the one who designed many of the components to work in the way that the architects wanted them.'

It was this marriage of standardisation with craftsmanship that Murcutt was exploring in his own work that caused the Maison de Verre to resonate. In addition, it made use of active façades in a series of hopper and louvred panels.

The Laurie Short House (1972–73) directly preceded the Marie Short House. While it is Miesian in its metal-framed, rectangular structure, the two houses do have elements in common. 'When you look at Laurie's house, it has two wings and a corridor down the middle. In Marie Short's, one wing extends beyond the other to produce a verandah in the corner,' says Murcutt. 'This was an articulation that went further in Marie's house.' In the Laurie Short House, he also introduced metal venetians and a brise soleil to modify heat and light levels. This responsiveness to climate was to find fuller expression in his next project.

Marie Short, Laurie's mother, had bought land near Kempsey, in rural New South Wales, a seven-hour drive from Sydney. She had asked Bill Lucas to undertake some additions and alterations to an 1890s two-bedroom farmhouse, but when she saw her son's house, she approached Murcutt. Initially, Murcutt responded to the brief for alterations, but when they received the construction estimate from builder Bill Brenton, Murcutt said to Marie, 'Instead of spending so much money on the old house, why not build a new one?'

Her brief to Murcutt was poetic. 'She wanted it to be as cool as standing under a mulberry tree in summer and, as the tree loses leaves, as wonderfully warm in winter with the sun coming in. Marie really was a critical client in my development – she spoke thoughtfully and was incredibly perceptive.'

OPPOSITE Murcutt used flyscreening extensively to keep insects and rodents out, but also to allow maximum ventilation and a sense of openness.

OVERLEAF, LEFT PAGE The master bedroom, part of the 1980 addition, is in keeping with the original.

OVERLEAF, RIGHT PAGE Exterior view of the master bedroom. The offset of the pavilions is clear, as is the perfectly calibrated relationship of the water tanks to the house.

The siting of the house was immediately evident to Murcutt. 'It was very clear that you are connecting two bodies of water. One was the lake, which is fed by three springs, and the other was the bend in the Maria River, and you can capitalise on both views.' The landscape always informs us, he often says.

A part of the brief that never eventuated was the potential to dismantle the house and move it elsewhere on her land. 'I designed it so that it bolted together and you could take it apart in two wings, and put it on a truck.'

As it's so far from Sydney, site visits could only happen every three weeks. Relying on local labour, Murcutt realised that simple structure and detailing would ensure the best result. Marie Short had been collecting top quality timber from a local sawmill, and with this combination of factors, the design came quickly. 'I left the site on a Sunday and came back the following Friday with the drawings half-done because I knew the available materials and the brief.'

The house consists of two offset pavilions. In the original plan (Murcutt bought the house in 1980 and modified it), the axis of living/dining area faces the river to the west, with its orientation north; two bedrooms and a winter sitting room form the southern wing. Each pavilion has a wide verandah at one end. The house is about six metres above flood level. It is on stilts another 800 mm above ground level to ensure heavy rains do not splash into windows, open for ventilation, and creatures seeking higher ground can't easily come in. The pavilions are joined by a wide central gutter, which was originally the only guttering. With the later inclusion of rain tanks at the end of each pavilion, edge gutters were added.

Murcutt used flyscreening extensively to keep insects and rodents out, and for ventilation and a sense of openness – especially on the verandah adjoining the northern orientated living area. This becomes an extension of the living space, with the low penetrating winter sun enabling it to be used all year round.

Murcutt failed the 'sun and shade' course at the University of New South Wales, and, as someone who knows the positive driver failure can be, made sure he understood it absolutely. This house is an example of how climate is managed – the way it responds to the sun as the day and seasons pass; how cool breezes from the north-east are welcomed in summer and westerly winds are minimised in winter. Metal sun screens over glazed louvres, of Murcutt's design, line the northern roofing of the living/dining area and the winter sitting room, and regulate the sun entry seasonally. Glass louvres are used on the southern side and venetian blinds in aluminium and timber allow further control.

The roof emphasises the connection to the Australian vernacular and plays into the skill set of local builders. Everything Murcutt specified was available onsite or could be readily sourced locally or from catalogues. The simple, local hardwood post-and-beam design, modular frame and the interior lining of native hoop pine boards ensured the quality could be delivered and the building's integrity maintained. The effect is Nordic, enhanced by Murcutt's longstanding appreciation of the furniture and design of Alvar Aalto and Yrjö Kukkapuro, and the lights of Arne Jacobsen and Poul Henningsen. 'Every architectural student should have, as an integral part of their education, the whole history of furniture, of light and lighting,' says Murcutt.

Talking about Aalto, Murcutt says, 'I saw longevity in his ideas. It was about light, prospect, refuge and space. He understood materials, the relation of materials to spaces.' He could be talking about himself. In 1992 Murcutt received the Alvar Aalto Medal from Finland and, in 2002, the Pritzker Prize for architecture. The jury noted that he was an exception in a world of 'celebrity starchitects'. Murcutt has had the self-possession to take his own path and, in the words of Thoreau, has undertaken to 'do ordinary things extraordinarily well'. It is nothing short of what his father, Arthur, would have expected.

IWAN IWANOFF

HE KESSELL HOUSE

1975

There is no doubt that the material is intrinsic to the building's intent. The concrete feels organic, becoming weathered over time, which links it with the landscape.

PREVIOUS PAGE The façade is signature Iwanoff. The concrete blockwork remains original and unpainted, as Iwanoff intended.

THIS PAGE The detail shows how the blocks locked together, sometimes to form a simple design and, at others, to create a more complex pattern.

OPPOSITE The design of the approach to the house has a sense of gravitas. The blocks create asymmetrical columns on either side of the steps – formal and repetitive on the left and intricate and totemic on the right.

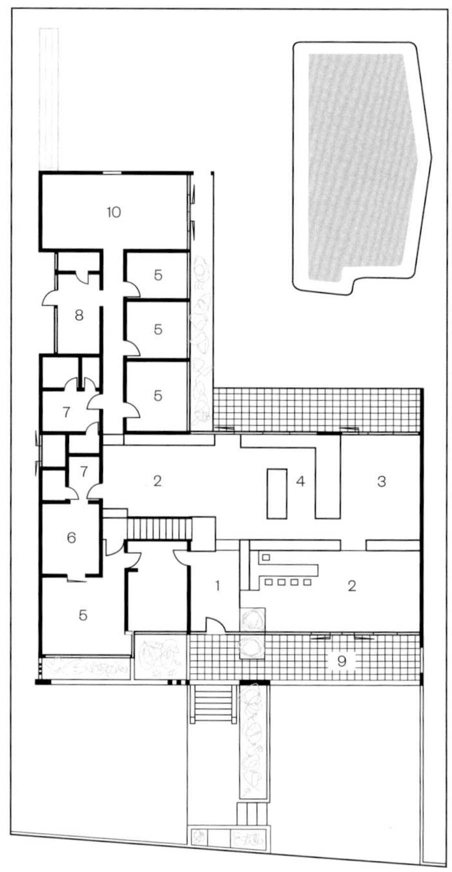

1 Entry
2 Living
3 Dining
4 Kitchen
5 Bedroom
6 Dressing room
7 Bathroom
8 Laundry
9 Terrace
10 Rumpus

'We would take that despised outcast of the building industry – the concrete block – out from underfoot in the gutter – find a hitherto unsuspected soul in it – make it live as a thing of beauty – textured as the trees.' These words were spoken by the great American architect Frank Lloyd Wright in the Twenties as he considered the structural approach he would take for his client Alice Millard's second house. Wright came up with an ingenious system in which precast concrete blocks interlocked, while the surface of the blocks created pattern and textural interest on the building's façade. Fifty years later, this concept was to resonate with the work of Perth-based architect Iwan Iwanoff, who also found beauty in the concrete block. Not all the 200 or so projects he designed in his career were built from this material, but it is the work for which he is best remembered.

Iwan Iwanoff was born in Bulgaria in 1919, and studied architecture during the Second World War at Munich University. His artistic sensibility was expanded by the course's strong emphasis on drawing, sculpture and design, and balanced by classes in structural engineering, which honed his practical skills. In the foreword to the exhibition catalogue *The Art of Architecture – The Architectural Drawings of Iwan Iwanoff (1919–1986)*, Iwanoff expert Duncan Richards points out, 'It was focused on training based upon a body of well established traditional design procedures and craft skills. The ultimate aim of the training was to develop and internalise semiautomatic "intuitive" judgments of visual order and visual coherence.' And what emerges strongly in his later work is this combination of crafted detailing within a rationalised structure. 'In my practice, the most exciting thing has always been the relationship between art and architecture,' Iwanoff said. His sketches of proposed buildings for clients were loose and lyrical with all the seductive powers of a romantic portrait. His plans, on the other hand, were intensely detailed, with every architectural element carefully delineated and described.

After working in a Munich architectural practice between 1948 and 1950, with Emil Freymuth, Iwanoff took the radical step of moving to Australia with his wife, Linda. Initially, he worked as a labourer in a local Boral factory which produced precast concete blocks until, through Bulgarian community connections, he met architect Harold Krantz. Krantz had a reputation for assisting migrant architects with the complexities of adapting to their new

culture and, in many cases, hired them to work for his practice, Krantz and Sheldon. As with other migrant architects featured in this book, the Board of Architects was often reluctant to recognise qualifications gained overseas, and careers could be stunted as a result. Apart from a year with Melbourne architects Yuncken Freeman in the early Sixties, Iwanoff was employed by Krantz and Sheldon until the mid Sixties when he was legitimately able to establish his own practice, The Studio of Iwanoff. However, right from the outset, Krantz had agreed that Iwanoff could undertake private projects, and his first independent commission was completed in 1951.

Much of Iwanoff's success came from his dedicated approach to clients and their requirements. He did not initially impose his views, instead learning as much as he could about what was wanted and how their lives operated. In his own words, he would 'swallow...more or less...and digest, and digest and digest...once you have all this the rest comes automatically'. The outcome would be a home that would more than satisfy his clients, and his reputation for empathy and understanding brought additional commissions. In this instance, Dr Kessell and his wife approached Iwanoff on the recommendation of previous clients, Dr Kessell's sister and her husband, Esther and David Schenberg, who owned an Iwanoff-designed house in Floreat, Perth. (The Schenbergs also commissioned a second house and a commercial building.)

Initially, the Kessells were not keen on the idea of a concrete block house, but Iwanoff was able to persuade them of its appropriateness. It is a house that Iwanoff himself had earmarked as significant and it would gratify him to know that the original concrete façade is still intact. To his great disappointment, many of the exteriors of his blockwork houses were subsequently painted, which he felt 'ruined the play of light' and turned them into 'something harsh and banal'.

There is no doubt that the material is intrinsic to the building's intent. The concrete feels organic, becoming weathered over time, which links it with the landscape. The decorative element created by blockwork is subtle, in the one soft shade of grey, while the interplay of solids and voids gives it sculptural depth. When painted, the surface becomes precise and delineated, robbing the building of its quiet power.

Like Wright before him, Iwanoff sought to transform this everyday building material, with its connotations of industry and economy, into something richly textured and beautiful. In the decade since he built his own concrete block house (1965–67), his use of the material had become more elaborate and the Kessell House is a fine example of his ability to balance intricate decoration within the context of structural restraint.

His detailed plans left nothing to chance, but the nature of the building work was intense. It was very different from the more conventionally constructed houses of the day, requiring specialist tradespeople who understood they were involved in the creation of something out of the ordinary. Iwanoff was known for his passion for his work, his hands-on approach and ability to infuse both clients and colleagues with enthusiasm. He told Duncan Richards the touching story of paying an unscheduled visit to a building site on a Sunday, where he found the builder proudly showing his wife and children the quality of the work he was doing there.

In the Kessell House, Iwanoff creates an intriguing sense of approach to the front door. The house is set back from the street behind a low tapering wall that follows the fall of the land. Steps from the driveway lead to a walkway, and another set of steps leads to the porch, which is flanked by asymmetrical supports – one of simple square concrete block columns, the other totemic and complex. Set into a surround of glass panels in the deep porch is a boldly black-and-white patterned melamine door. Welcome to the world of Iwanoff.

PREVIOUS PAGE The bar area is a tour de force of sculptural elements. The cutaway pelmet houses a fluorescent light which, through the five circular holes, illuminates the area below. The back wall of the bar has a sliding screen which opens up to access the kitchen behind.

OPPOSITE The elaborate room divider goes some way to explaining why the cost of the interior joinery exceeded that of the building shell.

The Kessell House is a large, single storey, four-bedroom family home arranged in an L-shape. To the left of the entrance is the bedroom arm, complete with a dressing room and study, both adjacent to the master bedroom. Three additional bedrooms, another bathroom, a laundry and a rumpus room at the rear (with access to the swimming pool) have all been accommodated in this section. To the right of the hallway, in the more public area, is the living room which contains a spectacular signature Iwanoff bar. Iwanoff's personality has been described as gentle, shy and friendly, but his work, as this bar reveals, has all the hallmarks of exuberance, with its carved pelmet, circular lightwells and the dramatic cutaway curve of the bar itself. Professionally, he was no shrinking violet.

The movement through an Iwanoff house is designed to sustain interest. Richard Black, in his article 'Eastern Block' for *Monument*, observes Iwanoff's ability to manipulate interior space. 'There is also a spatial character to the houses that is derived from the use of continuous flowing space to unify the living areas. This would be modulated by screen partitions, built-in cabinet work and sometimes through the articulation of the ceiling and floor plane. So the living areas have a permeable quality where one is always aware of adjacent spaces and activities, avoiding the feeling of separation that would have resulted from traditional walled-in rooms.'

A case in point is the sculptural timber room divider separating living and dining spaces. Another Iwanoff pièce de resistance, it is designed with a cabinet at floor level to anchor the unit and visually balance the speaker boxes that sit on either side of an integrated air conditioning unit at ceiling level. Perspex was a favoured material and the black sliding door on the cabinet provides a sleek contrast to the timber. Together with the bar, this piece is the hero of the house in terms of dramatic impact, but throughout the less public rooms, more subtle joinery is employed. It has been recorded that the detailed interior execution cost more than the building shell itself.

As observed by architectural writer Ian Molyneux, there are 'sunscreens, stairs, balconies composed in an abstract expressionistic, sculptural manner, requiring an enormous amount of supervision by the architect'. Iwanoff's commitment to the building as a whole, inside and out, meant that the project was fairly protracted and there were many on-site revisions. In addition to specifications for built-in furniture, there were wallpaper and curtains to consider, and Iwanoff accompanied the owners to help them choose items that would enhance the overall scheme.

His commitment to his projects and perceptive approach ensured enduring relationships with his clients, often visiting them and contributing ongoing ideas for their houses. When Iwanoff joined a group of architecture students on a tour of his houses in 1983, Duncan Richards, who was present, recalls, 'What came across so strongly was the pride and pleasure of the owners in their collective efforts with the architect in creating these homes.'

IAN COLLINS

HE COLLINS HOUSE

1976

'The building process was long and drawn out because no builder wanted to undertake the project, and so every weekend possible I was helped by friends: an orthodontist, the boat-builder and a biochemist.'

IAN COLLINS

PREVIOUS PAGE The Collins House, as seen from Sydney's Mosman Bay. Built in an area typified by Federation red brick houses, the Collins House stands out with its clean modernist lines and fibreglass construction.

THIS PAGE The house is characterised by the lozenge-shaped windows and doors. Shown here is the front door, with its linear black frame.

OPPOSITE This large picture window is a single piece of glass which was positioned with a great deal of difficulty, given the slope of the site.

GROUND FLOOR

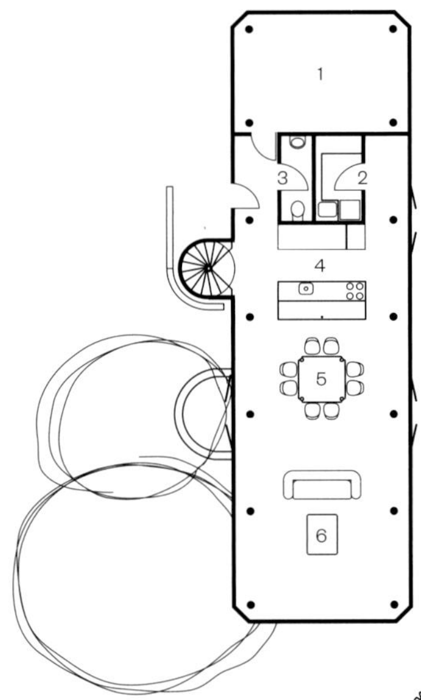

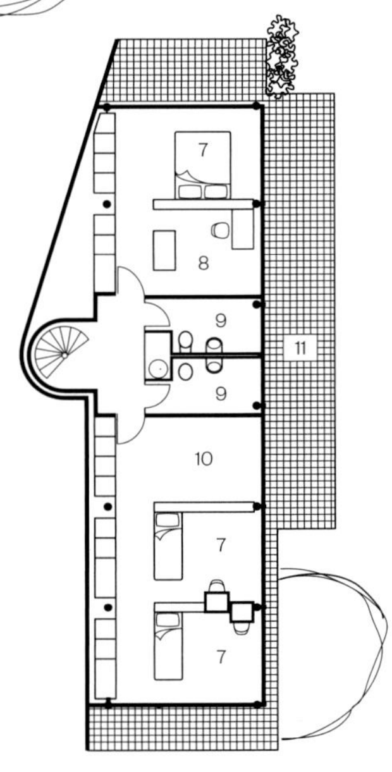

LOWER GROUND FLOOR

1 Garage
2 Laundry
3 WC
4 Kitchen
5 Dining
6 Living
7 Bedroom
8 Study
9 Bathroom
10 Playroom
11 Balcony

There is no mistaking the Collins House. Sited above the ferry stop in Sydney's Mosman Bay, it is a light, white modernist beacon in a sea of traditional Federation terracotta and brick. From a distance it is easy to see the outline of the house's simple form and the graphic ship's hatch windows, but the material with which it is constructed is not evident until close up: the shell of the Collins House is made entirely of fibreglass.

Ian and Rosanne Collins, both architects, lived there for more than 30 years and recall with clarity the process of finding the land, designing the house and building a home for themselves and their two daughters. 'It was Rosanne who first saw the site in 1968, and was smart enough to realise it wasn't big enough for developers to build a block of flats,' says Ian Collins. The site is small, steep and awkward, but its enviable location and outlook encouraged the couple to buy it, realising that with two architects in the family, a building solution wouldn't be too hard to find.

'Initially, we submitted a plan just to get council approval for a building on the site,' says Collins. At that stage, the idea was for a brick and timber house with a degree of structural complexity. Although council passed the plan, Collins began to rethink his design, and conversations with a friend, structural engineer Alex Osborne, persuaded him to move towards 'the biggest rectangle I could build on the site'. When the Collins purchased the land, a cream-coloured apartment block was scheduled to be built close by, and a neighbour had a modern garage, which freed Collins from any sense of obligation to conform to a Federation context.

'I was looking at the work of American architect Richard Meier and admired his use of inter-penetrating volumes. I didn't want to do a Meier-style house but he did open my eyes to new possibilities,' says Collins. Two other forces were at play – one negative and one positive. On the negative side was Collins' experience with the bricklaying trade. 'I was working in the Department of Public Works, alongside Ken Woolley and Peter Hall, and later my job was to supervise various projects. We went through a period of problems with bricks and bricklayers and I thought if I could be spared the need for that particular trade, it would be an advantage.'

At the same time, Collins' passion for sailing brought him into contact with a yacht builder who constructed Olympic-class boats. He had the capacity to

mould large-scale fibreglass panels, large enough, in fact, to be used to build a house. There were two mould shapes: a flat piece 1.5 metres wide by 3 metres high, and another forming the corner panels. The process was slow, as the boat-builder, Phillip Maloney, could only produce one or two panels a week. 'We'd put them on the roof of our Ford station wagon and bring them one at a time from Lane Cove to Mosman,' recalls Rosanne. They were stacked onsite, waiting for the weekend workers to hang them in place. 'The building process was long and drawn out because no builder wanted to undertake the project, and so every weekend possible I was helped by friends: an orthodontist, the boat-builder and a biochemist,' says Collins. 'We would hook the panels in place, fixing them to the roof, as a proper curtain wall might.'

While fibreglass may be considered a lightweight material for house construction, there was nothing insubstantial about the core structure itself. The sandstone bedrock was locked in place by rock bolts, and three thick concrete slabs were supported by sealed tubular steel columns. 'The firm of structural engineers Taylor Thomson Whitting oversaw the building and one of its principals, Dick Taylor, who had a boat moored at Mosman Bay, would call in regularly and check how we were doing.'

One of the defining features of the house is the lozenge-shaped windows which, again, reference boating. On the living level, the windows are like pairs of ship's hatches, made by inserting a shaped piece of pineboard in the standard fibreglass mould to create the window frame. 'The reason this shape is used in boats is that the seal is strongest without corners, so these windows are frameless and seal with a neoprene gasket.' The most impressive window is the wall of glass with rounded edges at the northerly end of the living area. 'I had designed it as five glass panels with fine mullions, but when the glazier saw it, he said that for the same price he could provide one large piece,' says Collins. Adds Rosanne, 'It took half a dozen men to carry it down the slope.'

While upstairs the view is chanced upon through pairs of windows, downstairs in the bedroom/bathroom level, it is completely embraced. 'We used a window system recommended by another sailing friend, the architect Richard Leplastrier. It's a sliding system of floor-to-ceiling glass opening up to the terrace. Richard also recommended the Vola taps in the bathrooms.' As the long side of the house faces west, it does get hot, and one of the original devices for cooling was to pool water on the concrete roof, designed with an upstand for the purpose.

Curves recur throughout the house, and the circular staircase between the levels is set in a white concave stairwell. The stair treads have been filled with fibreglass which has gained a patina over the years, giving it the appearance of tortoiseshell.

Right from the outset there was a different vision for the interior design of each level of the house. The living/dining/kitchen area was tiled in black, and the original wall treatment was of ply panels covered in black felt. 'I recall reading a book from Anthony Powell's 12-volume *A Dance to the Music of Time*. There was a description of a party in a room which was totally black, and the faces appeared to float...the idea stayed with me,' says Collins. 'The interior lining panels were pinned to the wall so that the black felt surface could soon be replaced, but it stayed, and we used the panels as a pin board as well as a background for artworks.'

Downstairs was light and bright, with white ceramic floor tiles laid in the bedrooms, and continuing out onto the terrace linking the two spaces. The girls' room with its white laminate cupboards and white walls was originally decorated with primary red furniture and bedspreads. 'If you look at the floorplan of the building, it doesn't read like a normal house. It is hard to tell where areas begin and leave off.' This is particularly true of the bedroom level,

PREVIOUS PAGE A bank of white cabinets separates the dining area from the kitchen. The monochromatic colour scheme and bold choices of mainly Italian furniture make a confident design statement. The Seventies marble table is by Italian architect Mangiarotti and creates a sculptural centrepiece in the open-plan room.

OPPOSITE The staircase, designed in steel with fibreglass treads, connects the entry level of kitchen, dining and living areas with the bedroom level below.

THIS PAGE The Caori coffee table was designed by Vico Magistretti for Gavina in the early Sixties.

where the children's room was partitioned by a row of Artemide bookshelves rather than a traditional stud wall. Hence, the house had the ability to evolve as family circumstances altered.

Decoratively, the interior made a strong statement – the couple started collecting quality furniture in 1964 when they bought the Eames table and chairs for their first marital home in Greenwich. The open-plan living area, with its monochromatic palette, showcased many classic furniture pieces from the Sixties and early Seventies. These include the Anfibio sofa bed, which was designed by Alessandro Becchi in about 1971 for the Italian company Giovanetti; the Caori coffee table, from around 1962, by Vico Magistretti; lights by Artemide and Flos, and the magnificent black marble Eros dining table, designed by Italian architect Angelo Mangiarotti, in about 1971.

'We have copies of *Domus* magazine from 1958,' says Rosanne. 'It was a fantastic inspiration to us.' In fact, Collins is the first to admit that the sweeping curve of the stainless steel on the kitchen benches was influenced by an article he saw in it. 'My mother had stainless steel kitchen benchtops in her cottage, so I knew the properties of the material and that it worked well, but the design inspiration came from a feature on a Mangiarotti kitchen,' he says.

Storage was considered from the outset. Floor-to-ceiling cupboards run the length of the retaining wall on the lower level. 'There is even a space at one point where you can walk through the cupboard into a "secret passage",' says Rosanne. Storage was something close to their hearts as, for many years, Rosanne ran a shop selling imported Elfa storage systems, which they used in their own home, along with modular furniture and Marimekko fabrics.

The Collins House is a one-off. While the nature of its design and materials delivered fast construction, marketing the concept was not something Collins considered. 'The fibreglass was not cheap, because it was for this use only,' he says. 'In addition, we had some costly excavation which is normal in this area. The house probably ended up costing the same as a brick equivalent.' Rosanne, an architect in her own right, acknowledges the house was her husband's creation. 'You see,' she explains. 'I was the client.'

THIS PAGE The galley kitchen combines white cabinetry with curved stainless steel benchtops. Open on both sides, with a view to the water, the kitchen is part of the main living area, but hidden from view by tall cabinets so as not to interfere with the clean lines of the overall space.

OPPOSITE The view into the master bedroom is framed by mature trees.

DARYL JACKSON

E JACKSON HOUSE

1976–1977

'Rather than harking back to the comforting history of farmhouses, it attempts the extraordinary – to transform, through scale reduction, the planning and forms of the larger and influential educational buildings of the day, into the typology of the house.'

GRAHAM JAHN

PREVIOUS PAGE While there was an initial thought of siting the house high on the hill with views of the bay, the seclusion of the setting, with its relationship to the creek, was finally selected.

THIS PAGE An overgrown trellis delineates the garden and orchard, separating it from the surrounding bushland.

OPPOSITE The pattern-making of the sunlight and shadow on the layered façade adds to the sense of a prism.

Daryl Jackson quotes American philosopher and art theorist Susanne Langer in his book *Daryl Jackson: Selected and Current Works*. Here, she unpicks the act of perceiving a work of art from the 'intuition of the whole presented feeling' to how contemplation allows the gradual revelation of complexities. This description is entirely appropriate, in that it mirrors the experience of seeing, and understanding, Jackson's holiday farmhouse in Shoreham on Victoria's Mornington Peninsula.

At first, the eye takes in the landscape of ancient gums and pines, the creek and the ridge beyond. Then follows the appreciation of the rusticity of the house itself, achieved through its weathered timbers, bush poles and corrugated iron, and the way in which it references farm buildings in the area while retaining its own distinctive character. As Jackson comments, 'It is a vernacular vocabulary, but in an urbanistic form.' With discussion and greater contemplation comes a new level of understanding. How the concept of the expanded Australian 'lean-to' developed from the appreciation of the simple pioneer cottage already on the land, and how, as Jackson says, 'the spatial revolution, perhaps modernism's crowning achievement, remains a keystone to my compositional tactics. Cubism in particular.' What you experience at first sight is undoubtedly confirmed, but often in ways you had not quite anticipated, which surely is the purpose of all good art.

Jackson has always liked a 'big' idea. 'I studied Walter Burley Griffin in my final year at RMIT, and understood Frank Lloyd Wright through Griffin. It wasn't so much Wright's organic modernism, but his "flow of space" modernism that influenced me, especially in this house.'

His teachers at RMIT were returned servicemen; he was educated 'along Bauhaus lines, which tended to be purist and narrow'. He, thus, benefited from the mentoring of architects Kevin Borland and Peter McIntyre. 'Ernest Fooks taught us planning and design, which focused on the arrangement of new towns and the new European vision. I resolved to go to Europe, to the source, and explore this urbanistic thinking, and how Europeans had laminated cities, one layer over another over another, over a long period of time.'

Jackson and his wife, Kay, left Melbourne in 1960 for London, where he worked with Chamberlin, Powell and Bon, a progressive firm best known

for the Barbican Estate, a controversial development in the Brutalist style. Jackson also contributed to the expansion of the campus at the University of Leeds and recalls, 'sitting on the train from London to Leeds discussing architecture at a philosophical level; Chamberlin, Powell and Bon were very much part of a renewing British Movement, their peers being Denys Lasdun in London and Geoffrey Bawa in Ceylon. London exuded an internationalism not prevalent in 1950s Australia,' he says.

Summers were spent travelling in Europe and North Africa. 'The work of Le Corbusier was a focal point, as was the modernism coming out of Milan – that of Gio Ponti and Carlo Scarpa,' says Jackson. He was also able to explore first-hand the European sensibility of reinterpreting old buildings by adding the new, and hence the reshaping of cities over generations as one building layered into another.

Returning home via the States, and a stint working for Paul Rudolph, he had a chance encounter with Robin Boyd, then at the height of his influence, who was impressed that Jackson seemed to know so much about Australia. 'I explained that I had been educated at RMIT and Melbourne University, and had read all his books.' (Jackson was, many years later, to become chairman of The Robin Boyd Foundation.)

In 1965, he set up a practice with Evan Walker in Melbourne, taught part-time at RMIT and became director of *The Age*/RAIA Small Homes Service, which had been founded by Boyd in the late 1940s, to provide architect-designed, low-cost plans for new homes. Jackson continued this work, interviewing clients, recommending suitable house types and producing a weekly column to promote the work of the RAIA in *The Age*.

A seminal project for Jackson was the Harold Holt Memorial Swimming Centre, opened in 1969, and which he worked on with Kevin Borland, his early mentor. 'Borland always understood the basic premise of design is about social exchange. He had a very strong socialist mindset,' says Jackson. Indeed, Emma Borland said in an essay on her father that, 'During the war, at the age of 17, he was on the second ship to enter Hiroshima after the atomic bomb had been dropped...He seldom spoke about it but I sensed the pain he bore as a result. He understood the need for "give and take" in life.'

Jackson was clear on the logistics of working together successfully. 'You have to be on a wavelength where the object becomes empowered beyond the mind of the individual,' he says. 'I had an overlaying sequence of thinking about geometry, about positives and negatives. I would structure stuff and Kevin would de-structure, and then we would debate. If you look at the Harold Holt pool, you will see the confluence of two minds working together.'

Confluence is an important concept for Jackson, especially in large, multi-faceted projects where there are many viewpoints. 'Confluence is really where all forces that make the stream come together,' he says, but admits it relies on his ability to 'dial back' certain aspects and 'dial up' others in order to achieve clarity. The Harold Holt Memorial Pool was an award-winning project which helped propel Jackson's profile, and other significant commissions quickly followed. While Borland and Jackson did not collaborate again – 'I think it was because we genuinely wanted to present ourselves as independent' – they remained close, working in adjacent terrace houses nd meeting frequently.

To escape at weekends, the Jacksons bought a farm block on the Mornington Peninsula. Jackson's understanding of the landscape, and the power it commands, rendered him realistic about the task in hand. 'The house had to contend with the landscape, with the pioneer timber

PREVIOUS PAGE There is a tremendous sense of openness as the terraced nature of the landscape is mirrored internally in the untreated timber atrium.

OPPOSITE The interior spaces, such as the generous dining area, are open and link visually, making the house suited to extended family gatherings.

THIS PAGE The construction has the no-nonsense approach of its rural context with the rusticity of bush poles, which Jackson describes as 'the poor man's concrete post'.

slab-and-mud lean-to shed and a 120-year-old cottage, with a marvellous white pre-Captain Cook eucalypt, on a hillside dropping away to a creek.' As a starting point, his scheme evolved from what was already there – working into what existed in the European tradition, but in a quintessentially Australian context and form. 'Building new to sustain the old became a leitmotiv in his work,' writes Patrick McCaughey to describe his approach in the broader commercial context, but it is also true in this personal, domestic project.

Jackson first stabilised and restored the cottage of stone slab, sticks and mud, which was virtually falling over after 30 years of cattle trampling through it. This sparked the idea for the house, 'of abstracting from the lean-to shape, the humble back porch or filled-in verandah to become the whole dwelling', he says. Combined with his ability to arrive at what he describes as 'primary situations', such as finding the essence of the house via the landform, this gave him a strong sense of place from which to create. Jackson is tuned into scale and the relationship of the structure to the landscape, how it integrates into the composition of the garden on one level and addresses the ridge and the valley at a larger level. He calls it a 'topographic composition'.

When it comes to influences, Jackson cites neither the machine age modernist aesthetic nor the dedicated organic school of Wright, but instead Alvar Aalto's humanising use of natural materials, his spatial understanding and unashamed regionalism which manifested in his desire to harness and reinterpret tradition. Aalto's philosophy resonated with Jackson's pluralist view that there wasn't just one prescribed path to follow, that it is possible to have modern architecture in a spectrum of ways. 'Understanding just how to juxtapose international or universal knowledge against distinctive local content was one of the key concerns of this era in my career,' he says.

The farmhouse is approached via a long track, lined with majestic eucalypts of the stringybark family, which recalls the tree-lined private roads to many a traditional Australian homestead. Initially, Jackson admits, there was a temptation to site the house higher up the hill where there are views of the bay, but that would have meant looking out over other properties as well. Eventually, the 'compulsive orientation' of the present site prevailed, with its views of the creek and rolling hills, and its more secluded positioning.

Jackson's building is linked to the land in two ways. He explains: 'A trellis sunshade becomes a fence separating garden and orchard from bush. The line it creates makes an important horizontal link between the house and stable.' The entrance to the house is via a broad timber bridge creating an anticipatory journey to 'the heart of the house'. Structurally, its openness is immediately evident. A series of platforms linked by open-tread staircases and the two-storey, glassed-in atrium reveal his preoccupation with geometry. 'My interest in Cubism is based on ideas of taking apart and transforming, of reconstructing and opposing, with elements being redefined and renewed by the changing set of relationships,' says Jackson. He admired the work of Picasso in this period with his ability to fundamentally alter the literal, representative nature of art by abstracting from life to produce a shift in perception and alter the accepted order of things.

Yet the feeling of the house is by no means sharp and fractured. Jackson manages to sidestep the angular through his choice of materials, by the way in which the house has been fabricated, and through his ability to balance his passion for Cubism with another 'ism'. 'The key point about expressionism is the inner vision, portrayed as content. It uses the world of feelings and emotions as much as any rationale or functional stance,' says Jackson. 'These two threads are the constant, endemic to my work throughout my life.'

THIS PAGE The master bedroom is one of the few enclosed rooms in the house.

OPPOSITE The wall of glazing in the master bedroom makes the landscape an important aspect of the interior. Jackson strove to combine universal knowledge with distinctive local content, and impart a strong sense of context.

THIS PAGE Jackson refers to 'topographic composition', illustrated by the terraced structure of the house as it steps down the site.

OPPOSITE Mindful of what existed on the site, one of Jackson's first acts was to restore a 120-year-old pioneer cottage of stone slab, sticks and mud.

The interior spaces are visually linked: standing at the bottom of the staircase, at the base of the atrium, it is possible to see into the living area and up the staircase to the workroom level. The terraced landscape is mirrored internally as well as externally. There is a multiplicity of viewpoints adding to what Patrick McCaughey calls 'the prismatic quality of the structure'. Similarly, the landscape is coaxed into the building. The atrium, with its interior planting, is an interim space, inside but mimicking out with its expansive glass wall, allowing full view of the creek beyond. The only private, enclosed space is the master bedroom, with its window to the more intimate view of the old orchard.

Although it is conceptually sophisticated, it is built in a spare and spartan manner that suggests the no-nonsense approach of its country context and the make-do philosophy of rural Australia. Jackson points out, 'The space enclosed is layered from light to dark, like the bush itself, the exterior breaking down the effect of harsh sun via a surface patina of trellis (canvas in summer) shadow, the interior forming deeper recesses.'

The walls were formed with 75 mm-thick planks of yellow stringybark from nearby Gippsland, cramped together vertically, with a form of foam in between to compensate for movement as the timbers acclimatised. 'Battens were added later to close up the gaps,' he says.

The timber, untreated inside and out, is the defining material of the house, and the patina it has developed gives the house its immense character. Add to this the external and internal use of bush poles ('a poor man's concrete post,' Jackson says), corrugated iron, extensive timber trellising and an exposed brick hearth, and it is the sense of rusticity that dominates. The furniture echoes this: an old Swedish table, cabinets and chairs, collected and handed down, sit comfortably next to modern pieces.

It is an accommodating house, in terms of the family's needs, evolving over the years. It has places for separation and congregation in equal measure. As I interview Daryl and Kay in the living/dining level, their son and grandchildren are working on a project on the workshop level above. 'At the time, there was no sense of, "I am making this for a three-generational family," but I am always conscious of where you can make the next move,' says Jackson.

It has always been a family place; the children kept and rode horses there, and family weddings have been held on the property. A cubby house was constructed from leftover building materials. There's a rose garden, a substantial dam and a tennis court, not to mention ancient trees to climb and a dilapidated old pioneer cottage as part of the composition.

The importance of Daryl Jackson's practice both in Australia and internationally cannot be underestimated. He has more than 100 awards to his name, is a RAIA gold medallist, holds an Order of Australia, an honorary doctorate at Ballarat University and, among his academic commitments as a professorial associate at Melbourne and Deakin universities, found time for many years to be a director of Essendon Football Club.

Along with confluence, there's another word he likes – serendipity. He still delights in the fact that the girl he met when they were both children became his wife, and shares 'comparative values and an understanding of where each other is coming from'. He also appreciates the serendipity of the land purchase and the evident pleasure the house has brought, and continues to bring, their extended family.

'My architectural concerns are to express space, structure, light and human associations in tectonic form but also, like Borland, to know what's essential and what's inessential,' he says. One senses, that for Jackson, this final statement is true as much in life as it is in architecture.

THE PH

BARRIE MARSHALL

LLIP ISLAND HOUSE

1983–1990

'The house in no way connotes residence or domesticity. In its context it lurks like a stealth bomber, hidden and subversive.'

HAIG BECK AND JACKIE COOPER

PREVIOUS PAGE Marshall's intention was that the views through the openings of the low-lying house would become the very essence of the building.

THIS PAGE The house was designed to barely register its presence, and read merely as 'a single plane on the oceanfront'.

OPPOSITE The narrow entrance to the compound feels monumental, creates a sense of anticipation and is in sharp contrast to the open space beyond.

OPPOSITE The entrance to the house is made from galvanised steel with a three-metre-high sliver of a wall leading to a galvanised portico and door. The house is narrow (5.4 metres), and so the view of the ocean is clear from the entrance. The blade wall masks a washing line, which is fixed to the side facing into the courtyard.

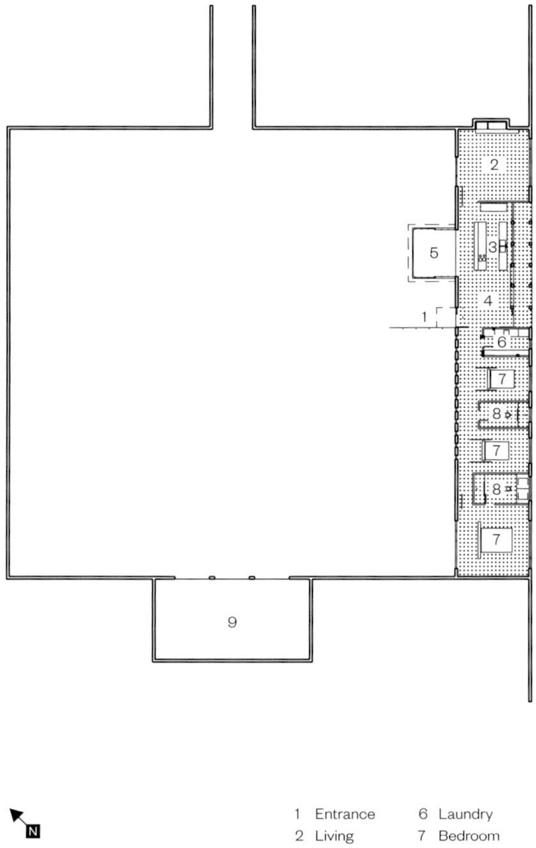

1 Entrance
2 Living
3 Kitchen
4 Dining
5 Sunroom
6 Laundry
7 Bedroom
8 Bathroom
9 Garage

As an architect, Barrie Marshall has an ability to create a sense of anticipation. The sinuous sculptural forms in canary yellow, and the seemingly precariously tilting columns in fire-engine red that line the freeway into Melbourne say something significant about how the city sees itself; it is about art and sculpture, it is about being daring, and demanding that you think differently. Denton Corker Marshall is the firm of architects behind this commission and Barrie Marshall, one of the founding partners, sees the entrance to Melbourne project as 'one of the best things we have ever done. It worked because we are interested in urban stuff, big sculptural forms and movement.'

On a different road and a different journey, the anticipation is no less intense. I had seen photographs of the Phillip Island House, two hours south of Melbourne, in a 1997 issue of *Architecture Australia* and, with only hand-drawn directions and a landline number (Barrie never answers his mobile, his assistant told me), I set off to see the house the locals call 'the bunker'.

Phillip Island is most famous for its motor racing, and is a popular holiday spot for Melburnians wanting a weekender – something fibro in the Fifties but more substantial and suburban these days. The Phillip Island House is located at Kitty Miller Bay on the south of the island where houses become less frequent and give way to low-lying, scrubby native grasses and windswept open farmland. Without the map, and the benefit of daylight, the house would have remained hidden, its grass roof blending into the surrounding landscape. The entrance is through a narrow gap in a fortress-like concrete wall, opening, dramatically and unexpectedly, to an enormous enclosed courtyard sheltered from the prevailing winds.

Barrie Marshall was not born to architecture and readily admits it meant nothing to him until a maths teacher at high school suggested he consider it as a career. 'I was brought up in Clayton, in a working class Australian family where none of the kids had been to university,' he says. 'I had never been inside an architect-designed house or even really knew what an architect was.' He applied for both architecture at Melbourne University and engineering at Monash, and chose the former. 'Just as well, as I would have made a terrible engineer,' he says.

'It was a big intake that year, maybe 130 students, and they all seemed to come from private schools and know about architecture, name-dropping

Mies van der Rohe and Le Corbusier. I was just 17 years old, so it was quite disconcerting for me as I wasn't from that background. Fortunately I was good at drawing and that made it easy for me to be accepted.'

Both his future partners, John Denton and Bill Corker, were in the same year – John in his immediate set of friends and Bill in another group. In 1966, in their third year of study, Barrie and John, along with some fellow students, set off to Europe on the last journey of the migrant boat *Flavia* to Italy. They ended up in London, living in Earl's Court, and working in various practices to gain broader experience. Six months later, they were on the road in a Kombi van, with 'Melbourne University School of Architecture' emblazoned on the side, taking a tour of significant buildings around Europe and the Middle East. 'John [Denton] and John Peck knew what they were looking for – I just went along for the ride,' says Marshall.

Post university, he worked for Eggleston, MacDonald & Secomb in their Melbourne office and subsequently for himself doing perspectives for a couple of years. In 1971, he and his wife, Raine, returned to London, where he worked for Powell & Moya until one day, towards the end of 1972, a phone call came from John Denton saying that he and Bill were setting up a practice with Grahame Shaw and would he come back to Australia and join them.

'When we started, we didn't have a great deal of work,' says Marshall. 'We had a landscaping partner, Andras Kelly, and John and Bill were both planners. That kept us going, but we didn't do any building work of note except for a sea pilot station on Western Port Bay, which wasn't bad.'

Gradually, their fortunes changed. DCM won the competition to do the City Square, which was a mixed blessing (it was later demolished), but helped raise their profile, and they were shortlisted in the competition for the Australian Parliament. Another opportunity came their way when establishment architects Yuncken Freeman were dismantling their practice and one director, Robert Peck, was given the Hong Kong office. 'He was a young business-y sort of guy who wasn't a designer and never pretended to be,' says Marshall. 'He had approached several architects to partner him without success, but when he came to us it seemed like a good opportunity to expand. I spent three months in Hong Kong to get the design side restarted.'

They became PDCM, and Robert Peck's connections got them into the competition for a significant office block, No 1 Collins Street, Melbourne, which they won. Next came the project that catapulted them into a whole new league.

The Australian Embassy in Beijing 'had all the big guns going for it – Seidler and John Andrews – and I think we got it partly because Richard Johnson, [principal architect with the Department of Housing & Construction], liked our rigid, austere design and knew that he could be involved and work with us, in a way that would not have been possible with the others.'

Marshall is aware that they were nobodies on the Australian architectural scene at the time and they hadn't earned their stripes either commercially or in the academic world.

'There was a sense of "who are these guys and what have they done?"...and I can see from their point of view we would have been these bloody upstarts,' says Marshall. But these 'bloody upstarts' were on a roll, with the commission for the Australian Embassy in Tokyo followed by another prestigious Melbourne office block, 101 Collins Street, in 1981.

While professional life continued apace, Marshall's private time was spent at Phillip Island. He had been going to Kitty Miller Bay spearfishing and skindiving since his childhood and, indeed, it was on Phillip Island that the 16-year-old Marshall met his future wife, Raine.

'She was camping with her family at San Remo – we were more upmarket in a fibro shack – and we met through friends of friends,' says Marshall. 'Fifteen

OPPOSITE Modular stainless steel benches, designed by Marshall, sit between the sunroom on the left and the wall of windows to the ocean on the right. The rigorously monochromatic interior of concrete, terrazzo and stainless steel allow the views to be the hero.

THIS PAGE 'Penguin' windows in the north facing wall throw varying light patterns according to the sun's angle.

years later, we bought a block of land at Silverleaves, and I built a tiny, two-storey, timber cube with the help of my brother-in-law. But over the years we could see Silverleaves becoming more suburban and when this block on Kitty Miller Bay came up we bought it.'

The four-hectare site sits between two headlands facing the ocean, and has the advantage of being the only area on Phillip Island's southern side that is protected from the direct sea swell. Having bought the land, an even more desirable block came up for sale on the headland. 'We put a deposit down on it and left for a six-week trip, leaving arrangements in the hands of the lawyers. We also put this land back on the market,' says Marshall.

While they were away, the whole deal fell through and his plans for a cave-like dwelling buried into the headland had to be put aside. 'It was probably just as well as it would have ended up even more expensive than this place.' Luckily, no-one had bought the Kitty Miller Bay site.

In terms of design, Marshall was clear what he did not want. 'I decided that, no matter what, the wrong thing to do was to make the house an object, that no matter how fine, how elegant, how cleverly executed – a butterfly perched on the crest of the dunes – it would have been the wrong thing to do.'

So in a plan that would have made Frank Lloyd Wright proud (his architectural philosophy was that building and site should work as one), Marshall set out to make his house as much a part of the landscape as possible. 'I didn't want to hide it, just to make it fit,' he says.

And it is around this idea of 'fit' and connection with nature that Marshall's concept grew. The dark concrete he chose links with the black granite rocks on the beach, the single-storey, low-lying building reads like a 'cliff in the landscape', and the grassed roof blends it seamlessly into the surrounds. The house is barely there.

This sense of integration into its site is furthered by the structure – a trapezium from the southern elevation. The house hugs the dunes on the western end so that the manmade structure blends into the natural one. 'From the ocean side I hoped it would read as an abstract composition: not an intrusion but a natural sculpture,' says Marshall.

Initially, Marshall's design was larger, with a colonnaded façade, and there was a plan for a concrete shell with a timber lining. When the quote came through in the region of $600,000–700,000 he revised the scale and the interior scheme, and just made a start. His priorities were always to have sun in as many rooms as possible and to exploit the views.

'I shifted to a simpler statement: a wall with punched openings,' he says. 'I started thinking of views from the inside. The views through the openings would become the very essence of the building.'

He also did something he could not do professionally – he allowed the interior demands to dictate the positioning of the window openings, with little regard to their external appearance. Each room has a placement according to its needs – full-length in the living space, sill-height when sitting in bed in the master bedroom, just above eye-level in the bathroom, and to floor-level up against the sunken bath. By abandoning his initial plan for a double skin, concrete became the material used outside and in, creating a dark frame that distils and concentrates the emphasis on the rugged view.

Marshall had worked through his desire to build in timber in the house in Silverleaves and, having seen the effectiveness of concrete in some of his commercial projects, it became his material of choice. Fortunately, through luck rather than design, Phillip Island has a concrete works. But instead of using Portland Grey concrete, which weathers to a dirty brown, Marshall opted for a black (dark grey) concrete that would achieve the more natural 'blotchy' effect he was after.

The other interior materials were no less compromising than the concrete: black terrazzo flooring, galvanised steel panels, aluminium, zinc and glass. Yet Marshall insists, 'I didn't choose these materials to be provocative, they arose out of practicality and also perhaps out of a sort of naivety. It was a holiday house, and I didn't see why not.'

The resulting use of this palette of materials is, as described by George Michell in *Architecture Australia*, 'ruthless elegance' and, as its dark tones combine with the manipulation of light, it becomes an immensely photogenic house.

The design was now resolved to be 'one long, singular volume', with rooms that were a 'series of subdivisions'. Large pivoting doors helped define the space, so the house could be opened up, or closed down as required. Marshall wanted the interior to be unrestricted by beams, so the 5.4 metre span became the achievable working width for the concrete wall-to-wall slabs.

A builder, Rob Needham, and his family were housed nearby, and for about a year he worked to get the building to a basic shell. 'At this stage there was no courtyard,' says Marshall. 'I worked on the insides for about a year and then we got a caravan and I worked for three or four months, but it took another two or three years to get it to where it is now.'

Marshall not only designed and built the interior fittings, he also designed individual pieces of furniture and fixtures. The double bed, in the master bedroom, with its myriad legs is now gently mocked by its creator as being incredibly impractical (impossible to get a brush to sweep under), and his stainless steel cubes for washing, set in the centre of the bathroom, he now sees as an 'exercise in making a lot of space less'. Yet, whatever his concerns, it does the job he set out to do with sunlight and views dominating.

The last piece of the design to be finalised was the courtyard. 'The site was a big, bare open field, and I had this idea that I could make this little world that looked out to the sea and, in time, I could turn it into anything at all – a rose garden or a vegetable garden,' says Marshall. The dimensions of the courtyard are directly related to the house – 33 metres square, and the wall height is 3.6 metres above ground level. This is determined by the height of the ceilings (2.7 metres) and the 700 mm that was added for the slab and the earth and grass cover. In the east wall, there is one external opening, which is three metres wide for access, and a roomy garage in the west wall, 'for all that crap you collect – mowers, trailers, wheelbarrows, timber, firewood, sailboards, boat, car etc', says Marshall.

The relationship of the house on the courtyard side is different from the ocean side. This northern wall attracts afternoon sun and the slim (300 mm) windows in the corridor (or 'penguin windows' as John Denton called them) create a play of light on the corridor floor that, according to Marshall, 'allows visual contact into the courtyard without long views into it'.

The sunroom is the only intrusion into the courtyard space and it takes on a different character from the rest of the house. It is a mix of aluminium sheeting for the floor and ceiling, and glass panels, both fixed and opening, on the three sides of the structure. While sun might drift in and out of the other rooms of the house, here it is an all day long affair.

This house is entirely personal. Never entered for awards because Marshall felt it was not quite finished, it is a combination of a medieval walled world and spare modernist edifice linked to nature and embracing the visual spectacle of its surrounds. From the ocean, it registers as an abstracted black line, from the land it disappears into the scrubby landscape, and from the sky, on Google Earth, it is hard to spot. In knowing what he didn't want, Marshall created something, in his own words, 'quiet and elemental with no architectural form on the outside'.

OPPOSITE The sill height in the bedroom is calibrated to match the eye line when sitting up in bed so that the view can be enjoyed. The bed with its dramatic steel bedhead was designed by Marshall, although he now criticises it for its impractical 'sea of legs'. The raw, unadorned walls and minimal lighting emphasise the 'ruthless elegance'.

THIS PAGE The morning light causes the white powder-coated panels in the bathroom to glow.

THE

KEN WOOLLEY

ALM BEACH HOUSE

1984–1985

'The generating concept of the design is the idea of a journey along a path that commences at the lower part of the site, winds up through the steep landscaping, climbs through the three levels within the house, branches off the living room to give access to open and covered terraces connecting with rock shelves in the cliff face and continues up the site beyond the house.'

JENNIFER TAYLOR
Architectural historian

PREVIOUS PAGE The exterior dining area, adjacent to the main living space, makes the connection between the secure wall of the cliff face and the house.

THIS PAGE Ken Woolley's love of the glassed-in verandahs of his childhood family holidays influenced the design of the banks of windows facing the view out towards Barrenjoey Head.

OPPOSITE The weekender, a sensitively designed timber tower, sits on a steep site 200 metres from the ocean. The entrance can be seen tucked under the trellised deck area. The sandstone cliff face is integral to the character of the site.

I interview Ken Woolley, and we photograph his Palm Beach weekender, in the final week of his 25-year ownership. We sit overlooking Barrenjoey Head, on one of the three decks, which not only form a distinctive part of the house plan, but also illustrate something of his determination as an architect to find new solutions. 'One fairly unusual idea on a steep site like this is to put the balconies at the back and side of the house, instead of on the view side,' says Woolley. 'The cliff wall is part of its character, and all the spaces are connected to the ground – it creates a different class of space.'

And, indeed, there is no sense of the precariousness often felt on a balcony high above ground level. These spaces are anchored, each offering a different experience: there is a sheltered courtyard, a covered area that acts as an outdoor entertaining room and a third platform to enjoy the view and take the sun.

Woolley is no stranger to awkward, steep sites, as his own award-winning houses (Mosman, Paddington and Palm Beach) all had this problem to overcome. The Mosman House (1962) was one of the most significant houses of its time, as it represented the quintessential Sydney School style. Of timber, brick and tile, its central idea was a garden terrace stepping down the slope; the crafted detail was extraordinary.

Woolley's tendency to do things differently has often attracted criticism. 'One of the things that used to be said about me was that my buildings are too diverse, too different,' he says. 'My response is that they have all been approached fresh and I am trying to find what the building ought to be rather than trying to represent myself.'

One suspects he has never been afraid to be different. He grew up in Sydney in a family of modest means, sharing a house with his grandmother. His mother was artistic and musical, and fostered his interest in art; his father was a craftsman who worked for a period as a fine art printer. The discipline of printing with seven colour plates gave him an ability to spot if something was a fraction out. It's something Woolley has never forgotten.

'As a child I was always making things. I was the leading exponent of making cubby houses, multi-storeyed structures out of wooden fruit boxes,' he says. 'I made plans of the air raid trench and the vegetable victory gardens.'

When the family bought their first car, they had driving holidays around Australia, one trip taking them as far as Townsville. They stayed in country

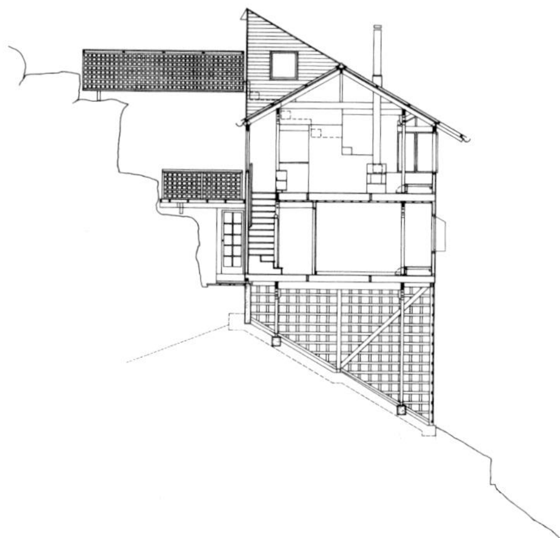

SECTION

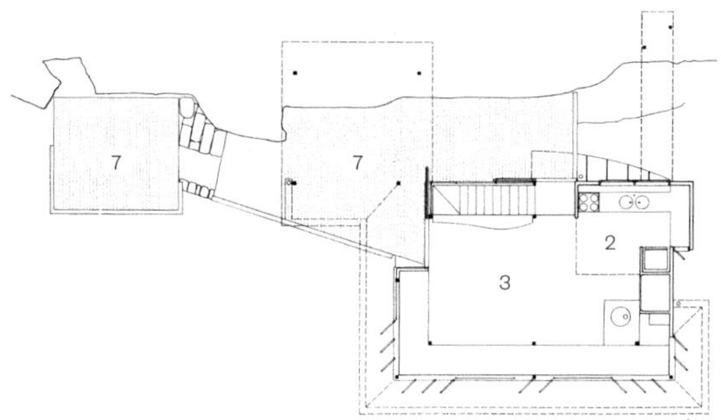

UPPER LEVEL

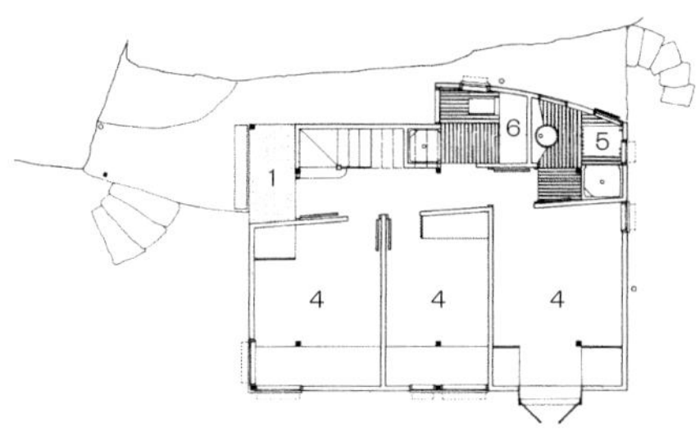

LOWER LEVEL

N

1 Entry
2 Kitchen
3 Living
4 Bedroom
5 Bathroom
6 Laundry
7 Deck

pubs and Woolley remembers the rows of beds lined up on the four-metre-wide covered verandahs where he slept alongside the commercial travellers. As he got older, these trips became a chance to observe, and record, Australian vernacular architecture. His drawings were executed with an early type of felt pen, crude and thick 'like a thumb nail dipped in tar', according to Woolley, giving his impressions a bold, distinctive appearance.

He went to Daceyville Primary, a selective feeder to Sydney Boys High, where he studied Russian, Latin, French and English to Intermediate level, and enjoyed the parallel universe of hanging out with his local 'golfing gang' and fostering ambitions to be a professional golfer, as some of his friends did.

The impetus to become an architect came from his mother, 'a very intelligent woman, rather thwarted by circumstances, who felt that architecture was a profession for someone who could draw – it became a sort of family assumption'.

Through a family friend, Woolley was introduced to the Government Architect, Cobden Parkes. 'He was a very affable man and was aware that we didn't have any money, so he encouraged me to apply for a traineeship,' says Woolley. At 16, he was seconded to the Government Architect's Branch of the NSW Public Works Department. Assistant Government Architect Harry Rembert ran the design room; Peter Webber was the first trainee to be taken on, Woolley the second. He was, at first, limited to running errands and elementary drafting, along with holiday stints in country offices such as Bathurst until, at the age of 18, he was allowed to work in the city office. By then, Woolley was getting good results at the University of Sydney (he was top of his year from 1950) and Rembert realised he had stumbled on a valuable resource. 'They recruited the top student three years in a row [Peter Hall followed Woolley], and the Public Service Board became enthusiastic and increased their intake,' says Woolley.

As a very young man, Woolley worked on large commissions, including the Chemistry School at the University of Sydney with Harry Rembert and Peter Webber, and undertook his first solo commission for the Chapel and Sisters' Home, St Margaret's Hospital, when he was 22. Although young, Woolley acknowledges that he was 'a fairly demanding person, and I made sure that I got what I wanted. There isn't a lot of point otherwise.'

In the postwar period, building was booming and Woolley admits that he had tremendous opportunities through the Public Works Department. 'It had the best work. It had the entire State building budget for schools, police stations and government offices. When I joined it in 1952, there were six in the department; when I left in 1964, there were 25.'

Scholarships allowed him to travel. In 1953, he went to Melbourne where he met Robin Boyd, Peter McIntyre, Roy Grounds and John and Phyllis Murphy, Neil Clerehan and Kevin Borland. 'They took us around all their buildings. Melbourne was the star place because of that lot.'

Graduating in 1955 with first class honours and the university medal, travel overseas opened his eyes further. In 1956, with the funds from the Byera Hadley Travelling Scholarship to pay the return passage to Europe, he met up with Peter Webber in London, and they visited Finland and Alvar Aalto's office. 'Here were the clues as to where modernism was going to move ahead, out of the International School,' says Woolley. 'Le Corbusier was also moving into a new period and I visited his just completed Jaoul houses. The people who lived there saw me hovering at the gate and called me in for a glass of wine and a tour.'

While Webber returned to Sydney, Woolley started working with architects Chamberlin, Powell and Bon on the Golden Lane Estate, a bombsite near St Paul's Cathedral. Having just won the competition for the Barbican development, their reputation was in the ascendancy. Travelling through France, Austria, Spain and Italy, Woolley sent back detailing for the St Margaret's Hospital chapel dome via airmail letters and arrived back in Sydney as construction began. The following

PREVIOUS PAGE The dining and kitchen area is warmed with a woodburning stove in winter and cooled with ceiling fans in summer. The simplicity of the timber interior with its exposed one-wall kitchen acknowledges the idea that a holiday house can have a different sensibility from that of an everyday residence.

OPPOSITE The staircase of irregularly stacked boxes doubles as storage space. For children, the climb is the start of a journey to a special sleeping platform and the outdoor bridge beyond.

THIS PAGE The cupboards recall old meat safes in their design, with mesh panels fixed behind the timber grids.

year came the commission to the Government Architect and T.E. O'Mahony for Fisher Library at the University of Sydney, with Woolley as design architect, a major undertaking given its context. Architect Philip Cox, a student at the time, felt that this was 'the most contemporary building in Sydney, in front of the neo-gothic of Blacket's grand university'.

The next phase of Woolley's career took a very different tack. In 1958, he and Michael Dysart won the Taubman's Family Home Competition through *The Australian Women's Weekly*, which led Woolley to contemplate 'the whole process of economy'. Three new designs for the Lend Lease Carlingford exhibition (a public exhibition of architect-designed project homes by well-known names) followed in 1961. Through this, Woolley met Brian Pettit and Ron Sevitt, who were in the process of setting up their own company after the collapse of Sunline Homes, a big player in the project homes market.

Pettit & Sevitt set itself apart by declaring itself, according to Woolley, 'absolutely modern with no compromise towards the more conservative mindset'. There was certainly a market among those who wanted an alternative to the standard builder offering, but couldn't afford a bespoke architect-designed home. Of the 4000-plus Ken Woolley-designed houses throughout Australia, most were executed under the Pettit & Sevitt brand, with the 'Split Level' and 'Lowline' proving the most popular.

Jennifer Taylor comments: 'Perhaps Woolley's major contribution to Australian architecture has been the role he played in raising the quality of the average suburban house – an outstanding achievement by any standard.' Woolley saw the houses as akin to product design, and met with hundreds of clients to discuss modifications, which often informed future design development of the homes. 'By the end, we had 20 different versions developed over 15 years,' he says. All this experience did not go to waste; in 2010 a revived Pettit & Sevitt released three of the designs, rethought for a contemporary market, and introduced 'Hillside', designed specifically for steep sites.

In 1962, Fisher Library won the Sulman Medal, and the Mosman House the Wilkinson. It was time to strike out. There would be enough money generated from Pettit & Sevitt to justify leaving the Government Architect's office. This coincided with an approach from the University of Newcastle to design a Union building and, almost simultaneously, prestigious firm Ancher Mortlock and Murray asking him to become a partner.

Woolley has made it clear that while he approaches each challenge with a fresh eye and a new set of solutions, he is cautious of 'wandering into innovation for its own sake'. His creative process is to formulate a strong central idea by establishing the ground rules of purpose, resources and client needs, and discovering what has the potential to satisfy. 'As Picasso said, "I don't seek, I find," and as you head towards the realisation of an idea you discover things – a whole set of subordinate ideas,' says Woolley. 'Some of these are in the direction of the building and some are in the artistic expression of the building. The problem is balancing your developmental ideas with your central idea.'

While living in his Wilkinson Award-winning Paddington House (1980), which he describes as a 'modern and personal townhouse', he began to look for a weekender. 'We looked all the way up the coast, at farms and so forth, and eventually decided that travel could be the killer and that we couldn't do better than here.' The site was, he says, 'unviable', but he set about searching for the idea, exploring what differentiated a holiday house from a permanent residence. 'This is a place to play, like camping or on a yacht. There are different expectations of privacy and space.'

The land was steep, with a watercourse running through it. 'I liked the notion of having a small footprint, and the idea evolved of a tower-like house, which would in itself be a staircase up the cliff, terminating in a bridge at the back.'

Memories, experiences and philosophical ideas also influenced him. Childhood holidays were spent at Lake Macquarie, in a cousin's cottage,

on the water and with a jetty. 'I have always had some affection for a typical timber house with a glassed-in verandah.'

He also refers to Harry Rembert's weekender in the Blue Mountains. 'Harry was a very good architect who did some outstanding public buildings, but it was his weekender that was a great influence on me.' Built in the Thirties and added to in the Forties, it was clad in fence palings, with the interior walls lined in Caneite, low-density fibreboard made from cane fibre. 'All the rooms here are lined with a similar low density fibreboard, just as Harry did.'

Another influence was the work of the California-based architect and academic Christopher Alexander, who wrote, among other things, *A Pattern Language: Towns, Buildings, Construction* and *The Timeless Way of Building*. Alexander studied building types, posed theories as to why windows with small panes are a good thing, and developed a language of scale that maintained the smallest detail should be only 6 mm in order to have the necessary range of scale in a building. For Woolley, he provided an interesting move out of the direct modernist identification style into a more free style while still maintaining connection to purpose.

The decision was taken to construct the house in timber for both aesthetic and practical reasons. 'Nowadays we would use a crane or inclinator with a builders' kit, but those weren't around in the Eighties, so that was one reason for keeping the structure lightweight.'

Given the steepness of the slope and the unstable ground, Woolley conceived a ladder-like concrete base, made up of a series of beams laid on the ground (rather than cut into it), following the slope and providing a base for the column supports. The concrete frames are tied to the rock and locked in with four metre rock bolts.

'We tried to remove some of the double purposes of structure by having this internal post and beam frame which runs right down through the house, one metre from the external perimeter walls,' he explains. 'This holds most of the load and the one-metre zone is used for seating, storage and the stairs.' It is described in *Australian Architects: Ken Woolley* as the timber frame version of the thick wall concept.

The house is formed in three layers, vertically. There is the living area on top with windows spanning three sides, rather like the closed-in verandahs of his childhood; the bedroom layer, with small windows and externally clad in hardwood timbers, and the lower section, which has lattice panel infills and bracing.

Internally, the living space is of open construction with beams and rafters visible. The detailing is simple and honest – surface-mounted bolts; ring-pull openers for cupboards, recalling a ship's chandlery; mesh panels in kitchen cupboard doors echoing meat safes, and tiny dowels providing a resting place for timber vents above casement windows. According to Woolley, the importance of detail is the same as that of a word in a poem, and so they must not be replaced by others in the building process.

Woolley describes himself as diffident, and what is important to him, as an architect, is judgment. As he says, 'The underlying sensibilities that lead to the judgments involved are what count – the feeling of what is right – of appropriateness and harmony.'

A playful element is found in the box-like stairs, from the living area to a tiny loft space, popular with his children and grandchildren, and out across the bridge that leads to the rocky plateau above. The garden has been landscaped, native trees and bushes planted and the lantana removed. The house sits comfortably in its natural setting, the cliff face forming a secure wall for the outdoor space, the bridge ingeniously linking it to its site. The house won the Wilkinson Award and the Robin Boyd Award in 1987, with the jury comments that 'Ken Woolley's quiet imagination has made a lovely place, with care and deep thought to be found everywhere...it is safe to say Robin Boyd would have loved it, but then it is also a place any sensitive person would love.'

PREVIOUS PAGE An influence on Woolley was his long-held appreciation for mentor Harry Rembert's cottage in the Blue Mountains, with its walls of Caneite. The material, shown here in a bedroom, creates a warm enclosure emphasised by the small, precise, window.

OPPOSITE Connection to the site is made clear by the walkway linking the house to the cliff, so that the escarpment becomes part of the character of the house.

THE

ROBINSON CHEN

ILDEBRAND HOUSE

1988–1990

'Where we might typically expect the holiday beach house as a lightweight affair, suspended mid-air by stilts and columns, periscoping outwards towards the view, this beastie bunkers down anchoring into the ground, securing its hold on the landscape.'

ANNA JOHNSON
Monument

PREVIOUS PAGE The audacious curves of the Hildebrand House present a challenging façade in a small coastal town of predominantly fibro and timber holiday houses.

THIS PAGE A curved, rendered wall draws the visitor into a gravelled courtyard. The red door is a promise of what is to come, as the interior makes use of a finely tuned palette of colour.

OPPOSITE The living area is simply furnished with modernist pieces and an anglepoise lamp repainted a vibrant yellow. The room is lit naturally via the wall of windows facing the creek and the skylight, which illuminates the rear of the room.

OPPOSITE The dining area, adjacent to the partitioned-off kitchen, illustrates the subtle geometry of the interior walls and the success of the nuanced colour palette.

OVERLEAF, LEFT PAGE The sculptural concrete stairs lead from the bedroom and bathroom level, where you enter the house, to the living and dining level above.

OVERLEAF, RIGHT PAGE The corridor to the bedrooms and bathroom is dynamic, with panels of solid colour and curved and angled walls. The recessed strip lighting adds to the effect.

The more I'm exposed to architect-designed houses, and attempt to understand what sets the great apart from the good, the more I realise the power of the architect/client relationship.

For many houses in this book, the architects are their own client and have to satisfy only themselves. Yet in every instance where an enlightened client has commissioned the work, the resulting building is a pure product of that relationship. It can be intense, collaborative and prolonged, such as Richard Leplastrier and the Palm House. Or it can spring from utter trust and minimal involvement, in which the client gives a brief and signs off on a scheme, as in the case of Melbourne architect Kai Chen with Denis and Janice Hildebrand. In both instances the vision and integrity are retained, and the houses, through lack of creative compromise, achieve a timelessness and, often, a greatness.

What has also endured is a tremendous friendship. I meet Chen and the Hildebrands over lunch and they tease and quip and reminisce. This house, refurbished in about 2009 ('We ran everything past Chen,' says Denis Hildebrand), still delights them all.

The Hildebrands, no strangers to commissioning architect-designed houses, had engaged Borland & Brown Architects (Kevin Borland was a leading Melbourne architect and part of the intellectual Left) to undertake a renovation of their Frankston house. They met Chen, a student at the time, who was working on their kitchen detailing. They liked him, remembered him and looked him up when they were planning to build in Somers.

Chen had come to Borland's office by way of an education in Malaysia and Melbourne University. He is honest about his failings. 'I have always preferred to learn by doing, and at university I had a disconnect between the teaching of subjects such as chemistry and physics, so I struggled.' One day, while looking at houses in the Melbourne suburbs of Eltham and Warrandyte, he came across one that interested him and, emboldened by curiosity, knocked on the door. 'The couple were very generous. We went in and spent the day there and I was so smitten by the house – the Colvin House (1974) seemed to me like early Gehry – that I knew I wanted to work with Kevin Borland,' he says.

At the time the area was bush with unmade roads and septic systems, 'with the rainwater tank very much integral to the house design. Quite a number of Borland houses were owner-built and this was one of them,' recalls Chen.

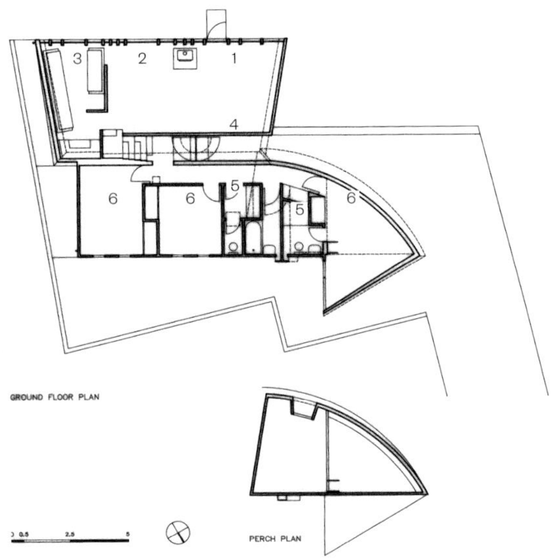

N

1 Living
2 Dining
3 Kitchen
4 Entry
5 Bathroom
6 Bedroom

He joined Borland's practice as a fourth-year student in 1978, staying for his fifth year and a year after graduation. It was late in the practice by that stage, and many talented architects, including Morrice Shaw and John Kenny, had already worked there. 'Borland was very socially minded and he injected a sense of conscience and community into how we worked and thought,' says Chen. 'He was talking about community long before it was fashionable and his practice attracted a particular type of architect and client.'

Borland was always at the forefront of Melbourne's architectural scene. He assisted with *The Age* Small Homes Service (previously run by Robin Boyd and, later, Neil Clerehan), which gave the public access to architect-designed houses at an affordable rate. Through this, he met a couple for whom he designed the Rice House (1952–53), using a system called Ctesiphon, whereby concrete is thinly spread over hessian and chicken-wire stretched across timber formwork. This house is made up of a series of arches, and, given the postwar scarcity of materials, made good use of very little.

Borland was part of the winning bid (with Phyllis and John Murphy and Peter McIntyre) for the radical Olympic Swimming Pool (1952–56). A member of the Communist Party, he saw the Preshil School (1962) as a key project, as the input of students was sought as part of the democratic design process.

While many of these projects were finished by the time Chen joined the practice, the culture continued and the spirit of community dominated. He considered this first choice of a major mentor highly significant. 'You could end up a very different person and a different architect if you made the wrong choice at this early stage. To this day, I feel I owe everything to Kevin.'

After graduation, Chen, 'unemployed and unemployable', set up on his own. In an attempt to make ends meet, he wrote about architecture for *The Age* newspaper and interviewed Ian Robinson, who studied with him at university. They formed Robinson Chen in 1980.

While no longer together (the Hildebrand House was at the tail end of their partnership and completed by Chen), he is proud of their accomplishments. 'We were better together than either of us is apart. People who worked with us would say the same. We were incredibly linked, the work was intuitive, rapid and the product of a close understanding.'

The Eighties was a period of intense innovation, multiple projects and award-winning work for Robinson Chen. For example, the Peel House (Mikado) in Rye (1982) won the RAIA Merit Award for Outstanding Architecture (New) and the President's Award for Young Architects in the same year. With its cubic form and distinctive sliced corner entrance, it is described on the Victoria Heritage Listing website as 'a fine and early manifestation of the Deconstructionist branch of post-modernism'.

In 1987, Denis Hildebrand approached the firm to design a beach house on land in Somers, a small coastal town on Victoria's Mornington Peninsula. Located on Merricks Creek, looking towards Western Port Bay and Phillip Island, the site was originally that of a general store servicing Lord Somers Camp, a summer camp engineered to bring together boys from a cross-section of society, and after which the township was named.

'We saw a photo of the creek in an estate agent's window and yet, when we came to the address it wasn't visible,' says Denis Hildebrand. 'Only when you walked through the site did you see it and it felt like something of a surprise.'

This sense of delayed gratification is something that Chen took to heart in the planning of the house. 'It was to be a sanctuary for Denis and Janice, so we took more of an introspective view of things and tried as best we could to tuck the building into the topography,' he said. 'It was the joy of burrowing into the ti trees, feeling the water, smelling it but not seeing it until the last minute, and then finally arriving at the beach...that drove the project.'

The first proposal was for a two-storey, L-shaped house, but its siting was deemed too close to the creek. Back at the drawing board, this scheme emerged. 'When we drew the damned thing up, it looked weird: the elevation was odd-looking but we liked that, it seemed to come from some other place, and the fact that we didn't fully understand it didn't worry us,' says Chen.

The Hildebrands, however, did seem to understand it. 'Immediately we saw the layout, we could see the quality. It was like a little diamond – small and tight with many facets to its exterior,' says Denis.

It was clear when it came to building that traditional processes would not apply. 'The integration of the structure, the servicing, the crafting, the building and the plan all had to come together,' says Chen. 'The engineers worked out how we would build it and then we had immense freedom.' Appearing at first as off-form concrete, the construction is, in fact, timber framed, with bracing plywood inside and out. A layer of cement render, applied over galvanised mesh, acts as a skin. While the materials had altered, the method is not significantly different from the Ctesiphon system Borland used on the Rice House. One of the Hildebrands' requests was that it be 'built like a brick dunny', to withstand strong winds. Using a team of builders and carpenters, who had worked with Robinson Chen over the previous 10 years and were no strangers to new ways of doing things, the building went up over a 12-month period. What emerged is known to locals as 'The Somers Opera House'.

Facing the street are curves and angles; a low wall partially masks the small bedroom windows, so there is little interface on the building's public side. It is a dark, dense object; the only aspect denoting domesticity is its scale. The front door, timber and painted fire engine red, is tucked away at the end of a curved wall. Here begins a journey into colour and geometry. Part of the appeal of the house is the way it treats opposites, so they support, rather than detract from, one another. The exterior is sombre and sculptural while the interior is a nuanced play of colours, textures and light. The street façade contrasts with that of the more conventional waterside one, with its full-height sliding doors set in a horizontal window wall leading out to the garden and creek. The view is fragmented by strong vertical columns, set at rhythmic intervals, an effect achieved, Chen says, by channelling Le Corbusier's monastery at La Tourette.

These columns are treated in the same way externally and internally, and echo the texture and colour of the exterior, linking the two façades. Yet again, there is that play of opposites, and Chen points out, 'The house is radical from the street but when you look back from the creek, it blends into the surrounds.'

Chen talks of his 'intuitive response to the site'; the two characters of the house are defined by the natural landfall, which formed two levels – lower to the north, stepped up to the south. The ground floor holds three small bedrooms (one with an ensuite) and a bathroom. The corridor wall slopes inward as it curves towards the master bedroom and is illuminated by a series of five fluorescent tube lights sliced vertically into the wall. Strongly coloured joinery and masonry in ochre, teal and mauve combine with the geometry of angled doors and tilted lines to give this zone its distinct character.

The stairs linking the bedroom level with the living/dining and kitchen floor are a beautiful example of off-form concrete, designed with pleasing irregularity and sculptural sensitivity. At the top, the turn into the main area reveals the view and makes a sudden connection with the natural world. 'The reward at the end of the journey,' as Chen puts it. While this level is more conventional in its dimensions, and conforms more often to right angles, again colour plays a key role. The ceiling is painted navy blue and floats like a night sky. Chen wanted to create the feeling of camping under the stars – as though one had thrown a tarpaulin over a crevice between rocks on a beach, and is living by the borrowed light of the moon and the stars. The experience makes

THIS PAGE The oblique angle of the external wall in the hallway is reiterated in the narrow bathroom, with the exterior wall leaning outwards by around 10 degrees.

OPPOSITE Bedrooms are sparsely furnished, but the interest comes through the mix of wall textures and the slices of light, both natural and artificial.

OVERLEAF Looking back from the creek onto the upper level, housing the living and dining areas and kitchen, it is hard to reconcile the two 'faces' of the house. From this aspect it sits discreetly on the site in a modest and measured way.

a clear distinction to that of being in the city. It is a primal notion and is a far cry from the halogen light-studded ceilings of many contemporary houses.

The combined management of light, colour and texture is remarkable. 'Ian and I were interested in colour – initially in the Mexican palette of Luis Barragán – and the amazing effect it could have on strong form,' says Chen. 'But for this project I had moved onto muted colours and this scheme emerged. It is unique and I haven't used it since.'

Smooth matt walls contrast with a textured effect achieved by pebbles dragged through the render and coloured to mimic concrete, albeit with a metallic sheen. This rawness, set against the precision of the painted surfaces, is made more apparent by the narrow strip of natural light seeping through the gap between the ceiling and the back wall. 'You are very conscious of the render, and the different light patterns throughout the day, but particularly in the late afternoon as the sun sets,' says Chen.

The kitchen is set behind a coloured partial wall, which neither reaches the ceiling nor spans the entire breadth of the space. One side is the open entrance and, on the other, a lowered cabinet painted a glossy black allows visual access. The geometry is one of squares in a mix of colour (grey and red) and scale; narrow your eyes and it becomes painterly, like the work of the Russian constructivist artist Kazimir Malevich.

During my research I came across a photograph of Kai Chen standing in front of the just completed Hildebrand House in 1990. It was in an article by Davina Jackson in *Vogue Living* showcasing the young Turks of Australian architecture; she notes that his 'methods result from a combination of oriental intuition, deep contemplation and sensitive intelligence'. The Hildebrand House was to bring him even greater exposure when a year later, in 1991, it was prominently featured in the Australian Pavilion at the Venice Biennale.

'Neville Quarry was the Australian Commissioner and wanted to feature the house in the exhibition,' says Chen. 'John Gollings took one black and white exterior photograph and blew it up so that it filled the back wall at the end of a passage. You couldn't miss it.'

Denis Hildebrand and Chen made the trip together and there was much excitement when Neville Quarry arranged for his friend Frank Gehry to visit the pavilion. Denis was there with his movie camera to record the famous architect walk up to the work, walk away and return for a thoughtful second look. Architect Jean Nouvel came with Jack Lang, the French Minister for Culture, who wondered out loud as to the location of the front door.

'The Biennale was an extraordinary time, with incredible people interested in the work and magazines worldwide picking up on it,' says Chen. It is a shared anecdote, which both architect and client enjoy in equal measure, and forms part of their shared history. The collaboration continued: Chen later worked with them on a property in the Melbourne suburb of South Yarra.

As Borland did earlier, Robinson Chen nurtured a new generation of successful architects – Shelley Penn and Kerstin Thompson among others. Of her time there, Thompson says, 'Chen was remarkably astute. He had the ability to quickly find your strengths and capabilities and to draw out your best. This was most marked with Ian Robinson. Ian would create these wonderful 3-D drawings and models and Chen would draw up the plan in red pencil, creating beautiful layered sketches as he worked and reworked the lines.'

Kevin Borland said that 'architecture is not for the faint-hearted'. In the Hildebrands, Chen found clients prepared to brave the process and in doing so they won the prize – a 'diamond of a house' – one that they continue to enjoy as much now as they did when it was first built. When I met them I commented that it was not a house designed with an eye for resale. Denis smiled and agreed. One suspects this distinctive house is theirs for life.

GABRIEL POOLE

E GARTNER HOUSE

1989–1990

'Poole's is a fanciful architecture of freedom. He drives to dissolve the wall and create an unbounded architecture that suggests the wish for the occupant to participate directly with the immediate environment.'

JENNIFER TAYLOR

Architectural historian

PREVIOUS PAGE The complexity of the design of the roof is both beautiful and logical, with the pleasing symmetry and the play of convex and concave curves designed to let light in and water run off.

THIS PAGE The covered walkway, accessed only from the garage, ensures privacy and creates a sense of arrival to the house.

OPPOSITE The sleeping pavilion of Gabriel Poole's groundbreaking Gartner House sits on an elevated position on Queensland's Mount Tamborine.

While stalwartly denying he has an architectural philosophy, one only needs to spend 10 minutes with Gabriel Poole for it to come across loud and clear. It is more that he and the philosophy are one – it does not sit on the surface, but is intrinsic to who he is in all matters personal and professional. As architectural historian Jennifer Taylor said to him, 'Gabriel, you have been blessed with a great talent, you should recognise it comes from a higher place, that it does not really belong to you, and that you have a duty to share it.'

There is a cinematic quality to his life and work. His personal story is quintessentially Australian, and he is the first to admit that he has created great challenges for himself throughout his career. It is clear that these challenges have produced great ingenuity. During a period of financial hardship, he was engaged by Peter Sachs, a friend and managing director of Sachs and Co., who wanted to explore the idea of demountable housing for remote sites in Papua New Guinea. While the project itself came to nothing, Poole developed a system that initiated the first of what he called the quadropod houses – '105' Noosa Valley (1983) – all lightweight prefabricated buildings, of which the Gartner House is a fine, albeit later, example.

A rebel as a child, Poole grew up in Queensland, the son of a Melbourne GP of Irish heritage and an artistic mother, Zelma, who designed the family house in the coastal town of Cleveland. 'Mother was incredible. She was a "bush girl", and she knew the importance of ventilation. She designed a bush seat around the verandah, something I used frequently when I started to design. A lot of my understanding came from her,' says Poole. He was skilled at carpentry, and tells the tale of becoming so frustrated when making a wooden boat that he smashed it with an axe and let rip with a full-on temper tantrum. His mother calmly handed him another bit of wood and recommended he start again. 'It was she who first demonstrated to me the quality of gentleness and love, and instilled in me the ability to perceive and appreciate beauty. She also taught me to hang on, to persevere and keep going when the going got tough.'

His time at boarding school during the war was deeply unhappy, made tolerable by learning to box and understanding the value in taking an 'offensive' position. Poole's father has been described as formal and distant, illustrated by the fact that only one of his children at a time was allowed to join him for the evening meal. He was, by all accounts, proud of his son's boxing ability and

OPPOSITE The dramatic ceiling is the defining feature of the Gartner House: internally, the effect is of two great sailcloths draped to form a roof. This sense of lightness and insubstantiality is made more evident by the broad strip of Perspex that runs the length of the room.

arranged matches in the holidays where Gabriel was required to fight much larger boys in the local pub. He hated fighting – 'I was always scared' – but managed to become a schoolboy boxing champion. His schooling was not a success, and he says he couldn't get out of there fast enough.

At 17, at his own request, he was sent to Gatton Agricultural College where he continued to rebel and provoke, and left after only a year. 'Nobody knew how to handle me. I was a rogue...I must have been really unhappy to be that belligerent,' he says. Running out of options, his mother turned to her friends the Bells, who owned Camboon Station, a 50,000-hectare cattle property on the Dawson River in Queensland. Poole describes Minette and Bill Bell as a second family and acknowledges their tough love shaped his character for the better. He recalls turning up to the property like 'Roy Rogers without the gun' in a city boy approximation of country clothing – pristine RM Williams boots and moleskins – for his job as a jackaroo. Bill Bell asked him whether he had ever ridden a horse. 'To my reply of no, he said, "Well, that horse over there has never been ridden, so you can both start together."'

He stayed in the old homestead and, as Bruce Walker, author of a book on the life and work of Gabriel Poole, notes, in his lightweight constructions 'many of the principles and materials used in the design of the old homestead were to be incorporated: corrugated steel, curved roofs, open living areas with minimal walls and pavilions connected by covered walkways.'

The work was hard, the climate tough and the physical demands on the jackaroos were greater than others working on the property. He stuck it out for three years, the last two as overseer at Camboon before moving to Cracow and Lisburn Stations. While the experience was the making of him, he had the clear realisation it was not what he wanted to do for the rest of his life.

Again, his mother helped shape events. A friend offered accommodation in a rundown gardener's cottage in return for Poole renovating it. 'With the skills I had learnt in the bush, and the sensitivities learnt from my mother, I rebuilt the hut, lined and painted it, and designed and built a new kitchen.'

Several cutting-edge young Queensland architects, John Dalton, Robin Gibson and Don Winsen, were at the party to celebrate the cottage's completion. They were impressed by Poole's innate abilities, and offered him work. 'At the time, I was studying for an entrance exam to get into medicine, but these guys seemed to think they could train me up,' he says.

Poole had an old Morris Minor and, as Gibson couldn't drive, would chauffeur him around building sites, listening and learning as he went. 'Gibson lumped responsibility onto me,' he recalls. He was a great teacher, drawing out of Poole what he thought was wrong with a particular job, and pointing out to him what he had missed. At the same time, Poole went to Brisbane Technical College, where things went less smoothly. 'I was up with the top in final year design, but they failed me in my finals in that subject all the same, just to show me that they could,' he says. 'I did challenge them during the course and tell them that they were untalented idiots, so that was their revenge.'

In 1964, Poole travelled to London, working for architects Jim Cadbury-Brown and later Powell & Moya, designing the nurses' quarters for the Wythenshawe Hospital. He tells of visiting the buildings of Le Corbusier (La Tourette and Ronchamp) and how, with particular Poole determination, he climbed into the scaffold-clad Villa Savoye and took a personal tour of the building during its renovation. While Le Corbusier's mantra of houses as 'machines for living' did not resonate with Poole's humanist streak, he did admire much of the architect's conceptual thinking. The use of *piloti* (columns which elevate the building above ground level) impressed him, and he used them in his Le Corbusier–inspired house for the Fosters in Buderim (1971). More importantly, the idea of elevation above the site became the basis of his

OPPOSITE The sense of structure, where everything is visible and has a purpose, characterises Poole's quadropod architecture. Developed to be portable, there is a transparency of method and honesty of intent. This section shows a guest bedroom on the lower floor.

OVERLEAF A beautifully realised drawing by Poole of the Gartner House.

thinking as he developed the lightweight quadropod style of building. Alvar Aalto, however, did resonate, and Poole later introduced his work to Lindsay Clare, for whom it became a formative influence.

Returning to Australia, he considered a partnership with Robin Gibson before deciding to move in his own direction. In the first house Poole designed for his family in 1962, the Sherwood House, the Miesian preoccupation of Gibson's influence is evident. It is a flat-roofed, U-shape house of concrete block and fibro cement, planned around a courtyard. His concerns for ventilation and airflow are already at play. By 1967 he had sold Sherwood and, on a block bought from his father-in-law in the Brisbane suburb of Graceville, built a timber post-and-beam house using prefabricated elements. Ventilation was addressed by a gauzed verandah to the north (a device used in the Camboon homestead) and innovative skylights, with canvas covers, which could be raised in summer for airflow. In winter, the canvas was removed and the skylights lay flat and returned to their original function.

His first clients, the Shirens, took a punt on a young architect who delivered a mixture of tradition and innovation. The design used a colonnade of telegraph poles and a tiled pitched roof (most unfashionable at this period) to form deep eaves, while construction adopted prefabricated elements.

The Dobie House (1972), perhaps his best known from this period, illustrated an important development. The site, on Buderim Mountain, was steep and unstable; his approach was to bore four deep holes into which he inserted steel poles to support the base platform. From this point, the prefabricated walls were tilted into position. With little disruption to the land, he managed to site this modest holiday house with the full span of its majestic view. Stylistically, it took its cue from Eames and Ellwood, as Poole comments, 'They did very fine sort of steel architecture and floated their buildings over gullies and hills'. Sadly, the Dobie House has since been demolished.

While Poole maintains his primary devotion was to housing, he did have a period in the Seventies where his Sunshine Coast office worked with developers designing commercial buildings and apartment blocks. He tells of being interviewed by Jennifer Taylor, who had been following his work. 'What are you doing interviewing me?' asked Poole. 'Gabriel, you are going to be famous, so you had better get used to it,' she replied. Yet a difficult period was to follow, and the recession of the early Eighties was to see Poole, carrying substantial financial exposure, declared bankrupt.

Two things carried him through: the tremendous support of his second wife, Elizabeth, and the ability to draw on the lessons he had learnt from his mother and Bill Bell. 'It really was the turnaround in my life because I started concentrating on quality architecture. I thought, "Well, if I'm going to be involved in architecture, then I am going to do what I like",' he says.

With necessity the mother of invention, Poole set about developing a building system for Peter Sachs, who wanted a prefabricated solution that could be carried through the jungle of Papua New Guinea and built without the requirement of heavy machinery and with limited skilled resources.

While it was never used for this purpose, Poole successfully used it in his housing. While the '105' Noosa Valley House (1983), for his family, was the first to exploit this technology, other quadropods followed: the Allan House in Dayboro (1984) saw the system refined, and this tiny, elegant house, nicknamed the Samurai House because of its Japanese influence, sits on an Eiffel Tower of legs in the middle of a horse stud farm. The Gloster House was a collaboration with architect Michael Gloster, and utilised Poole's '105' system, and the Noble House (1985–86) at Noosa Heads was on a site so steep that it rendered traditional building impossible. Each time, Poole adapted, learnt and added to the core idea of the system. As Elizabeth said,

'Gabriel never does the same house twice. The site and the client mean each house is an individual solution.'

In 1990, the Pooles' own house, the Tent House in Eumundi, took the architectural world by storm. Friend and architect Lindsay Clare had sent it as part of the Australian submission to the Venice Biennale and he persuaded Poole to enter the house for an RAIA award. Poole had boycotted the institute for decades after a dispute over process, so it was a major rapprochement for him to enter. In return, they gave the Tent House the Robin Boyd Award. The ensuing publicity generated 3000 enquiries – none of which resulted in a commission. The downside was that his work was associated with fragility and impermanence. As Jennifer Taylor said, his drive to 'dissolve the wall and create an unbounded architecture' had emotional appeal, but ultimately the challenge of living that way was too much for most people.

There were, however, clients for whom his work had strong and lasting resonance. Angela Rawnsley had been shown the Noble House by a friend and knew it was exactly what she wanted. She approached Gabriel Poole to say she wanted a house but didn't have the money – just yet. Two years later she came back. 'I had bought the land, two blocks in Mount Tamborine, so overgrown with lantana that I didn't even know I had a view until I propped a ladder against a tree and climbed up,' she recalls. 'The real estate agent recommended I get a goat to control the vegetation.'

'Good clients get good houses,' says Poole. Rawnsley, an artist, had a few stipulations and then left the rest to him. The house had to accommodate a living/dining room, a kitchen, a bedroom and a studio on one level and two more bedrooms, bathroom and laundry on the lower level.

She had a Chinese screen that was to form a pivotal part of the living room; she needed light, and she 'liked the roofline of a hotel in Noosa that Gabriel had designed'. It was to be a custom-made house to suit her requirements. Rather like Virginia Woolf's *A Room of One's Own*, this was to be Rawnsley's 'House of Her Own'. She was at a stage where she had to only suit herself.

She didn't like cooking – the kitchen is small. She wanted seclusion – the house is approached via a bridge accessed through a lockable garage. She wanted an open house with breezes – the house is sited for maximum airflow. 'The site is extremely steep and drops over the edge of the cliff to the floor of the valley some hundreds of metres below, with views to the north-east over the Gold Coast and the Pacific Ocean,' says Poole.

Without the quadropod system, and its reduced footings with only slight disturbance to the site, and the ability of the system to calibrate the platform to get it square, it would have been impossible to build. Poole's brother Simon, a steel fabricator, built the structure to platform level and then a builder friend of Angela Rawnsley took over from that point.

'By this time, I was separating quadropods into towers and using the space in between to install staircases,' says Poole. The internal staircase spans the width of this space with Perspex risers providing visibility of the terrain below.

The roof, however, is the defining feature of the Gartner House. The cross-section shows the Oriental feel of the sweeping Custom Orb corrugated steel that peaks above both the living room and the master bedroom. In each instance, the ridge becomes a strip of Perspex, which acts as a light source but also, when viewed internally, enhances the feeling that the roof is afloat. While the interior is refined, the exterior blends with the setting as rough hewn weatherboards and corrugated steel become lost in the tropical rainforest.

Once, after a glass of wine, Rawnsley steeled herself to call Poole and tell him, 'I love this house – it has changed my life.' While the RAIA Gold Medal (which Poole received in 1998) is the ultimate accolade from his peers, Rawnsley's statement must surely be the ultimate accolade from a client.

WOOD MARSH

T

E GOTTLIEB HOUSE

1990–1994

'The game here is one of geometric forms. An elliptical raw concrete drum, a glass cube, a slab of concrete resting on parallel concrete walls. Each precisely arranged, the composition a study in sculptural abstraction. This is stark architecture; outwardly unwelcoming and impenetrable. There are no windows to the street.'

JOE ROLLO
Concrete Poetry

PREVIOUS PAGE The Gottlieb House is an exercise in abstract forms and geometric shapes, its impassive concrete and glass façade giving nothing away to the street.

THIS PAGE The entrance to the house is through a large-scale steel door with the glass cube hovering overhead.

OPPOSITE The atrium echoes the exterior in form and materiality. The light from the skylight illuminates the space and changes the mood with the time of day and the seasons.

OPPOSITE The study space, with table and chairs designed by Wood Marsh, makes a connection with the garden through large floor-to-ceiling windows.

OVERLEAF, LEFT PAGE The huge entertaining space has a museum-like quality, yet its relationship to the garden enlivens the space.

OVERLEAF, RIGHT PAGE Materiality is used to denote the structural elements of the house: the roughly rendered section in the ceiling, broken by slices of glazing, echo the bedrooms above.

When Roger Wood mentions, in passing, the de Chirico-esque nature of the Gottlieb House, it makes immediate sense. As architects who draw on the art world for inspiration, rather than that of their own profession past or present, the reference is fitting, given the Italian artist's penchant for enigmatic architectural vistas, often including a featureless tower. 'The lack of immediate legibility leads to uncertainty about scale and refutes domesticity,' says Wood.

The brief the Gottliebs gave the architects included but a few mandatory requests, of which anonymity was primary. 'Be big and don't give anything away from the street, they said, and beyond that they left it to us,' says Marsh. Set on a flat block in the Melbourne suburb of Caulfield, the house is surrounded by a stylistic mixed bag of inter-war homes. 'Suburban subdivisions are something we grew up with, but we always think they need challenging,' says Wood. 'When applying for a planning permit for this, the council said that we had to address the context that we were building in. So I looked at the context and said to the planner that I thought it was somewhere between Tel Aviv and a James Bond film.'

With its austere monumentality and refusal to give any clues of domesticity, it is no wonder that during construction, neighbours thought the Gottlieb House was a new squash court or a mini-power station. As pointed out in the ABC television series *In the Mind of the Architect*, the house was indeed 'thumbing its concrete nose at convention'.

Both Roger Wood and Randal Marsh graduated from the Royal Melbourne Institute of Technology (RMIT). After a brief spell working in other architectural firms, they established Biltmoderne with Dale Jones-Evans in 1983 and together designed the Choong House in Eltham (1985–87). It was radical in its design, won the 1987 RAIA Merit Award for Outstanding Architecture, Residential (New), and Wood comments that it contains certain core themes that have remained in their work. 'The idea of converging blank walls to a door or an opening is something we are still doing, and was a device we used in the Port Phillip [Estate] Winery.'

Even earlier, though, in 1985, Biltmoderne had won the RAIA Merit Award for Outstanding Architecture, Commercial (New), with their project for

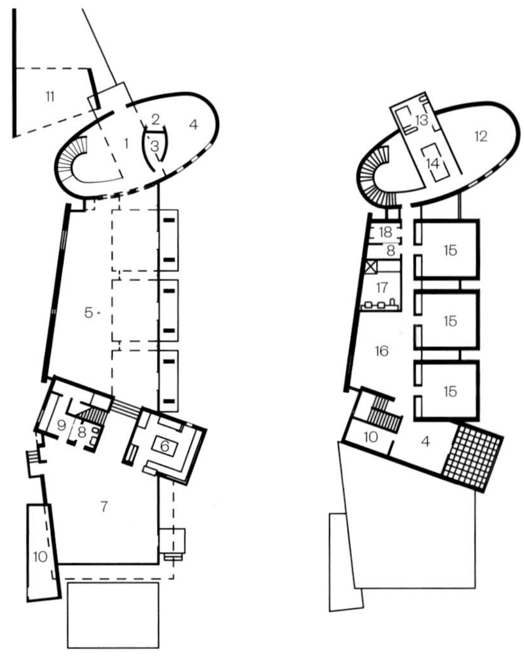

GROUND FLOOR PLAN

FIRST FLOOR PLAN

N

1 Entry	10 Plant
2 Cloak	11 Carport
3 Powder room	12 Master bedroom
4 Study	13 Ensuite
5 Living/dining	14 Robe
6 Kitchen	15 Bedroom
7 Family	16 Living
8 WC	17 Bathroom
9 Laundry	18 Store

Inflation Nightclub. For a period in the Eighties, they were the architects to go to if you wanted a cutting-edge nightclub design, and they worked on a series of spaces – Subterrain, Chasers and The Metro in Melbourne. They exploited theatricality through use of sets and lighting – both natural and staged – and were at pains to avoid 'evenness' in their work by embracing the movement through dark to light, and managing the flux of space and form. This was a fertile and inventive period when they were also designing furniture, theatre sets, installations and interiors. In 1984, they designed the film studio, McCrae and Way, in South Melbourne and it was here, in 1987, that Joe and Pesa Gottlieb, while visiting, first saw their work.

'It was such a strong, honest structure with a great use of space,' says Pesa. 'There wasn't a square room, yet everything worked. Joe only ever saw the façade, but it was enough to convince him.'

Prior to the Gottliebs, Wood Marsh had designed a string of houses on suburban sites around Melbourne. The most notable was the Kyritsis House (1988), in Eaglemont, in which geometry, weight and abstraction were the defining elements. 'It's part of a body of work that deals with perspective and composition,' says Marsh. 'The basic form is made from two tapered blocks on the ground floor and a third bridging block.' It presents a somewhat daunting façade, not only in its dense sculptural form, but also in its cladding materials: bluestone tiles and roughly textured cement render. Graham Jahn, in his book *Contemporary Australian Architecture*, observes, 'the simple heavy massing...stands defiantly against the "lightweight" conception of modernism as the product of minimal frames, floating planes and transparent walls. This building avoids such delicacy, preferring instead substantiality.'

Key for the Gottlieb House was the sense that Wood Marsh had moved beyond what they termed as the 'standard domestic configuration' and were primed to take their thinking to the next level. Pesa Gottlieb acknowledges they were naïve about the process. 'We just picked up the phone and said that we would like them to design a house for us. It was that simple.' Wood Marsh, who had set up their own practice in 1987, were delighted. 'We were commissioned in November 1989 and, by January 1990, there was a recession looming,' says Marsh. 'It was our first really big budget house, a full-on commission with clients who seemed to be up for anything. It was perfect.'

As well as privacy, the Gottliebs, who had three boys, had a few other stipulations that allowed the project to flourish. They wanted an entertaining area big enough to invite 350 guests to their eldest son's bar mitzvah, four bedrooms and a low-maintenance solution. 'We were young when we were doing the house and, fortunately, at the time we could afford it,' says Joe Gottlieb. 'Everything they described during the design process was built exactly as promised and without compromise.'

It became Wood Marsh's first 'complete' building, with a sense of unity throughout. 'The materiality of the building is exactly the same internally as externally,' says Wood. Externally, it presents as a massive elliptical concrete drum with a silvery, gridded glass box grafted onto the façade. Right from the outset, a dynamic is set up. The concrete form is industrial and massive, while the light-reflecting glass box (which Wood Marsh likens to a flash bulb) that protrudes over the large stainless steel front door is a finer, more precisely engineered aspect of the composition. To the street, it feels challenging and monolithic, especially in the setting of the surrounding Brady Bunch–style houses. 'We are keen that our buildings aren't defined [from the exterior] as a house or art gallery or restaurant. It is a theme that runs through our work,' says Wood.

To step inside is an awe-inspiring experience – something normally achieved in public or religious spaces rather than domestic settings. 'The theatrical quality of the work is to do with our understanding of scale and how people react to it,' says Wood.

The elliptical drum in raw concrete forms the atrium. To the right, a soaring curved staircase (its shape emphasised by a custom-made stainless steel handrail) leads to the main bedroom and ensuite. Cut into the ceiling is a circular skylight throwing an ovoid of sunlight by day, moonlight by night, into the heroically spare interior. To the left, a roughly rendered curved wall conceals a small guest bathroom and study space beyond. This area echoes the curve of the bedroom above, with the two levels sharing lights – what forms a ceiling light in the study becomes a floor light above.

From the atrium, 'you can see there is a spine, albeit curved and twisted, that runs through from the front door to the slice of green in the garden at the rear of the property', says Marsh. 'It clearly illustrates the transition through the space.' The atrium leads directly to an enormous (20 metres by 10 metres) rectilinear living and dining space. It is essentially a monochromatic but soft, light-absorbing interior – pale green onyx crushed into the terrazzo flooring gives the impression of scattered autumn leaves, while gold fabric-covered sofas, that Wood Marsh designed specifically for the house, and the artworks the architects chose ease the restricted material palette.

Animating this large space are slices of light, dragged into the building as the sun moves across the north-facing long elevation. The ever-changing light effects, and the connection to nature between house and garden, continue to delight the owners.

The transition to the family living area from the more formal space is made by an artificial rise in level and a move through a corridor of charcoal-coloured stacked slate. A series of textural, visual and scale cues throughout the house mark the move from public to private space. 'The family living area and bedrooms are compressed in scale, they have lower ceilings and hence are more intimate,' says Wood.

The house is circulatory in nature, with stairs, of markedly different character, at either end. From a door in the family room, its walls painted dark charcoal to create a sense of enclosure, the stairs lead up to the boys' bedrooms and bathroom, another seating area and a corridor to the parents' quarters.

From there, a left turn leads to the curved staircase down to the atrium entrance. This sense of the circulatory is literal, but Wood explains that the sculptural form means that, from any point, there are different views, with the layering of sequential forms, of external and internal vistas, of the interplay of light and textures within the building. It is both serene and, paradoxically, without a dull moment.

'Early on, our investigations into geometry were to do with getting away from the rectilinear, the obvious corner and the flat elevation,' he says. 'The ideas that inspire us are often about not seeing everything at once but requiring the viewer to move around, like one would a sculpture, in order to understand it fully.'

As with many groundbreaking aspects of the design, there was the challenge of finding the right tradespeople for the slate walls, the formwork and the glass work on the box. Joe Gottlieb recalls that the recession meant few on the team, including the architects, had other jobs at the time, and so the house received a rare level of attention to detail. As Joe Rollo commented in his book *Concrete Poetry*, 'There is a kind of rigour in design in this house you seldom come across in residential architecture. All has been considered, every opportunity has been explored and you are left with the impression that no detail has been left unexamined.' It is bespoke in every sense of the word.

Wood and Marsh are both design architects, and when asked if the design scheme came easily, Marsh is unequivocal. 'It did, because all our work is an ongoing dialogue about design, so nothing is ever laboured.'

THIS PAGE The bathroom mixes the luxurious and industrial: leaf-cut marble, terrazzo, glass, mirror and stainless steel.

OPPOSITE The bedhead in the master bedroom conceals drawers, accessed from the dressing room behind. The floor lighting, at lower left, doubles with ceiling lighting in the room below.

OVERLEAF, LEFT PAGE To the left of the entrance, a guest bathroom and study are tucked behind a curved, roughcast render wall.

OVERLEAF, RIGHT PAGE The view along the north-facing wall shows how the first floor bedrooms sit over the main entertaining area, and how it links to the drum form at the front of the house.

'We did, however, have some debate around the kitchen as neither had used one in their lives,' recalls Pesa. The result, however, is generous in cupboard space and working surfaces, with angled windows providing views to the side of the house.

With three boys in the family, robustness was paramount, and the architects recall, with a degree of pride, the time they visited to find a basketball hoop had been installed in the main space, not to mention the bar mitzvah for which the entertaining area was designed – not only were there two punk bands and a bar, but guests exceeded the 400 mark.

The patina the house gains as the years go by is viewed by Pesa and Joe as adding to its character, but its fundamental solidity, level of craftsmanship and forward-thinking design mean that it has neither dated nor decayed.

The main ensuite is a case in point. Located in the glass box that spans inside and out, it has a rare combination of drama and taste. An expanse of leaf-cut marble forms the back wall, a circular skylight creates a moving light source and the elegant stainless steel wall cabinets nod to the industrial. The shower sits above a magnificent marble trough, which was designed to double as a bath (but was never used that way), and mirrored walls provide endless reflections. It is a bathroom that has endured both stylistically and functionally.

The adjoining bedroom, with its raw concrete interior, has been given a touch of luxury with an over-scale padded bedhead, designed by Wood Marsh, which accommodates drawers accessed from the other side of the wall, and subdued lighting from a series of floor lights around the perimeter of the room.

Pesa Gottlieb admits that her friends have begun to tell her they now understand what she and Joe were doing back then, and neighbours no longer approach them with paint charts making helpful suggestions for exterior colours.

'In the beginning, we were such a focus of attention,' she says. 'I was making coffee one morning, not long after the house was finished, and there were five men in black suits standing in the garden. Ignore them, they are architects, Roger assured me.'

Just as you cannot judge a book by its cover, you clearly cannot judge a house by its façade. Industrial, forbidding and intriguing to the street it may be, but inside there is beauty, joy, art, connection to nature, to light and the changing seasons. It is a robust family space that takes entertaining in its stride and is undaunted by a basketball game or a bucks' night. It is another example of Gabriel Poole's maxim that clients get the houses they deserve, and maybe the serendipity of architects finding the clients they, in turn, deserve.

Wood Marsh challenged the notion of suburban architecture with the Gottlieb House; it provided a base for later work, both commercial and residential and, as such, is pivotal. Their first large urban design project, the Eastern Freeway, owes a debt to the Gottlieb House in its use of concrete walls, and the later warehouse conversion, the Taylor House (1997), employs the same restricted (and non-domestic) palette and materiality, and has a similar sense of the unexpected.

Through their remarkable partnership, Wood Marsh have been able to shape the city of Melbourne with groundbreaking projects, from the Australian Centre for Contemporary Art (ACCA) (1996–2002), a structure in Corten steel that is as much sculptural object as building, to Yve (2007), a building of such sinuous curves it redefines the words 'apartment block'. While they do not chase awards, the foyer of their office is running out of wall space to accommodate the number of framed certificates. As self-described mid-career architects with a long way to go, they had better nominate another space.

THE M

ANDRESEN O'GORM

OOLOOMBA HOUSE

AN

1995

'With its belvedere seeming to hang in the treetops, inviting both the breeze and the ocean, the house is essentially a landscape pavilion closer to a Japanese moon viewing platform than a suburban cottage.'

PETER TONKIN

Architect

PREVIOUS PAGE The easterly, long side of the house, with outdoor staircase leading to the belvedere and the north-facing ocean view, embraces a garden of banksia and fish fern.

THIS PAGE The louvred windows in the bedrooms ensure through breezes.

OPPOSITE The entrance to the house shows how the walkway was constructed around the tree.

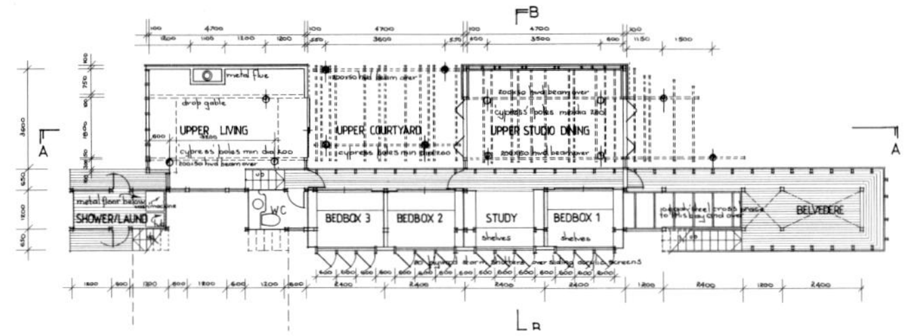

UPPER FLOOR PLAN

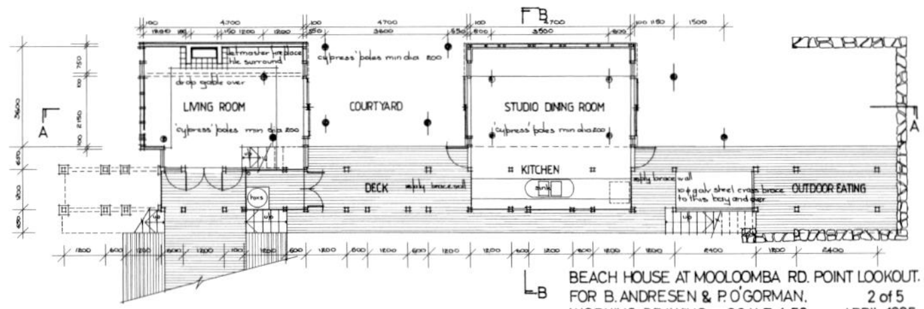

LOWER FLOOR PLAN

Brit Andresen's reputation precedes her. Long before I have the opportunity to interview her, I hear only good things from peers and students alike. Glenn Murcutt admired her work; Timothy Hill of Donovan Hill had been inspired by her teaching, and had worked with her on the property adjacent to the Mooloomba House; even friends who have simply toured the Highgate Hill House in Brisbane enthused. Despite a relatively small body of work, Brit Andresen and her late husband, Peter O'Gorman, garnered international attention and, in 2002, she received the RAIA Gold Medal (the highest award in Australian architecture), the first time it had been awarded to a woman. Her acceptance was coupled with sadness, as O'Gorman had only recently died and all their work, both academic and design projects, was the result of collaborative thought. 'We would keep looking, keep thinking, keep talking – these are the ways of sharing insights. It wasn't planned, it was just driven by one another's interest and conversation about architecture,' Andresen says of their partnership, which spanned more than 25 years.

The house they designed and built together is a summary of many of their shared philosophies and how, as Andresen noted, 'by engaging in poetic abstraction as well as the pragmatic', they created a building where 'inside–outside boundaries become eroded and illusive, forming rooms, alcoves and a belvedere which are both inside and out'.

There are three townships on North Stradbroke Island, which lies off the south-eastern coast of Queensland – Dunwich, Amity Point and Point Lookout, a tourist destination on the surf side of the island where whale watching is a holiday pastime. Andresen and O'Gorman bought land in Point Lookout in 1985. 'It has always been a tightly held area,' says Andresen. 'We might have preferred to be further from neighbours and the road, but this was a north-facing block and that's so difficult to find.'

Sitting at a table in the nest-like belvedere looking out to sea, Andresen explains the thinking behind the house and the long journey, both geographically and intellectually, to get to this point. While born to Norwegian parents in the small town of Sandnes, she has little memory of it. From the age of five until she left home at 17, after her school Leaving Certificate, she had an Australian upbringing. Her father, an engineer who initially worked on the Snowy Mountains Hydro-Electric Scheme, brought his family out by boat in 1951. They

PREVIOUS PAGE The sand courtyard sits between the more enclosed and sheltered 'cave' room, and the double-height living and dining area. The design combines regular rhythmic patterns with the seemingly random.

OPPOSITE The narrow walkway above the kitchen is used to access the 'bed boxes', the small enclosed bed spaces.

THIS PAGE While the majority of the house is of open, light, single-skin construction, the winter room is more conventional, dedicated to the seasonal change and to lower temperatures.

moved around, but Andresen's teenage years were spent in Sydney, and she went to Hornsby Girls' High School. 'Some of the strongest feelings and love of the landscape come from growing up on the North Shore, because at that time you could walk out the back door and into a gully of native bushland,' she says.

At 17, she travelled to England via the United States. 'I remember being intrigued by buildings such as the newly built Eero Saarinen's airport terminal in Washington, DC.' However, at that time, her primary interest was in biological sciences and art but, encouraged by a wonderful high school teacher, Barry Fulton, she developed an interest in seeing and thinking about the physical environment, and an ability to trust her own judgment. She found the models and drawings of architecture student friends curiously engaging, and by the time she had received her exam results was ready to apply to (and be accepted by) the Architectural Association in London.

At the time, her father had accepted a post in India, and her parents were keen for her to move back to Norway to study. Andresen attended NTH Trondheim where she qualified as a *Sivil Arkitekt* in 1969. 'My Norwegian was of the 200-word variety when I arrived, but I could pick up the language easily enough,' she says. 'What was more difficult, initially, were the cultural nuances.'

Educationally, she was exposed to areas of interest that have stayed with her to this day. 'I loved learning about architecture from the beginning. I just soaked it up,' she says. 'We studied the history of timber buildings in Norway, some of which were over 1000 years old. Learning about history was another way of making up for not having the Norwegian cultural experience.'

It was also a time of rich and varied influence. Visiting lecturers and part-time teachers from the UK, America, Sweden and Finland came to Trondheim, and students travelled in small groups to Milan and Rome. 'We looked at Italian streetscapes – which were so different from those in Scandinavia – the way streets were furnished by architecture, and the ways in which people used public space,' Andresen recalls.

A Dutch-Norwegian scholarship to explore alternative approaches to multiple housing involved a move to Holland, shortly followed by an invitation from John Hix (who had been a visiting teacher in Trondheim) to go to Cambridge University to participate in an event and studio teaching at the school of architecture.

At Cambridge she met Barry Gasson, also a part-time lecturer, and together they put forward a competition submission for the prestigious Burrell Collection in Glasgow. 'The brief was beautifully put together and it was exciting to work on,' says Andresen. 'But none of us expected to go through to the short list.' When they did, they involved John Meunier (Gasson's partner in their joint architectural practice) to assist in the development of the project. It was a momentous achievement to win the competition in 1972.

The first half of the 1970s was a fulfilling time for Andresen – teaching in Cambridge and at the Architectural Association, and travelling to Glasgow to develop the plans for one of the most exciting public works in Britain at the time. Then, in 1976, came an economic downturn, and the museum project was shelved. Colleagues began looking for jobs overseas and one friend drew her attention to a teaching job at the University of Queensland. 'I had an interview in London and I remember the interviewers, who were English, all but dissuading me from going, implying that I would be better off staying in the UK.'

Undeterred, in 1977 Andresen drove across the New South Wales border into Queensland, and was struck by the Queenslanders. 'These timber houses with their big roofs and wide verandahs, with filigree and batten work, were so different from Sydney houses, and I imagined that the architecture school must be housed in one of these,' she recalls. She was surprised to discover the school in a concrete structure not unlike those she had left behind in England.

When she arrived, there were no women teaching there, but a growing number of female students. Undaunted, she set about plugging the gaps as she saw fit. 'I did a lot to try to increase student expectations in the first few years. I saw that students didn't assemble work in portfolios, didn't hold an end-of-year exhibition or have an exhibition space or produce an end-of-year publication,' says Andresen. 'I was fortunate to find interested students and colleagues who collaborated on these initiatives.'

Peter O'Gorman, who was keen for the school to move forward in the same way, was one of the first people Andresen met, when the head of the department suggested they might like to work together in the first semester. It signalled the beginning of a long and fruitful partnership in both life and work.

After doing some building work with his uncles during his teenage years, O'Gorman, Brisbane born and bred, had decided that, while he enjoyed the building process, his real interest was in learning to design buildings. He enrolled in Industrial High in Brisbane because it taught geometrical drawing, then a requirement for entry to the architecture course at the University of Queensland, in which he enrolled in 1958.

On graduating, he won the A.E. Brooks Travelling Scholarship that took him on a trip to compare the organic growth of Greek villages with the Danish model of planned social housing. The rest of Europe followed, through Denmark and Finland into Russia, across Siberia and then to Japan.

'Travelling overseas became an important source of ideas and learning about architecture,' says Andresen. 'You can't really know enough about a building or public space from a book – you have to experience places and see them in their wider context. Travelling informed our teaching, research and our work together.'

Their first joint project was an extension to a small cottage in New South Wales. 'It wasn't so much the idea that we would form a practice – we just started designing together and our practice evolved,' says Andresen.

By the time they worked on the Deer Park, a tourist lodge, they had known one another for three years and found it interesting to work on a non-residential scheme. 'Peter taught me to design with the local hardwood, a material that the local carpenters know how to handle. We both studied American Arts and Crafts architect Bernard Maybeck – we enjoyed his sense of humour – and so thought we could raise a smile with shaping the ends of beams as abstracted animal heads to decorate the Deer Park hunting lodge.'

Professor Philip Goad has described their residential commissions as a 'laboratory for three things: refining the use of Australian hardwood as a building material; the use of mathematical proportions and harmonic series as ordering devices; the constant search for an appropriate creation and definition of space'. All find full expression in the Mooloomba House. They had bought the land more than 10 years earlier, but as they didn't have the funds to build, they even contemplated selling at one point. O'Gorman felt the only way to get on with it was to take a year of unpaid leave, make a start and make something small. The other persuasive factor was that Graham Mellor, a joiner and carpenter they had worked with for many years, was available. 'He understands what is involved in making a house where the construction is made fully visible,' says Andresen.

They debated having elements built on the mainland and sent across, but Mellor preferred the control of working on site. Therefore, the design had to work well within the construction skill set and the tools available. Glass for the double-height windows, for example, came in sections which were joined with lead came; doors were made on site rather than in a factory, and appliances kept small so that they could fit in the car if they needed repair.

The house sets out to satisfy basic human needs of shelter: sleeping, cooking, bathing and relaxing, but finds solutions to satisfy the soul as well.

THIS PAGE The simple 'bed box' design is in keeping with the easy lifestyle of a holiday house.

OPPOSITE The measured design evokes a Japanese love of craft through the narrowness of the staircase and the depth of each stair tread.

OVERLEAF The belvedere is intentionally confined, and the sense of a nest enhanced by the use of woven timbers in the balustrade.

'Peter and I often talked about the human appetite. Humans like sweet things, but not all the time; we like salt, but it is unbearable in huge quantities. It is the same when things are just too utilitarian; it doesn't fully satisfy the appetite. The utilitarian gives answers, but the poetic creates wonder, and architecture involves the inclusion of these two, often competing, qualities.'

Because Andresen believes that architecture is experienced mostly below the level of consciousness, the Mooloomba House introduces design with many opposites: enclosure and openness; rhythms of regular geometry against the seemingly random; untreated bark contrasted with smooth planed and pigment-stained boards; standard issue and custom made; transparency and solidity. All are held together in a balance in which each underscores the significance of the other. There is a sense that every aspect of the house has been deeply considered, assumptions about what a house should be have been questioned, and solutions expressed honestly and directly.

Its siting defies the norm of directing the focus towards the view, instead lying along the western boundary with 'floating' platforms and walkways wrapping around the banksia trees and fish fern to the east. It is only when one takes the external staircase to the belvedere that the ocean view is apparent.

Philip Goad describes the house as 'a long inhabited "wall" with two permanent "tents" attached'; the climate permits it to be formed by a series of screens and 18 mm–thick ply. It is complex to describe, and yet simple to understand when one is there, consisting of two primary rooms visually linked across a sand courtyard – one a small 'winter' room and the most conventional in the house, with plasterboard internally and fibre cement sheeting externally, to 'create a room that is more sheltered and cave-like', according to Andresen.

The structure surrounding the banksia court is an open timber framework with some areas enclosed by marine ply sheeting (2100 x 1200 mm) trimmed to achieve the proportions of the Golden Mean. Inside, the supports are locally sourced cypress poles, stripped of bark to give a smooth appearance, but maintaining all the character of a tree trunk. These are mirrored by the poles in the sand courtyard, but in this external space they retain their bark.

The primary and secondary frame of the house is revealed throughout, and is its most expressive component. Externally, around the courtyard, the rhythm of the frame is quite regular, at 600 mm, 1200 mm and 2400 mm spacing.

Staining with pigmented eucalyptus oil brings unity to the structure and enables the eye to register the line work of the timber framing painted black. Inside, the play of geometry, while seemingly random, is in parts based on the Fibonacci Sequence, and creates its own visual dynamism. It is this balance of relationships between competing factors – visual complexity with order – that Andresen believes contributes to the richness of the building. She acknowledges that with design, 'sometimes intentions are pre-planned and sometimes kept open to take advantage of opportunities'. Something that might be required for utilitarian reasons can present an opportunity to extend a poetic resonance. The battens around the belvedere are regular and functional, but weave into them sections of timber and you have a metaphor for a nest or basket, and the experience is subtly transformed.

The design choreographs with scale – narrow doorways and the galley walkway at bedroom level (only 600 mm wide) and four enclosed 'bed boxes' contrast with the double-height living area. The belvedere, looking out to a wide view, is a small, tight space and this experience of containment is something that Andresen and O'Gorman liked to explore. 'So much of our childhood imaginings take place under a table or in a "little house" and there is a lot written about the way those imaginings can carry poetics into later life,' she says. 'So we liked the idea of sleeping in a small space, a kind of tree house. Or this belvedere – it could lose these associations if it were large.'

There were several ways in which the economy of construction was addressed. The house is small, 65 square metres, in terms of internal space, but the ways in which external areas have been appropriated and the selective use of enclosure make it seem much larger. Costs were contained by keeping bathroom and kitchen elements to a minimum, and using standard ply sheeting and corrugated acrylic roofing (used as a wall in the main room) for the single skin structure, alongside locally sourced cypress poles. Wastage was also minimised and 'when we ran out of money we would simply stop work until we had more and could move on to the next stage', says Andresen.

The fact that they were their own client meant that they 'knew the kind of things we enjoyed, just simple things, and the fact that it was a holiday house brought freedom and a sense of adventure', she says.

One of the most beautiful things about the house is the changing play of light throughout the day, as it passes through battens and corrugated acrylic. At times it is soft and diffuse, at others it takes on the geometry of a Bridget Riley painting. The sense of transparency communicates itself through light and breezes, plus the ability to move through internal/external space both visually and physically with the greatest of ease.

The house has been likened to a sixteenth-century Japanese tea house and, certainly, there is a purity and simplicity achieved through deep thought and architectural understanding. Where the real strength lies is in its humanity, its ability to tune into the fundamentals of experience and to, in turn, delight.

Peter Tonkin and Ellen Woolley, in Peter O'Gorman's obituary in *Architecture Australia*, wrote that 'while his built work was never ordinary it celebrated ordinary values of (apparent but hard won) simplicity of comfort and humanity'. The Mooloomba House is testament to this most fundamental of truths.

THE

DURBACH BLOCK

ROGA APARTMENT

1996–1997

'The form of the penthouse is intentionally mute and sculptural, a tough response in a tough neighbourhood. This muscular exterior belies the smooth, calm and elastic interior, a distinctive mix of urban immersion and overview.'

DURBACH BLOCK ARCHITECTS

PREVIOUS PAGE As owner Daniel Droga points out, the apartment sits like a sculpture on a brick plinth, illustrating Durbach Block's ability to make buildings 'fit' the existing urbanscape.

THIS PAGE Both Durbach and Block voiced their appreciation of this perspective, which simultaneously takes in the exterior city view and the main sweep of the room, bisected by the powerful curve of the wall.

OPPOSITE The meeting of the original brick wall of the adjacent building and the sweep of the zinc cladding illustrates the successful dynamic of the pairing.

OPPOSITE Voids in the wall are practical – the doorway – and aesthetic, with the geometric treatment puncturing the wall's solidity, allowing a beam to cut through at ceiling height.

OVERLEAF View from the mezzanine level shows curved walls echoing one another, and steel posts and beams, emphasising the building's origins.

The genesis of any architectural project is interesting, and none more so than that of the Droga Apartment. Sometimes the client knows the architect by reputation, is a friend of a friend, or has seen a particular work that has stirred excitement. The Droga Apartment is the result of a series of events that make it a wonder it ever happened at all, let alone with the multi-award-winning outcome it has enjoyed.

Camilla Block happened to be travelling with her sister in India (visiting Le Corbusier and Kahn projects in Ahmedabad) near where Daniel and Lyndell Droga were getting married. Camilla ended up with an invitation to the wedding and, during a conversation, Droga mentioned that he found it awkward dealing with the architects he had shortlisted to undertake a warehouse conversion in Sydney's Surry Hills. Camilla defended the profession, pointing out that one wants an architect to be slightly antisocial, to devote time to mulling things over rather than putting their energies into being highly personable. Droga, impressed by her directness, engaged Durbach Block for the project. 'When I saw their work, particularly the Einfeld Apartment, the connection was immediate,' he says.

'Daniel was the first client to walk into our office and say he wanted a contemporary building,' says Block. 'Neil [Durbach] and I had been working together for five years; this project solidified our working relationship, gave us a name together and was the first building published under Durbach Block.' It also won both the Wilkinson and the Robin Boyd awards for residential architecture, scooping, respectively, the state and national prizes in 1997.

Both Durbach and Block have roots in South Africa. While Block was educated in Australia and returned to South Africa for two working years during her architecture degree, Durbach was educated in Cape Town, and his philosophy shaped by his time there.

While some architects are born to the profession, others have a road to Damascus moment when confronted with something truly great. This moment illuminates, with great intensity, the power of architecture. It also has the ability to transform a passive interest in the subject into a passion. Such was the case with Neil Durbach. He was something of a self-confessed dilettante, who decided early in life, because of his great facility for drawing, to be an artist. 'My mother wanted me to be a doctor, or at least study law,

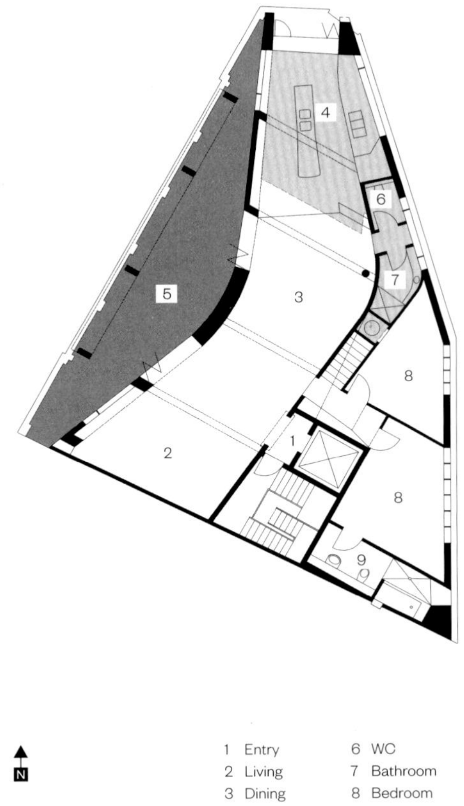

1 Entry
2 Living
3 Dining
4 Kitchen
5 Terrace
6 WC
7 Bathroom
8 Bedroom
9 Ensuite

but I liked the look of the architectural set with their sports cars and leather jackets,' he says.

After a schooling he describes as akin to a military camp, university was a liberating experience. Study at the University of Cape Town involved making movies and Marxist theorising rather than any serious study, but a trip during his fourth year changed all that. 'My father put me on a cargo ship to America,' says Durbach, and a visit to Louis Kahn's Exeter Library in New Hampshire crystallised for him what great architecture could do. 'I realise it is a cliché, but I had this amazing physical reaction to it,' he says. 'I gave up the frivolous stuff, and became addicted to architecture and worked obsessively.'

While Kahn's architecture carried great sway in South Africa, Durbach was to find other heroes, both locally and internationally. Close to home it was Roelof Uytenbogaardt, a practising architect and professor of planning at the University of Cape Town, who paid little heed to the colonial heritage and rigorously pursued abstraction. His emphatically sculptural buildings defined what it was to be progressive in Cape Town in the Seventies, and the students revered his uncompromising approach.

'His works were amazingly ahead of their time,' says Durbach. 'Although he studied with Kahn, he drifted into a more Corbusian oeuvre and produced these incredibly athletic, muscular spatial works.' For similar reasons, Durbach is drawn to the work of Le Corbusier and James Stirling. He admires Le Corbusier's willingness to subvert the expected, and in Stirling's work he applauds the expansive gesture, the materially massive and his lack of concern for the overly detailed. Durbach is drawn to a devil-may-care attitude, the broad brush and the big idea – he finds fussiness tiresome.

As a student, another pressing question was what it meant to be African and how architecture should manifest in that context. 'It was incredibly important at the time, and there were the two schools of thought,' says Durbach. 'Those that adopted a sort of postmodern adaptation of forms where everything looked African, and those that felt it necessary to understand the deep history and the connection with the land.'

It was to Australia in 1983 that Durbach 'dragged these complexities', inspired by movies of the time – George Miller's *Mad Max* and Peter Weir's *The Last Wave*. He felt their energy and rawness, and assumed they were the product of a land where risks were taken and conventions flouted. Another drawcard was a compelling image, in *Rolling Stone* magazine, of the architect John Andrews in his office, blue water visible through a window behind him.

What he found in Australia took him slightly by surprise. While culturally it was certainly more clubby and conservative than he had imagined, he also found the architecture to be 'lightweight' – psychologically, as it didn't spring from a place of considered conflict, and physically, as it had none of the muscular attributes he admired.

'What I saw seemed against the qualities I was familiar with,' says Durbach. 'Much of the work seemed overly detailed and precious, indulgent even, and I was used to a cruder but, to me, more intense architecture. The debate at the time was between postmodernism, and I was working for Ken Woolley on projects in that genre, or exploring what it meant to be Australian, as were Murcutt and some people from Cox Architects. While I was essentially uncomfortable with both positions, there was a sense that you had to choose a side.'

In the end, he stuck to his own path – the Australian aesthetic perhaps tempering his original predisposition, as he grew to appreciate the beauty in what he at first saw as insubstantial. He had success, along with Harry Levine (with documentation in association with Allen Jack + Cottier), in winning the additions to Tusculum, the nineteenth-century villa that is home to the RAIA, now the Australian Institute of Architects (AIA).

It was a challenging commission with the problems of how to marry the venerable old building with a contemporary vision, and how to fit an auditorium, a gallery and additional office space into a relatively small site. Given that it was the RAIA headquarters, there was also the pressure to deliver something notable that managed to articulate what the profession stood for. 'I will always admire Glenn [Murcutt] for choosing us, as we were young and not well-known,' says Durbach. With such a significant commission under his belt, did this put him on the map, I asked. 'No,' he replies, 'nothing seemed to put us on the map. We just started over again.'

With a recession looming, Durbach started teaching at the University of Sydney, where Lawrence Nield was a professor and Peter Stutchbury was teaching next door. He met interesting people, became more methodical, and honed his architectural philosophy. It was here that he met Camilla Block, and they started working together in 1992, forming a partnership in 1997.

Camilla Block had come to Sydney from Johannesburg with her parents at the age of 12, but went back as a fourth-year architecture student for a two-year stint in an architectural firm. 'It was interesting to discover that there was a deep down connection to the landscape and buildings of your childhood. It was like coming home,' she says. Workwise, she was thrown in at the deep end and came to understand clearly the direct relationship between what you draw and what you build. Near mistakes were averted and a steep learning curve took place. Her return to Australia was of her own volition. 'I immigrated with my parents the first time, and the second time I "immigrated" myself.'

In the early days for Durbach and Block, renovations and additions provided bread and butter, before commissions, principally from friends, for houses began to filter through. The Darling Point House (1992) was one, on a site so difficult to access, Durbach says it was akin to building a ship in a bottle.

'It's a house where the beauty of it creeps up on you quite slowly,' he says. 'While there is nothing really to see, the journey through the space is important. You travel from the ground to the sky, winding through rooms, to a roof terrace, across a bridge. The goal was to make a small house seem bigger.'

The project with Droga began as a renovation of the five existing floors of a brick warehouse in Surry Hills, near Central station – at the time, a rundown part of Sydney's inner city. After renting for five years, Droga had bought the building in 1995, as part of a co-operative with his brother and friends. The plan was that each of the partners would retain a floor, and Durbach Block would give the building an overhaul of plumbing, electricity, lifts, foyer and so on, and create a workable floor plan for a work and living space.

During the exploration of floor space ratio, Droga and Durbach Block realised that, by a canny reallocation of space from the five floors, more than a roof garden could be built on top. Block had admired the utilitarian beauty of the raw building they were working with, but now the project had the additional challenge of creating something distinctive and architecturally ambitious.

The internal debate in Durbach Block is an interesting one of context and how that, in turn, drives form. 'We strive to transform architectural language by getting inside it and understanding it, and in turn altering how people see it,' says Block. They walk a knife edge, anxious to avoid 'noisiness' but also desirous not to blend in. Theirs is not an anonymous architecture but rather one of 'fit', where they skilfully define the terms of what it means to fit.

The scheme utilised the floor space of the roof and, when examining the drawing of the elevation, the relationship to its brick base is clear. There are strong vertical alignments that anchor the penthouse and create a sense that, although contemporary, it has strong links to its base. 'There is a sense of permission to play above the parapet line,' says Block. 'The penthouse has been described as a lizard on a rock – it has an anthropological quality.'

THIS PAGE The staircase to the mezzanine is inserted between two dynamic walls: curved and cutaway to the left, and open to a deeply recessed window to the right.

OPPOSITE The kitchen steps up to the north and sits below the mezzanine level, while sharing its city view. The flare of the island and the apple green cabinets create a slightly off-kilter interior that rejects the convention of the straight line.

OVERLEAF The strong shadow of the brise soleil adds to the drama of the terrace and emphasises the counterbalance between its rectilinear structure and the muscular curves of the building itself. As Block points out, many of their buildings 'inhale' to create outdoor space, and this is a fine example of its effectiveness.

'The Droga Apartment was the first time we tried something as sculptural on that scale,' recalls Durbach. 'At first, we were thinking about using brick and in a more "boxy" arrangement. It was Harry Levine, looking at a model, who said, "What happened to all those curves you used to do?"' That changed the course of the project, but when they looked at the revised model, Durbach's reaction was, 'Oh my God, this is hideous,' and he felt the whole thing could be a disaster. The other major shift was the external cladding material. 'Daniel and I used to look at the building as we passed on the train, and one day he said, "Why don't we use a reflective material for the façade".'

Droga had remembered a photo in an architectural exhibition of a copper-clad power station in the German countryside. 'It was both protective and a foreign object in its setting.' In the Droga Apartment, the panels of zinc that turn golden as the afternoon sun hits the west-facing portion of the exterior give the structure a different dimension. 'We have made a number of buildings that seem to inhale to create outdoor space,' says Block. 'With your back to the curve of the terrace, in the deep recess, you feel protected.'

One imagines that something so radical would at least have raised an eyebrow in council. Surprisingly, the project was supported, in particular by Penny Day, a planner at Sydney Council, who gave a great deal of advice around what was possible, and was clearly key in unlocking the possibility of the penthouse level. As Droga points out, in a more salubrious part of the city, there would have been many more restrictions; its context gave it freedom.

The brief for the interior was a 'big warehousey sort of space', which Durbach Block delivered via a huge curved room with steel beams linking to the industrial roots of the building. 'The geometry of the site was a given, and we chose to make one stable shape to hold steady, and the rest – the bedrooms and bathroom – take up the exigencies,' says Block. This is made very clear by the plan, which the architects describe as three hinged bands emerging from the northern corner of the building. One band forms the terrace, the second the living space, which rises up to the kitchen at the north, and the third the service areas and the bedrooms.

This main space is animated by the approach to the internal walls. They are neither straight nor absolute – there are curves and cutaways – openings for function and openings for effect. Discussing a series of 13 projects in the Pesaro Architectural Monograph *Durbach Block*, Professor Philip Goad comments, 'Each project is characterised by inhabited walls that are bent, skewed, canted or carved into.' Durbach had a great deal of enthusiasm for the work of American architect Steven Holl and some of the cutaway devices in the Droga Apartment pay homage to his work.

The staircase, hidden behind one such wall, draws you up to a mezzanine level, which sits above the kitchen and shares the city view. For Block, the apartment's two main views are significant. 'From the terrace, it is the much flatter, horizontal view of the low inner-city buildings and the railway line, while from the northern windows it is a more vertical view towards the city towers.' Droga felt that the second storey was integral to the building's success. 'The height of the mezzanine gives it presence and a certain sculptural elegance, and creates the impression that the brick base of the original building is acting as an oversized plinth for the penthouse.'

Two things slightly alarmed the architects about the project. One was the level of building work it unleashed: the street was closed the whole time because of the crane, and there was scaffolding over the entire laneway. And the second was the publicity around winning both national and state awards in the same year. Durbach admits to being 'very unprepared' and inching out of frame in a TV interview. Why, I ask, was it so celebrated? 'I think in a messy part of the city it feels heroic,' he says.

SEAN GODSELL

THE KEW HOUSE

1996–1997

'Although apparently "modern" in its language, the house is primordial in its intent – rust, oiled secondhand boards, recycled decking and lack of "precious" detail combine with the rudimentary services to form a house which is elemental rather than processed.'

SEAN GODSELL

PREVIOUS PAGE The entrance, through native grasses, leads straight into the large-scale living room with two separate seating zones.

THIS PAGE The table is at the heart of family life – for working, eating and entertaining. It is large enough to accommodate it all, possibly at the same time.

OPPOSITE Sean Godsell's gridded steel box cantilevers out to the west. Reclaimed timber boards have been oiled, and the play of light from the steel grids adds to their character.

Sean Godsell was born to architecture. As a boy, he sat on the knee of his father, architect David Godsell, and watched him draw. He tagged along with him to building site visits, and even committed to paper in his neat six-year-old script, 'I want to be an Architect and draw all kinds of houses with my dad.'

David Godsell started his career in the Fifties in the offices of society architect Guilford Bell, and while they had fundamentally different architectural philosophies – Godsell was an advocate of Frank Lloyd Wright while Bell was more of a classicist – there was a great deal of mutual respect. Godsell was appointed site architect for Bell's large office building project, Feltex House, when he was only 26 years old.

However, in 1960 Godsell set up on his own with the architectural intent 'to embrace and enhance the beauty of the site on which the building stands for occupier and viewer'. His Wrightian ideals were to find full expression in his own practice, particularly with his Kennedy House (1964) and Chapman House (1965).

Sean Godsell grew up in Beaumaris, a beachside suburb of Melbourne, in a house of his father's design. 'Dad made himself a yacht, it was a very casual, very Australian existence. And, yes, we were considered to have the weird house.' The site was difficult and, like many architects' own homes, took a long time to complete, but the result was an arrangement of space that accommodated all the family's needs, including parents' quarters and the architecture office at street level.

Ask Godsell what he learnt from his father, and his answer is profound. 'I learnt from him the importance of the making, and crafting, of a building. It became unfashionable in the postmodern era but I am happy to see it is making a return. When I was approached by Japanese architectural magazine *GA* to write an essay on any part of residential architecture, I chose to write about the window mullion. Too many contemporary architects pick windows from a brochure. One of the ways an architect working on residential projects can express themselves is through mastery of the detail.'

He not only absorbed an appreciation of technical skills, but a fundamental core of philosophy that informs everything he does. Godsell Snr once said he 'would rather dig ditches to support his family than compromise his architectural integrity', and Sean Godsell's practice is underpinned by the

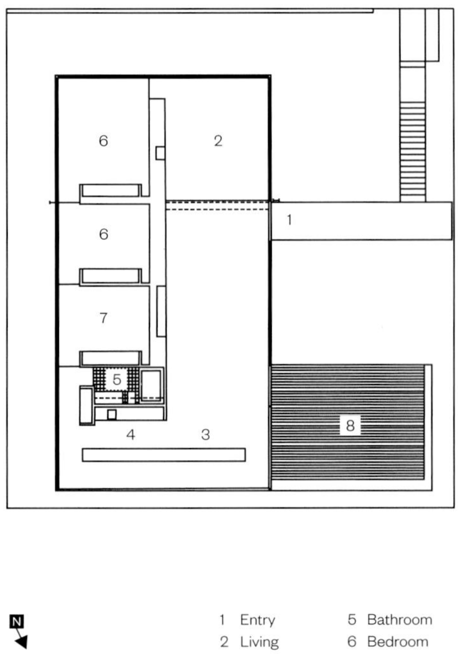

1 Entry
2 Living
3 Dining
4 Kitchen
5 Bathroom
6 Bedroom
7 Study
8 Deck

same stance. Hence, it is small and, as architectural commentator Leon van Schaik points out, he operates in an 'intensely individual atelier mode'.

Growing up around the practical aspects of architecture did have its drawbacks when it came to academia. 'So much was intuitive for me that I struggled in the first years of university to see it as an academic pursuit. I saw it to be about building and was impatient. I was playing Australian Rules footy professionally for St Kilda Football Club and thought I could wing it until I got to the juicy bit of the course and then concentrate,' he says. When he failed a subject by one mark, 'it was a kick in the pants'. It was engineering, the subject he thought he was best at, which 'made me realise I had to learn the theory if I was serious about what I wanted to do'.

After graduation, he was determined to be exposed to as much as possible, and to discover for himself what made the great buildings great. He travelled to Japan, where he admired the work of Shinohara and Ando; to Finland where he visited most of Aalto's buildings, and to France, to Le Corbusier's convent, La Tourette, and Villa Savoye. His observation that 'photos tell a thousand lies' was strengthened by what he saw. 'Photographs of architecture can be very deceiving, and when you see a building it can be completely different, either much better or much worse,' he says. 'I do feel my father's work would have benefited had he had the opportunity to see the buildings he admired first-hand.'

Godsell's education also developed by working in practices both in Melbourne and London during the Eighties. As a third-year student, he worked for Edmond & Corrigan, and in London worked for Sir Denys Lasdun, responsible for, among many other buildings, the Royal National Theatre on London's South Bank. 'I have witnessed creative people under duress. Lasdun was 73 when I was 26, and he was still terrifying, so emotional and passionate – I adored him,' says Godsell.

Returning to Melbourne in 1989, at the beginning of the recession, he was raring to go but had to wait. He worked for various firms and bided his time. In 1992, he built the Faraday Street House in Carlton for his wife, Annemarie Kiely, and son, Jack. 'I needed to do that, to build a house. And it is a classic first house with some good ideas and full of flaws,' he admits.

Other projects followed. Another house, an addition and gradually his work began to attract attention from the media and win awards and the recognition of his peers. It was the commission for the S Gandolfo house alteration (1994) from old clients of his father's that enabled him to form his own company in the same year.

When it came to building a second house for his family, Godsell and Kiely looked around Kew because that is where they thought Jack might go to school. 'It was Annemarie who found the land – a tiny garden subdivision of the house to the immediate north,' says Godsell. To him, as to his father, the site is of paramount importance.

'I struggle with every single building, and it takes a long time to get everything right. So there are always a number of variations on the idea. Now I realise that this is part of my technique. That I refine and refine and even when I am building I refine and refine,' he says. 'In the end, all I wanted was a very simple pavilion which caught the city views and gave us the possibility of having north-facing outdoor space or another building later on.'

Godsell regards his house at Kew as part of his early work, but recognises its contribution as a platform for his more mature phase. 'For me, it is a significant building, even though I know why and where it is derivative, and who the architects were that influenced me at the time,' he says. 'For this building, I looked at a number of architects who had produced cantilevered steel structures – Ellwood, Johnson, Eames and Breuer had all done them – and

I liked Jean Nouvel's Le Saint-James in Bordeaux. I admire his work a lot and think he is one of the truly innovative architects of the last 50 years.'

The house is modest in size. As Godsell says of the project, 'We were young and poor, and we built it on the smell of an oily rag, and there is something gauche about building more than you really need.' But adversity is the mother of invention and Godsell's solution of utilising standard dimension walkway grids in 350MPa steel, and rusting and oiling them, gives the simple pavilion a distinctive character. While the context is suburban, the bold cantilever (5.5 m) and the rusted surface treatment combine to give it a monumental feel. 'I find the way nature attacks a building interesting. Architects and builders are largely trained to resist nature. Rusted steel is a classic example. Explain to a builder how to rust steel and they look horrified.'

The plan is very simple and considered. The 170 square metre rectangle is bisected lengthwise; on the north side is the large living area and on the south a series of smaller rooms – bedrooms, bathrooms and a study. The kitchen is at the eastern end and a large seven-metre table runs its entire length.

'The divided plan shows the influence of Asia on Australia,' says Godsell. 'In this building it is contrived and deliberate, to highlight the possibility that Australian architecture could be influenced by the west *and* the east.' The living area has a sliding wall to separate the space and create two areas, just as in Japanese architecture a series of rooms is animated by operating screens. The house has no corridors and so has a continuous flow of space, which Godsell admits was easier with a small child than a teenager.

'The gesture to the west, the symbol of Australian life, was the table, because the kitchen is the focal point in the house,' he says. 'We don't bother about formal dining, hanging around in the kitchen is normal.'

As Godsell deems this house part of his early work, is there anything he would change? 'I think it is incredibly dangerous for architects to tinker with their earlier decisions, but the house was built in 1996 and I would like to bring it a new lease of life,' he says. So he has designed a separate building, sensitively sited to the north and constructed in rusted steel.

'We plan to rip out the bathroom and spend more money on it and upgrade the kitchen appliances. This is not a building I would ever want to leave. We have had some fantastic times here, and some wonderful architects such as Peter Zumthor and Rick Joy have visited.'

And one can see why. The space is beautiful, sunlit and comfortable. The rusted grids give a sense of enclosure while still enabling the view of the city in the distance. Behind the longest kitchen table in Melbourne, outside a commercial premises, is a wall of rusted steel with an aged patina that glows when the northerly light hits it.

Art works are propped casually against walls and the backs of sofas, a couple of Akari lights by Noguchi add a soft sculptural presence, while two timber sofas designed by Godsell, in the style of Donald Judd, sit on either side of an open fire. The recycled floorboards combine with the steel and glass to reinforce the sense that this is a robust house with genuine character.

It feels creative and nurturing, and would have been a great environment for a child to grow up in. A neighbour who, with an interest in psychology, implored Godsell to rethink his design for fear of the damaging effects on the mental health of his young son, need not have worried. Jack has been a doctor for a number of years.

Detail is careful and considered but never extraneous. Godsell is an architect for whom rigour and principle are everything. 'The creative process is about endless decisions, applying good judgment to each element, from the tap fitting to the external materials. There are lots of individual decisions, which also need to work collectively. You pay the price if they are wrong.'

PREVIOUS PAGE Godsell-designed sofas, inspired by Donald Judd, sit around the fireplace. Artworks are propped, not hung, giving the sense of a casually curated space.

THIS PAGE A Clement Meadmore sculpture is tonally compatible with the Corten wall.

OPPOSITE The way the light engages with the building externally and internally is one of its remarkable aspects. The bedroom is entered via a sliding door, and the geometry of light creates its own decorative pattern in the simply decorated space.

Knowing that with the Kew House he was still at the stage of 'figuring stuff out', Godsell had an awareness that the next house had to be great in order for him to make a leap professionally. Designed in 1998 and completed in 2000, the Carter/Tucker House did just that. It gained a great deal of recognition locally and internationally, winning awards in Australia, the UK and Best Building in the Region in the World Architecture Awards announced in Hong Kong in 2001. It also enhanced his reputation as something of a 'hard man' of architecture. 'Steel boxes were designed to go at the entry and some knucklehead had put a blow torch near them and the steel buckled. It was close to the end of the building process and I was so angry I went around the corner into the bathroom and whacked my head, like a Liverpool kiss, in sheer frustration,' says Godsell.

The other project that catapulted his career was the development of the Future Shack project, an emergency housing solution made from recycled shipping containers. Features such as height-adjustable legs for uneven ground and a parasol roof for shade that could be packed away and stored in the container itself illustrate the practicality of his thinking. 'I have two responsibilities as an architect: one is to be true to myself and be an artist of the utmost integrity, which is what I have tried to do; the other responsibility is to be a really vigilant and analytical observer of society – by doing so we remain relevant to society.'

He followed Future Shack with a design called Park Bench House in 2002 in order to provide the homeless with shelter. British style bible *Wallpaper** nominated Godsell as one of the people destined to 'change the way we live'. Not only was he the only Australian, he was the only architect on the list.

His stance hasn't always made him popular. He works as a sole practitioner with a small team. Because he keeps the scale small, he feels no obligation to take on projects in which he feels he cannot maintain the integrity of the work, giving him a reputation for arrogance. He knows how destructive the profession can be. 'It is very demanding. Most architects start out as sensitive dreamers, and a lot of us end up bitter and twisted because it is a form of artistic expression that is so vulnerable to other people's influence and input along the way – be it the client or the local authority.'

One feels that with Godsell, maintaining the rigour is everything and that when he looks back over his career, at his body of work, he wants it to be flawless. Does this create a pressure? 'Pressure,' he says, 'is kicking a goal in front of 50,000 people and hearing the collective groan if you miss.'

OPPOSITE While the house is clearly visible from the street, the rusted steel obscures its interior life.

THIS PAGE The rusted wall that spans the eastern end of the main living space has a very beautiful patina that responds to the varying pattern of light throughout the day. Sitting in front of it is a sculpture by Jan Learmonth.

STUTCHBURY&HAR

THE REEVES HOUSE

PER 1997–1999

'Stutchbury sits firmly within the Australian tradition of elevating the honesty and directness of the rural shed to a measure of structural and formal purity.'

PROFESSOR PHILIP GOAD

PREVIOUS PAGE The north-facing aspect opens to surrounding decks and landscape. The 'twisted' roofline manages light and breeze by rising to the east and turning down to the west to admit sun in winter and keep it out in summer.

THIS PAGE This is a room designed to be cool in summer, with large timber and glass doors leading to a generous balcony facing the view.

OPPOSITE A view back towards the glazed entrance, which is set between two heavy masonry walls.

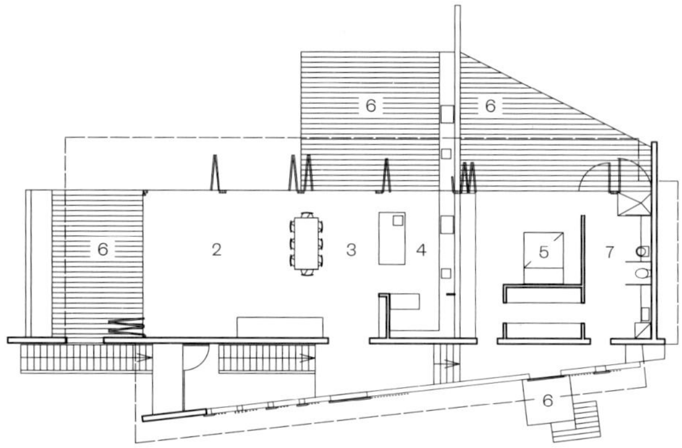

UPPER FLOOR PLAN

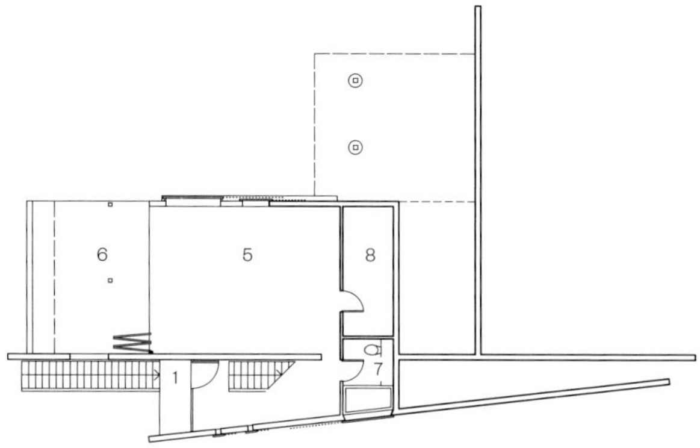

LOWER FLOOR PLAN

N

1 Entry
2 Living
3 Dining
4 Kitchen
5 Bedroom
6 Deck
7 Bathroom
8 Store

If ever an architectural practice were wedded to its geography, it is Peter Stutchbury Architecture. Not only is the fit topographical, it is a marriage that works intellectually, socially and creatively. The Peninsula, a finger of land stretching north from Sydney's CBD, is defined by its landscape of native trees, sandstone escarpments and water views: the Pacific Ocean to the east and Pittwater to the west. Stutchbury's office is in the beachside suburb of Newport. While to many it is the 'insular peninsula' (once you are there, why would you ever leave?), it has a long history of holiday houses for Sydneysiders wanting a place to relax only an hour's drive from home.

Property prices have risen dramatically since the Eighties – when Stutchbury bought his first block of land in Clareville in 1985, it was one of the cheapest suburbs in Sydney. Fibro cement beach houses have given way to architect-designed homes for clients with a desire to embrace the environment while demanding a high level of architectural sophistication. There are also those who live there full time – people with an appreciation of architectural merit and alternative thinking. It is among these two types of people that Stutchbury has gradually built up a client base that understands his open, honest architectural style and his innate ability to manage climate, site, materials and orientation.

From this point on the globe, his reputation has spread. In 2007, Japanese fashion designer Issey Miyake set his office the task of searching the world for an architect who could design a retreat on oceanfront land outside Tokyo. Miyake already had a Samurai and a Geisha House sited there for guest and staff use, and wanted a house for himself. The brief to find the architect was succinct – only five words: nature, function, environment, connection and wild – and with just these words to work with, and a search of 14 months, they found Stutchbury. The finished house is an exercise in refinement and is movingly beautiful. The palette of materials is spare, the detailing fine and the balance of innovation and tradition is matched only by the sensitive link to the site and the existing buildings. As Stutchbury told Miyake, 'Everything I have learnt is in there', and, in avoiding a modern, provocative work, he feels he has managed to create something timeless, as befits his client and the building's context.

All the layers of his life's experience led to this commission. Nature and a relationship with the land was a major part of his upbringing. His mother, Gwenda, went as far as articulating that she wanted her sons to have a city

education, but the knowledge of the country. So while they attended Knox Grammar, a Sydney private school, much of their holidays were spent on their aunt's property, Manuka, south-west of Cobar in central western New South Wales. 'The country is a legible place. A city might be open to very different interpretations, but the country and its buildings are very honest – they can't afford not to be,' says Stutchbury. 'For me, the bush experience was profound.'

This sense of 'letting the country do some talking in your life' is something he is keen to pass on to his own children. He also worked hard physically, and the discipline needed to survive gave him a respect for the land that has become ingrained professionally and personally. From the age of four, he would sit agog at the tales his uncle, Don Mosely, a long-serving missionary in Papua New Guinea, would tell of headhunters, cannibals and tribal life. And while it may be too obvious to link Stutchbury's passion for travel in later life to this early exposure to wildness and adventure, these stories must have painted a compelling picture of other worlds and other cultures.

Stutchbury holds the view that character is shaped in percentages: 30 percent is inherent, 30 percent is from your parents and 40 percent is developed. For Stutchbury, the sums add up. While there are no architects in his family, there is an assortment of engineers, artists, builders, surveyors, bridge designers. Add their skills together and you have an architect, he says. His mother is described as his 'guardian angel who shaped the softness and care and the understanding of people'. His father, Ernest, on the other hand, was primarily a practical man who lived and breathed construction, and ran International Combustion for many years, building power stations and shaping Australia's energy industry. The intuitive side has led Stutchbury to people whose work or philosophy he feels an emotional connection with and who, in turn, have shaped his outlook and approach. While Stutchbury is a self-confessed idealist, his father's emphasis on practicality has encouraged in him an ability to build and to think logically about structure and stability.

When it comes to the 40 percent of factors and people that developed his character, there is no shortage. While his schooling was sound, if uninspiring, he found life studying architecture at the University of Newcastle pleasingly free of social stratification. However, living in a farmhouse and surfing every second day, he still struggled with the discipline of study, and credits the faith, and teaching skill, of Eric Parker with leading him from being a student who repeated first year to one who graduated with honours six years later. To this day, Stutchbury praises what he learnt at university from watercolour artist Malcolm Parker; Gordon Appleby, part of the Sydney School of Architecture; and Ted Harkness, who pioneered studies into shade and ventilation.

While Stutchbury admired the work of Bruce Rickard and John Andrews, it was his relationship with Richard Leplastrier that allowed his architectural philosophy to flourish and find its true form. A friend of Stutchbury's had recommended he meet Leplastrier but, before he had the chance to do so, he snuck into his partly built Palm House. 'The beautiful terrazzo floor and the steel frame were the kind of architecture I dreamt about, and here it was being built,' he recalls. 'I wasn't there long when I heard the rumble of a VW pulling up and Rick and the client got out. I hid in the garden but listened for 45 minutes to the most inspiring conversation. It is just the most beautiful building in Australia.'

Meeting Leplastrier not long after at a friend's wedding, Stutchbury undertook a study of his work, which enabled them to spend time together. 'I would make models and drawings and stay with him at Lovett Bay – he had this little helper. He is a remarkable man who coloured my world and laid the foundation of my architectural thinking.' Leplastrier also introduced him to his drawing tutor at university, Lloyd Rees, who was also to become a friend of Stutchbury's and a strong role model.

PREVIOUS PAGE The deck by the living area faces the trees and water views to the west. The large-scale windows on the northern side of the room slide open to engage completely with the surrounding landscape.

OPPOSITE The living, dining, kitchen and bedroom areas are housed under one skillion roof. The indoor-outdoor kitchen was pioneered by Stutchbury for his client, who was a chef.

THIS PAGE The concertina doors, which extend the length of the north face of the house, minimise the barrier between inside and out.

Not all Stutchbury's influences were through academia or architects. His search was for a more primal understanding, shown through his thesis on Aboriginal people (*Australian Aboriginals*, 1977) and their relationship with the land. For several months, Stutchbury lived at Wilcannia in far western New South Wales. 'I would get up at 6am every day and draw Aboriginal tools, hand signs or boomerangs, and what washed through me was that how they lived in the landscape was sufficient to sustain them.'

As Nielsen Warren, his first employer at Quay Architects and, later, friend, wisely pointed out, it allowed Stutchbury to 'get in touch with values, the beauty of extreme economy, aesthetics unrelated to price. Accommodation in terms of acceptance, mutuality and the extended family.'

Two years later, he went to Papua New Guinea for 18 months to do a postgraduate study of the longhouse. 'I helped my uncle design and build a church in Port Moresby,' he says. 'I didn't get paid, but it enabled me to get around on a mission plane and stay in mission accommodation so that I could measure and photograph 45 different longhouses for my thesis.'

The buildings were an exercise in the elimination of wastage and made Stutchbury realise just how 'pure architecture a building could be'. The church was a refined building despite its elementary nature, and one of its key elements was the simple beauty of the twisted tapered roof, in turn a signature element in the Reeves House.

His career settled into a pattern of undertaking small buildings, or extensions, for a network of family and friends, predominantly in the locale of the Northern Beaches. He used the money to travel, and travel seriously: a year on an architectural scholarship backpacking through Africa, trips to Asia, Europe and eventually to his ancestral home, Scotland.

In the mid-Eighties, he bought land in Clareville, and built his own house in a 'series of experiments' with materials and structure. He wanted the landscape to remain free, so built a platform in the trees with a parasol roof. It's this, and his use of steel portal frames, that give the building a sense of lightness. He is aware of the freedom he experienced building for his then-wife and partner in the practice, Phoebe Pape, and their children. 'Sometimes you can only do it when it is for yourself. You are not scared of changing the poetry if you see something different, and the whole idea of composition can adjust.'

More than 10 years later, by which time his reputation had grown, a commission from the Reeves was to come his way. Their site was down the road from his own house, so the landfall and orientation were familiar, but the solutions were very different. Lloyd Rees had applauded Stutchbury's ability to surround himself with young minds and, in this instance, his collaboration with Sue Harper is proof of the benefits that could bring. Sue Harper had been taught by both Stutchbury and Leplastrier at the University of Sydney before working with Troppo Architects in the Northern Territory for six years, and Stutchbury for a further six years. This house was designed after she had set up on her own and she recalls the project with evident pleasure.

'We had an open-minded client, and the process of working with Pete's sense of invention was fun. But, most pleasing of all, there was a strong simple form and clear planning to work with, and the drama coming from one element – the twisted roof.'

'This was a very steep block with a water course running through it, and we had to deal with it both physically and emotionally so the qualities of the site were best maintained,' says Stutchbury. 'We have used the corridor entrance as a defining wall and tapered it from narrow to wide to express the flow of water which now runs down the side of it.' This masonry corridor not only provides a significant sense of entrance and introduction to the house but it turns on its head, or rather on its side, the manner in which Stutchbury

THIS PAGE The bedroom faces its own private deck and is contained by a partition wall that separates it from the corridor and adjacent bathroom. The roofline soars at this point.

OPPOSITE The long bathroom doubles as a dressing room, and is as near to showering outdoors as possible.

OVERLEAF, LEFT PAGE The slightness of the structure is achieved by the use of slim steel 'Y' supports, the extensive use of glazing, and the Perspex-filled gap between the top of the thermal walls and the roof.

OVERLEAF, RIGHT PAGE Masonry walls on the south side of the house make use of the properties of thermal mass, and enable the structure to turn its back on buildings to the south.

had worked with the balance of weight and lightness in his previous buildings, where the weight had more conventionally been at the base.

At the Reeves House, the use of rough masonry walls to the south, running perpendicular to the site, was a breakthrough for Stutchbury. 'I really learnt the lesson of thermal mass,' he says. 'It holds the heat in winter and discharges it into the house, and in summer the heat is dispersed through ventilation at either end of the corridor. Until this point, I hadn't understood that potential.'

The other major aspect of the house plan is how the siting works with the topography, and with the desire to balance openness with both visual and aural privacy. 'Our aim was to organise the building so that it connects most with landscape and least with urbanscape.'

With only small window openings to the south, the polycarbonate roof here ensures the area is always light, and the tapering has the effect of drawing you into the house. The mix of concrete and timber is used even in stair treads. It is this balance of materials, along with the twisted roof and the indoor/outdoor kitchen, that makes it, for Stutchbury, 'a landmark building, an honest building, expressing so many of the things that preoccupied the practice at the time'.

Harper concurs. 'I really like the clear definition of space. The northern side is the active side and the space between the two blade walls is a movement zone, with a subtle, soft feeling achieved by the light coming through the polycarbonate ceiling.'

While the entrance corridor feels solid, weighted and monumental, the main living area feels, by contrast, almost shockingly light and transparent. Above all else, there is the sense of openness of both the space itself and in the way internal and exterior spaces blur at the edges.

The living, dining, kitchen, one bedroom and bathroom are all contained under one canopy roof, with the minimal degrees of separation signalled by either changes in level – the bedroom/bathroom zone is one metre higher than the rest of the interior and behind a wall – or changes in flooring, as you move from the interior concrete to the blackbutt decking boards outside.

On this level alone, there are three significant outside spaces, each contributing to the connection with nature. The deck to the west, and the water views, extends the living space; the deck to the north is for cooking and eating outdoors (the original client was a chef); and the bedroom deck, again north, provides the ultimate in privacy and extensive garden views.

The slightness of the structure is achieved by the slim steel 'Y' supports, the extensive use of glazing, and Perspex-filled gap between the top of the thermal walls and roof, which enhances the feeling of lightness and allows for ventilation.

Stutchbury used a twisted roof on his award-winning Olympic Archery Centre (1999), but the Reeves House was the first time it was used on a residential building. The 'twist' tilts up to the east to allow in morning light, and down to the west to minimise the westerly sun; it pivots to the north to encourage the north-easterly breeze and has deep eaves to the north to admit sun in winter and limit it in summer. It is a parasol roof taken beyond the functionality of shelter to provide a solution to the climatic conditions.

Originally, Harper recalls, there were plans for a plunge pool off the bedroom and an open fire in the living area, which would have contributed to the sense of a connection to nature by pulling the elements of water and fire into the building envelope. The house is still remarkable for its ability to connect inside and out. In many ways, it pays homage to Leplastrier's Palm House in its openness to the garden and the merging of boundaries, allowing minimal shelter and living in the landscape to dominate as central themes.

Hence, a decade before Issey Miyake earmarked Stutchbury as the man to deliver on 'nature, function, environment, connection and wild' for his own residence, all the hallmarks are already here in the Reeves House.

DONOVAN HILL

THE D HOUSE

1998–2000

'Design is a bit like poetry – it calls up something that people recognise, and know, but can't quite put their finger on. The role of the designer is to touch those nerves.'

TIMOTHY HILL

PREVIOUS PAGE A winner of the Robin Boyd Award for residential architecture in 2001, the façade of the D House reads as a walled garden to the street.

THIS PAGE With conventional thinking turned on its head in so many ways in the D House, it is more than appropriate that there isn't a front door in the traditional sense, but rather, a gated entry.

OPPOSITE The timber screen pulls back to reveal a perfectly curated interior.

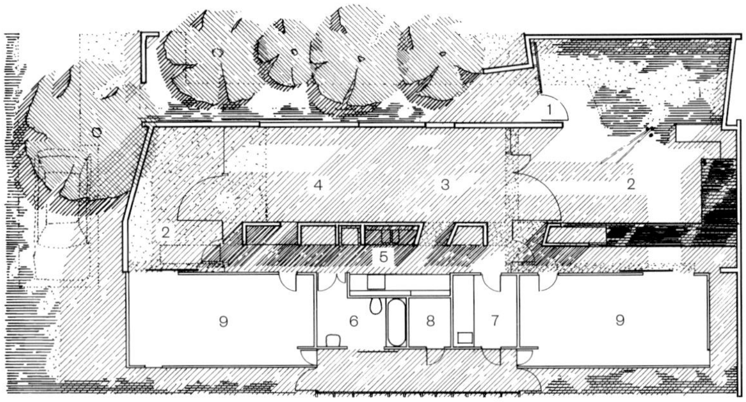

N

1 Entry
2 Courtyard
3 Dining
4 Living
5 Kitchen
6 Bathroom
7 Laundry
8 Store
9 Bedroom

Architects name their houses in different ways. Traditionally, they were named after the commissioning client. Bruce Rickard, for instance, designed the Curry House in 1967; when the clients came back for a second home, it became Curry House 2. It keeps that name for time immemorial, sometimes, one suspects, to the chagrin of longstanding subsequent owners.

There is also a penchant for naming after an aspect of the site (Frank Lloyd Wright's Fallingwater is a stellar example) and many of Peter Stutchbury's buildings use this nomenclature: Deepwater Woolshed and Springwater, for example. When I first started to explore the work of architects Donovan Hill, I was met with a sea of letters. The T House, the HH House and the C House.

At the end of my interview with the articulate Timothy Hill, I sheepishly asked, as though asking his star sign, the meaning of the letter D. The answer, like so many aspects of this exceptional house, both surprised and delighted.

'Each house has an initial that comes into being during construction – derived sometimes from the owner or the location – but, in this instance, the house developed a nickname. Local Italians used to sit under the trees and watch the builders at work,' says Hill. 'One day, a tradesman asked them what they thought, and they said that it was the kind of construction they would do in Italy, but for donkeys, not people. To them we were building a stable, so D is for donkey.'

Brian Donovan and Timothy Hill met at the University of Queensland and formed their partnership in 1991 in order to design a shop that sold stuffed animals and specialised in koalas. 'Our partnership is such a quintessentially Queensland thing – so frontier in a way. Our only meaty strategy, which we were barely conscious of at the time, was that whoever rocked up, we would make a go of the job. If they came along wanting a rumpus room, it was a starting point for dialogue. With no work behind us we had only the legitimacy of our thinking and we quickly learnt to communicate.'

From tutor Brit Andresen, originally from Norway, they learnt the ability to ask, 'What does it mean to people?' as a founding basis for making judgments, rather than simply, 'What does it look like?' 'Also being foreign, what she imagined in terms of architecture was a very big idea – to be alongside that captured the imagination, and to be part of the standard minimums she presumed was very valuable,' says Hill.

One of the newly formed practice's first commissions was the HH House, a low cost extension at the rear of a Queenslander in Brisbane's Highgate Hill.

OPPOSITE With the potential for uses other than that of a home (a consulting room, for instance), the bedrooms can be independently accessed. The wall of glazed tiles changes with the effects of light throughout the day.

OVERLEAF The blurring of lines between outdoor and indoor space makes sense in a climate where living outside most of the year is possible. A shallow pond separates the public living and dining area from the more private bathroom and bedrooms to the left.

Timothy Hill refers to these early houses as rehearsals in every way. The HH House does this on several levels. It uses unconventional materials. Tomato stakes (economical timber battens) are used to enclose areas, but still remain open and aerated, while irregular columns of rough and raw, off-form concrete create what Professor Philip Goad calls 'a monument to pleasing decay'. With its modern-day Venus de Milo sculpture perched on one of the concrete stacks, it is indeed an accurate description.

This notion of how buildings weather, gain patina and a rich mutable life was something of a preoccupation of the practice. Their next major project, the C House, was built between 1991 and 1998.

More than a decade after its completion, Hill felt it had only just evolved to a point where its maturity met their original intention, through the weathering of materials and the evolving nature of the landscaping. The slow burn of the construction period was enabled by a client who acknowledged, 'I am using a Japanese timetable,' and savoured the expertise of a small, dedicated team. 'With the C House we were inventing a new kind of language and practising with tradespeople. While it was our most refined rendition, it was also clearly the work of very young people, because you can count off the tributes – Aalto, Scarpa, Lutyens and Schinkel,' says Hill.

Goad describes the house as an 'elaborate landscape of walls, steps, seats, ledges and a long narrow pool'. It plays with sequential spaces where scale is in flux, intimate areas give way to grand, materials transform from rough to smooth, and timber detailing from ceiling to sliding screen declares its bespoke nature.

Hill is at his most passionate when he speaks of Lutyens and his 'magic' with a plan. 'We are plan-fascinated – we are interested in organising the plan rather than decorating the pavilion,' he says. 'Lutyens orchestrated the house to have a sense of arrival at defended territory, and he would over-sequence the approach to enlarge the scale of the house, which is something we do. He would also invent a site where there was none.' All this has tremendous resonance in the D House.

The D House is exceptional, because it overtly engages with its urban context in a way that no other house represented in this book does. Privacy is almost always the goal, with a range of strategies applied, including the choice of remote sites, fortress-like approaches and plans that turn their backs on their surrounds. But then, to be fair, none was ever imagined as anything other than a domestic residence. The D House was always different in its intent.

'One of the great legacies of Queenslanders is, with their generic plan, they can adapt to business premises, and are easy to re-service because they are suspended off the ground,' says Hill. 'They have a series of rooms unlike today's fashion for "ki-di-lis" (kitchen/dining/living all in one space), which have little flexibility.' Queenslanders, he says, have been used this way in inner suburban Brisbane since World War II, and so he was mindful, as much as anything, of 'building a good bit of urban infrastructure rather than simply tailoring a house for someone'.

As a practice, Donovan Hill seemed to be masters at holding the future in their gaze while operating in the present. They planned for how their houses weather and mature as much as for how their clients' lives shift and the demands on the spaces they live in alter. 'The main thing that happens to households is that they change. Mothers come to stay for extended periods of time, kids don't leave home, but don't want to be down the same corridor as Mum and Dad, or someone loses their job and needs to work from home. We raise the notion that their investment might be more versatile if their household is more versatile. Then it starts to gel.'

Fortunately, Hill's long-held view appealed to his client who was aware that, while a modest project, it represented the sum of her resources and so liked the idea that use wasn't limited to that of a house. 'She also liked it ethically, that if you were going to the trouble to make a building, it really ought to have another use and that she could lease it to a business if circumstances required it.'

The D House is in the inner Brisbane suburb of New Farm and has been built on a small 310 square metre subdivision. It is, as Hill says unequivocally, 'a dud site with no view and so we needed to ramp up the value of what is actually outside'.

He also needed to recreate the physical terrain, which has been cut and filled, calibrated and manipulated, 'totally contrived to seem inevitable'.

To approach the house is to experience Lutyens' extended sequence. The taxi dropped me off at what looked like a garden wall (albeit with a beautifully crafted timber shutter), and the approach is made through a small grove of trees, passing along the length of the house (slightly elevated from the street) to arrive at a gate.

'The difference between a door and a gate sounds slight, and looks slighter on the plan, but it makes for a graduated entrance, as it means you have arrived at the territory before you have arrived at the house,' says Hill. While I had no conscious appreciation of these strategies, there is no denying that it is extremely effective in setting up expectation by allowing visual slices of interior life to be seen and different physicality to be experienced, from the rise in the ground to the changes of light under the trees.

The idea of the garden wall helped Hill's concept for the house in a couple of ways. 'Homes often have atmosphere when they are a conversion of something else, a warehouse, for example, and it is hard to be the author of something initially. I needed a conceptual tool to get it moving. So I thought of the house as an enormous garden terrace with a tarpaulin over it, and that permitted me to think about the things that weren't "housey".'

In negotiations with council he also argued that a pleasing garden wall would add to the street appeal, that there was precedence in the area, and that the apparent absence of a roof would allow the roofs of surrounding houses to provide the edge to the sky, paying deference to the existing buildings. Two years of debate still ensued.

This small two-bedroom (200 square metre) house is in three zones – the main living area, with its shifting degrees of public/private life; the kitchen, positioned behind a masonry wall and part of the interior corridor spanning the length of the house; and the private area consisting of two bedrooms, a large bathroom and a spacious laundry/storage room.

'The house is planned very much like a piece of townscape. The main room is like the footpath because, as you are moving up and down in the house, exactly parallel to the footpath, you have the sense that we are all in the network,' says Hill. And he should know. He moved in as a lodger in 2000 and delights in the fact that, while not a chiropractor or therapist using the building, he does at least qualify as 'non-traditional family use'. Hence, he knows the house intimately. 'If I am working here, what I like to do is open it up and it becomes my office – I am with the world and it is a working day. If I am here by myself or the base household of two, it is often closed, but as soon as friends come over, we open it up and it becomes a setting for events.'

The window and its timber shutter help define mood and activity. As the only window in the building, it has a sense of consequence, enhanced by Hill's 'fiddling with proportion'. Despite its length of 3400 mm, it is only 1800 mm high and it makes a huge difference that it is set low in the wall. 'The Japanese and Chinese reduce the height leading into a courtyard. This act of synthesising from other cultures is a professional obligation. We only have the vernacular here, and that is colonial.'

Hill's other preoccupation is a quest for atmosphere. Friends who have visited this house enthuse about it and, I suspect, it is partly because it has

THIS PAGE The mix of materials – timber, tiles and concrete – illustrates the skill of mixing raw and crafted.

OPPOSITE Donovan Hill are advocates of built-in furniture, as shown in this corner of the living space. Hill also designed the copper wall light above the window.

OVERLEAF, LEFT PAGE The entrance to the kitchen is illuminated by the skylight. This is Hill's technique of often placing skylights where threshold decisions have to be made.

OVERLEAF, RIGHT PAGE At ground level, the meeting of travertine, pebbles, solid timber and slatted timber forms a very conscious floor surface arrangement to denote the movement from one space to another.

managed to capture this elusive quality. Hill's philosophy, born of practicality and planning, is that a sense of 'unevenness' creates character and, hence, atmosphere. 'This house is part fibro shack and part Italian marble. Some parts tighten up to be almost too small (some doorways are 450 mm wide) while other doors are massive and oversized,' he says. So large is mixed with small, rough with smooth, refined with coarse, expensive with cheap. 'Even the construction is uneven, with the shell of the building put up by a merchant contractor and the refined detail executed by another.'

Atmosphere is also about the manipulation of light and plays of perception around exterior and interior. Above the window is a small skylight, which causes the interior wall to become light, like an exterior wall, not shadowy like an interior one. There is another large skylight above the threshold where 'there are a lot of decisions to make', and hence the need for illumination. One of those decisions is, quite literally, where to put your feet. While the ceiling is one great 'tarpaulin' of oiled hardwood timbers, the floor is, in part, a mosaic of materials and textures made up of travertine, pebbles, solid timber and slatted timber. Hill explained that there is often a confidence in walking in interior spaces that is not true of exterior ones – hence the idea of creating a heightened awareness of the ground. 'This was one way of linking the building with the landscape. You have to plan where to put your feet, to map it like in landscape, and that slight hesitation comes from outside.'

The climate in Brisbane is hot and wet, and so the degree of openness befits the conditions. As light and surfaces mix up external/internal messaging so does the plan of the indoor/outdoor spaces. The main room is glazed at either end, extending the sense of space to courtyards open to the sky at one end and forming a significant outdoor room at the other. 'By offering the sky to the deep interior, it creates another type of transparency and connects it to shifts in light and hence to what is happening outside.' This lightness of being is further enhanced by the spare use of furnishings and, in particular, the built-in sofa with its lack of heavy base, allowing the eye to travel through to the courtyard beyond. Stools are used as side tables, and shelves are designed for the curated objects and paintings that are propped on them with consummate casualness. Before the domestic nature of the building was declared with a post box and number, a woman passed her card through the window asking if they would give her a call when they got more stock in.

The private rooms at the back, which are used as bedrooms, have considerable thought given to the ventilation and light sources. Doors in the corners of one room allow access, light, ventilation and a large opening to the courtyard. The other bedroom, with a large screen providing privacy, opens directly onto the outdoor courtyard with all the charm of a Japanese water garden. 'I had always rented dumpy old houses on the river, which can be big and blustery, and I wondered how it would feel to do the Japanese thing and miniaturise it,' says Hill.

He is an advocate of the laundry/storage room. He feels it not only helps them keep house, but also avoids the tyranny of endless cupboards becoming the dominant feature of the interior. It is typical of the approach to many things about the D House. It is a rethinking of how we live, placing priorities accordingly. Deciding what values are important and what are not. Asking how a building can make provision for future use and where the emphasis of labour and cost should be applied. Looking to provide comfort, be conscious of climate and create atmosphere. Exploring how to be private and still engage with the world. In Timothy Hill's words, 'This is what design is. Trying to account for the tremendous consequence of things that aren't aesthetic.'

And in doing what Brit Andresen taught him – to look towards what it means to people, and not merely how it looks – the aesthetic has emerged in a profound sense. While it is clearly the product of thoughtfulness, the effect is of that most sought after, but rarely achieved quality – the seemingly casual.

BIBLIOGRAPHY

Adlercreutz, Gunnel, Stutchbury, Peter and Leplastrier, Richard (essays) *Spirit of Nature of Wood Architecture Award 2004*, Building Information Ltd, Helsinki, 2004

Andresen, Brit, A.S. Hook Address, 2002 RAIA Gold Medallist

Archer, John, *The Great Australian Dream: The History of the Australian House*, Angus & Robertson, Sydney, 1987

'Architectural Steel Innovation with Bluescope Steel', *Steel Profile* No 96, September 2006

Art Works: Drawings by Ken Woolley, The Images Publishing Group, Melbourne, 2003

Barouch, Judy, 'Mirrabooka – A Real Thriller', The National Trust Website (www.nsw.nationaltrust.org.au)

Beck, Haig, and Cooper, Jackie, 'On Andresen & O'Gorman's Stradbroke Island House', *UME*, Edition 3, 1997

Bevan, Robert, 'Stage Craft', *Monument*, No 73

Bingham-Hall, Patrick (ed.), *A Short History of Melbourne Architecture*, Pesaro Publishing, Sydney, 2002

Black, Richard, 'Eastern Block', *Monument*, No 73

Blunck, Reiner, 'Il Clima Padrone', *Abitare*, Edition 265, 1988

Blythe, Richard, 'A Terroir of Terroir (or, a brief history of design-places), Architecture and Design, RMIT, 2009

Boyd, Robin, *Australia's Home*, Penguin, Melbourne, 1952

Burton Taylor, Jane, 'So Last Century', *Sydney Morning Herald*, April 13, 2006

Cuffley, Peter, *Australian Houses of the Forties and Fifties*, Five Mile Press, Melbourne, 1993

Daab, *Australia Architecture & Design*, daab gmbh, 2007

Davies, Alan, David Moore: *100 Photographs*, exhibition catalogue, State Library of NSW, Sydney, 2005

Day, Norman, *Heroic Melbourne: Architecture of the 1950s*, RMIT, Melbourne, 1995

'Documentation of Places for Entry in the Register of Heritage Places' (Kessell House, Data Base Number 06658) Register of Heritage Places, May 2004

Donovan Hill D House, Brisbane. *UME*, Edition 15, 2002

Drew, Philip, *Peter Stutchbury*, Pesaro Architectural Monographs, Pesaro Publishing, Sydney, 2000

Drew, Philip, 'Profile of Peter Muller' from the Peter Muller website (www.petermuller.org)

Drew, Philip, 'Radar Delight', *Architecture Australia*, July/August 2002

Dunphy, Milo, 'Growth of an Australian Architecture', *Hemisphere Magazine*, August 1962

Edquist, Harriet, 'Many Strands', *Modern in Melbourne: Melbourne Architecture 1950–75*, RMIT, Melbourne (http://users.tce.rmit.edu.au/E03159/ModMelb/mm2/lect/50_60_70/50_60.html)

Evans, Doug, *Kevin Borland: Architecture from the Heart*, RMIT University Press, Melbourne, 2007

Evans, Doug, 'Modernity, Progress and Place – at the Centre and at the Periphery: Melbourne Regionalism in the 1950s', *Modern in Melbourne 2*, RMIT, Melbourne (http://users.tce.rmit.edu.au/E03159/ModMelb/mm2/index.html#anchor142416)

Farrelly, Elizabeth, 'A Dreamhouse You'd Actually Live In', *Sydney Morning Herald*, June 22, 2004

Farrelly, Elizabeth, 'Hugh Buhrich's House' *Architecture Australia*, July/August 2004

Favaro, Paola, 'Interviews with the Canberra Architect Enrico Taglietti (At the Architect's Office in Manuka on 23 April 2003 and 8 October 2003)', *Architectural Theory Review 10*, number 2, 2005, University of Sydney, Sydney

Fromonot, Françoise, *Glenn Murcutt: Buildings and Projects*, Thames & Hudson, London, 2006

Fromonot, Francoise, *Glenn Murcutt: Works and Projects*, Thames & Hudson, London, 1995

Fromonot, Francoise, *Jørn Utzon, The Sydney Opera House*, Gingko Press Inc, California, 1998

Ghezzi, Sebastiano, 'Roy Grounds: Bibliographical Details', *Modern in Melbourne*, RMIT, Melbourne (http://users.tce.rmit.edu.au/e03159/ModMelb/mm2/modmelbprac2/rg/groundsbio.htm)

Giannini, Eli, 'About Face', *Architectural Review Australia*, Residential 2000

Glueck, Grace, 'Design Review; The Man Who Was Martha Stewart Back Before She Was', *The New York Times*, December 7, 2001

Goad, Philip, 'Grafts and Crafts', *Architecture Australia*, July/August 2004

Goad, Phillip, *Gruzman: An Architect and His City*, Craftsman House, Victoria, 2006

Goad, Philip, and Trimble, Judith, *Living in the Landscape: Heide and Houses by McGlashan and Everist*, exhibition catalogue

Goad, Philip, *Melbourne Architecture*, The Watermark Press, Sydney, 1999

Goad, Philip and Bingham-Hall, Patrick, *New Directions in Australian Architecture*, Pesaro Publishing, 2001

Goad, Philip (introduction by Glenn Murcutt), *Troppo*, Pesaro Architectural Monographs, Pesaro Publishing, Sydney, 2005

Hamann, Conrad, *Modern Architecture in Melbourne: the Architecture of Grounds Romberg and Boyd*, 1927–1971, Monash University, Melbourne, 1979

Haskell, John, 'Towards an Australian Idiom: the Architecture of Neville Gruzman', *Art & Australia*, Volume 23, Number 2, Summer 1985, pp. 231–236

Hayes, Babette, and Hersey, April, *Australian Style*, Paul Hamlyn, London and Sydney, 1970

'House at Rye, Victoria', *Architecture in Australia*, December 1964

Houston, Melinda, 'Get Inside the Art of Heide', *The Age*, July 19, 2006

Hyatt, Peter, Local Heroes, *Architects of Australia's Sunshine Coast*, Craftsman House, G+B Arts International, Sydney, 2000

Irving, Robert, *The History and Design of the Australian House*, Oxford University Press, Melbourne, 1985

Jackson, Daryl, *Evolutionary Modernism: Daryl Jackson Selected Works*, MUP 2006

Jackson, Daryl, *Daryl Jackson, Selected and Current Works, Master Architecture Series 11, 2*, Image Publishing Group, 2000

Jackson, Davina, and Johnson, Chris, *Australian Architecture Now*, Thames & Hudson, London, 2000

Jackson, Davina, 'House Boys', *Vogue Living*, November 1990

Jahn, Graham, *Contemporary Australian Architecture*, Gordon and Breach Arts International, Sydney, 1994

Jahn, Graham, *Sydney Architecture*, The Watermark Press, Sydney, 1997

James, Barbara, and Harris, Phil, 'The Sanctuary', *Architecture Australia*, March/April 1999

Johnson, Anna, 'Sea Shell', *Monument*, No 78

Johnson, Donald Leslie, *Australian Architecture 1901–51, Sources of Modernism*, Sydney University Press, 1980

Jolley, E., Colton, C., Ong, V., Chan, S.S., 'David McGlashan (McGlashan & Everist)', Modern in Melbourne, RMIT, Melbourne (http://users.tce.rmit.edu.au/E03159/ModMelb/mm2/modmelbprac2/dm/dmbio.htm)

Keens, Leta, 'Wall and Peace', *Belle*, August/September 2001

Ken Woolley and Ancher Mortlock & Woolley, The Master Architect Series, IV, The Images Publishing Group, Melbourne, 1999

Kennedy, Ken, 'Into the Light', *Monument*, Vol 1, No 4, 1994

Kiely, Annemarie, 'Take the A-Frame', *Belle*, August/September 2001

Leplastrier, Richard, A.S. Hook Address, 1999 RAIA Gold Medallist

Lewis, Jim, 'The Native Builder', *The New York Times*, May 20, 2007

Lloyd Wright, Frank, *An Autobiography*, Pomegranate Communications, 2005

McNeill, Barry and Woolley, Leigh, *Architecture from t he Edge*, Montpelier Press, Hobart, 2002

Maddex, Diane, *Fifty Favourite Houses by Frank Lloyd Wright*, Thames & Hudson, London, 2000

Mainwaring, John, 'Air & Rhythm', *Architecture Australia*, September/October 1998

Margalit, Harry and Goad, Philip, *Durbach Block: The Luminous Space of Abstraction*, Pesaro Architectural Monographs, Pesaro Publishing, Sydney, 2001

'Marshall, Barrie: Marshall House, Kitty Millers Bay, Phillip Island', *UME* in a box. Box 1, Portfolio 3, 1992

Mayoral Minutes, Woollahra Municipal Council, 'Tribute to the Life and Work of the Late Neville Gruzman, AM', May 9, 2005

Metcalf, Andrew, Canberra Architecture, Watermark Press, Sydney, 2003

Michell, George, 'Ruthless Elegance', *Architecture Australia*, July/August 1997

Miles, Martin, '61 Sullivan Crescent, Wanniassa (1980)', Canberra House (www.canberrahouse.com)

Miles, Martin, 'Enrico Taglietti Image Gallery', Canberra House (www.canberrahouse.com)

Miles, Martin, 'Roy Grounds', *Canberra House* (www.canberrahouse.com)

Miles, Martin, 'The Post-War Melbourne Regional Style', *Canberra House* (www.canberrahouse.com)

'Modern in Melbourne 2: Melbourne Architecture 1950–75: Practice Archives: Peter McIntyre: McIntyre Residence 1955', RAIA, Melbourne (http://users.tce.rmit.edu.au/E03159/ModMelb/mm2/index.html#anchor142416)

Mooloomba House, Timber Research Unit, School of Architecture, University of Tasmania

Murcutt, Glenn, A. S. Hook Address, 1992 RAIA Gold Medallist

Myers, P., Lassen, C., Durbach, N., 'Obituary: Vale Hugh Buhrich' *Architecture Australia*, September/October 2004

National Trust of Australia (Victoria) 'National Trust Launches Boyd Foundation' (www.nattrust.com.au)

Neille, Stephen, 'West Coast Cool', *Monument*, No 69

Nichols, John and Richards, Duncan, *The Art of Architecture: The Architectural Drawings of Iwan Iwanoff (1919–1986): An Exhibition of Architectural Drawings by the Architect Iwan Iwanoff From the Collection held by the State Archives of Western Australia* (April 15 to May 13, 1991) Alexander Library Building, Perth Cultural Centre, Perth, 1991

O'Brien, Geraldine, 'Houses that Russell, John and Keith Built', *Sydney Morning Herald*, April 25, 2003

O'Donnell, Marcus, 'Success without a Price', *Monument*, No 16

Paroissien, Leon and Griggs, Michael (ed.), *Old Continent New Building: Contemporary Australian Architecture*, David Ell Press in association with the Design Arts Committee of the Australia Council, 1983

Perren, Claudia and Ring, Kristien (ed.), *Australian Architecture: Living the Modern*, Hatje Cantz, 2007
'Peter Muller', *Architecture in Australia*, July – September 1955, p.76
Poole, Gabriel, A.S. Hook Address, 1998 RAIA Gold Medallist
Quarry, Neville, *Award Winning Australian Architecture*, Craftsman House in association with G+B Arts International, 1997
Reinmuth, Gerard (compiled by), 'Central Coast Houses Then and Now', *Architectural Review* (AR), Number 64, Winter 1998
Reinmuth, Gerard (ed.), 'Tasmanian Modern: Then & Now.' *Architectural Review Australia*, No 74, 2001
Richards, Duncan, 'A Temple for Suburban Living: The Iwanoff House, Lifford Road, Floreat Park, Western Australia (1965–1967)', *Transition 44/45*, RMIT, Melbourne, 1994
Rickard, Bruce, and Goad, Phillip, 'Radar Obituary: Vale Neville Gruzman', *Architecture Australia*, July/August 2005
Robin Boyd Award for Residential Buildings; Jury Verdict, *Architecture Australia*, November/December 2001
'Rose Seidler House', Historic Houses Trust brochure
'Roy Grounds House and Flats', *National Trust* (www.nationaltrust.org.au/pdfs/ntvic1.pdf)
Royal Australian Institute of Architects, 'RAIA Tour of Houses Designed by Bruce Rickard' brochure, 18 August 2002. Contains excerpt from *Contemporary Architects* by Muriel Emanuel, 1994
Searle, Geoffrey, *Robin Boyd: A Life*, Melbourne University Press, Melbourne, 1995
'Sir Roy (Burman) Grounds', *ArchINFORM* (www.archinform.net)
Stewart, Kate, 'Sheer Brilliance', *Interiors*, April/May 2003
Stuckey, Helen, '3 Projects', *Transition*, Issue 43, RMIT, 1994
Stutchbury, Peter, and Spence, Rory, 'Architecture & Place', *Architecture Australia*, January/February 1999
Swann, Graham, 'The Work of Neville Gruzman: Hills House, Turramurra, 1960 to 1983', *The Twentieth Century Heritage Society of NSW* (http://www.twentieth.org.au/People/Gruzman/Hills/Hills.html)
Tadi, Ettore, *Enrico Taglietti: Architect In Australia*, Lodigraf, Milan, 1979 'Taglietti's Unique Sculptural, "Organic" Style', *The Real Estate Times*, September 26, 1998
Tanner, Howard (ed.), *Architects of Australia*, Macmillan, Melbourne and New York, 1981
Tanner, Howard, *Australian Housing in the Seventies*, Ure Smith, Sydney, 1975
Taylor, Jennifer, *An Australian Identity: Houses For Sydney 1953–1963*, University of Sydney, Sydney, 1984
Taylor, Jennifer, *Australian Architecture Since 1960*, National Education Division, Royal Australian Institute of Architects
Tonkin Peter, 'Stradbroke Space Farm', *Architecture Australia*, March/April 1998
Urford, J.C., 'Excerpts from Volume 1...Abstract and Introduction', *The Architecture of Peter Muller*, 1993, from the Peter Muller website (www.petermuller.org)
van Schaik, Leon, *Design City Melbourne*, Wiley & Sons Ltd, Chichester, UK, 2006
van Schaik, Leon (ed.) *The Life Work of Guilford Bell, Architect 1912–1992*, Bookman Press, Melbourne, 1999
Walker, Bruce, *Gabriel Poole – space in which the soul can play*, Visionary Press, Australia, 1998
Wallace, Miranda and Stutchbury, Sarah (ed.), Place Makers – *Contemporary Queensland Architects*, Queensland Art Gallery, Brisbane, 2008
Walter, Betsy, 'Innovation and Open Plans', *Belle*, September/October 1978
Watson, Anne, 'Frank Lloyd Wright', *More Space*, Issue No 7
Weirick, James, 'Harry Howard: Landscape Architect, 1930–2000', *Sydney Morning Herald*, October 7, 2000
Whitelaw, Ann, 'Exotic Roofs, Three Levels, and Hilltop Views', *The Canberra Times*, July 2, 1968
Wilk, Christopher, *Marcel Breuer Furniture and Interiors*, Architectural Press, London, 1981
Wilson, Andrew (ed.), *Hayes & Scott: Post-War Houses*, Queensland University Press, Brisbane, 2005
Woolard, Steve, *Ian McKay 1961–1992: The Sydney School: Thirty Years of Development*, thesis, University of Queensland, Brisbane, 1992
Woolley, Ellen, and Tonkin, Peter, 'Obituary; Peter O'Gorman', *Architecture Australia*, January/February 2002
Woolley, Ken, A.S. Hook Address, 1993 RAIA Gold Medallist
Zemaitis, James, 'Russel Wright and Modern America', *Artnet*, New York

ONLINE REFERENCES

www.dentoncorkermarshall.com
www.gabrielpoole.com.au
www.woodmarsh.com.au
www.durbachblockjaggers.com
www.seangodsell.com
www.peterstutchbury.com.au
www.pettitandsevitt.com.au
www.exero.com/mastergate/secured/design/wooley.htm, 'Nationalism...never been a good source of good art'.
www.architecture.com.au, Australian Institute of Architects, Tribute to Ms Andresen by Lisa Findley
www.rmit.edu.au, RMIT, Modern in Melbourne
www.theage.com.au, 'No guts, no glory' *The Age*, September 2003. Words by Lisa Bragge
www.abc.net.au, 'In the Mind of the Architect'
www.ozetecture.org, Architecture Foundation Australia portfolio, Brit Andresen, Glenn Murcutt, Richard Leplastrier
http://www.lablog.org.uk/wp-content/060327-casi-studio.pdf
http://www.architecture.com.au/i-cms?page=6712
20th Century Buildings for National Estate Register - Tasmania - Australian Institute of Architects
http://www.heritage.vic.gov.au/admin/file/content2/c7/Post_war_study_Stage1_Vol2_ResidentialG.pdf
http://www.terroir.com.au/article_attachments/0000/0044/Reinmuth__G_2001___Then_and_Now_Tasmanian_Modern___No_74_LOW_RES.pdf

CREDITS

Cover image abstracted from Enrico Taglietti's Dingle House
273: Artwork by Akaram Zaatari
275: Artwork by Guo Jian
276: Artwork by Ingo Kleinert
277: Artwork by Darren Wardle and Akaram Zaatari
280-281: Artwork by Jeremiah Bonson
286: Artworks by Mick Namarari Tjapaltjarri, Stieg Persson (2), Melinda Haper and Fran O'Neill
289: Artwork by Carmel Seymour
307: Artworks by R. Schuurmans-Medek, Laura Frances, Peter Harding and Chris Battersby

CONVERSION GUIDE

1 hectare = 2.47 acres
1 millimetre = 0.039 inches
1 centimetre = 0.39 inches
1 metre = 39 inches
1 m^2 = 10.76 square feet
1 kilometre = 0.62 miles
1 kilogram = 2.2 pounds

Note: It took a number of years from first sketch stage to completion for most of the houses in this book. The year indicated on opening pages refers to the date of completion.

In 2008, the Royal Australian Institute of Architects (RAIA) became the Australian Institute of Architects (AIA). The organisation is referred to throughout the book by its historically accurate name.

INDEX

ACKNOWLEDGEMENTS

I am deeply grateful that these books have endured and merited a joint edition to bring together *50/60/70 Iconic Australian Houses*, published in 2007, and its younger twin, *70/80/90 Iconic Australian Houses*, published four years later.

I started out knowing very little about architecture, and regard each chapter, with its attendant research, architect interviews and visits to the buildings, to be my education on the subject. Hence I would like to thank each and every architect for affording me that privilege.

In addition, it took the homeowners to generously open their doors and let us capture the houses and share their stories of commissioning these houses, or living in them, in what many see as the role of custodian.

Since 2006, I have continued to work with photographer Michael Wee, whose images have a new design treatment by Evi O. Ditto Leta Keens, who has edited six of my books with this reworking as a seventh. Having this trusted and talented team makes what I do a great pleasure.

I would also like to thank Murdoch Books; in particular Lou Johnson and Jane Morrow, for having the foresight to give the books another incarnation, and to the production team, including Jane Price, for their steady hands and efficiency.

This book is a precious record – already the dial has shifted with houses represented here ruined by careless and insensitive renovation, and the death of five great Australian architects – Ian McKay, Neil Everist, Bruce Rickard, Ken Woolley and Enrico Taglietti. Here, their voices are loud and clear, and it is important that their work, alongside that of others, is able to be referenced and better understood through these pages.

Karen McCartney, May 2019

MIX
Paper from responsible sources
FSC® C008047

Published in 2019 by Murdoch Books, an imprint of Allen & Unwin
Some text and images were previously published in *Iconic Australian Houses 50/60/70* and *Iconic Australian Houses 70/80/90*, also by Murdoch Books

Murdoch Books Australia
83 Alexander Street, Crows Nest NSW 2065
Phone: +61 (0)2 8425 0100
murdochbooks.com.au
info@murdochbooks.com.au

Murdoch Books UK
Ormond House, 26–27 Boswell Street,
London, WC1N 3JZ
Phone: +44 (0) 20 8785 5995
murdochbooks.co.uk
info@murdochbooks.co.uk

For corporate orders & custom publishing contact our business development team at salesenquiries@murdochbooks.com.au

Publisher: Jane Morrow
Designer: Evi O
Editor: Leta Keens
Creative Manager: Megan Pigott
Editorial Manager: Jane Price
Photography: Michael Wee
Production Director: Lou Playfair

ISBN 978 1 76052 522 4 Australia
ISBN 978 1 91163 253 5 UK

A cataloguing-in-publication entry is available from the catalogue of the National Library of Australia at nla.gov.au
A catalogue record for this book is available from the British Library

Colour reproduction by
Splitting Image Colour Studio Pty Ltd, Clayton, Victoria
Printed by C & C Offset Printing Co Ltd, China